The New Revolutionaries

A Handbook of the
International Radical Left

The New Revolutionaries

A Handbook of the International Radical Left

EDITED BY TARIQ ALI

William Morrow and Company, Inc.

NEW YORK  1969

Copyright © 1969 by Peter Owen Ltd.
"Letter from Jail" by Eldridge Cleaver © *Ramparts*.
"How We Became Revolutionaries" by Paul Rockwell
copyright © 1969 by Paul Rockwell.

All rights reserved. No part of this book may be
reproduced or utilized in any form or by any
means, electronic or mechanical, including photo-
copying, recording or by any information storage
and retrieval system, without permission in writing from the Publisher. Inquiries should be
addressed to William Morrow and Company,
Inc., New York, N.Y. 10016.

Printed in the United States of America.

Library of Congress Catalog Card Number 79-79860

Dedicated to the people of Vietnam
whose heroic struggle against imperialism
has inspired revolutionaries throughout the world

Contents

Preface

The reason for presenting this book to the public is essentially a simple one. For too long the ideas of revolutionary socialists on the left of the traditional communist parties have been suppressed or distorted, both in the capitalist countries and in most of the communist world. In the West it has been against the interests of the ruling groups to permit the development of a Marxian alternative to Stalinism; while in the Soviet Union itself the bureaucracy is afraid that a penetration of critical communist concepts will result in an ending of its powers and privileges. Of late, however, a spectre has begun to haunt the communist parties of Europe: Leon Trotsky. The ice-pick that killed Trotsky did not succeed in killing his ideas, and a revival of the theories advocated by Stalin's most powerful and consistent opponent are now seen by many as a Marxist alternative to Stalinism.

A streak of Trotskyism, therefore, runs through this volume. For this I make no apologies. Its validity as a political credo has stood the test of time.

I would like first of all to thank the contributors themselves for their support, the editors of Intercontinental Press and of the following publications, in which some of the articles in this volume originally appeared: *The Black Dwarf, Granma, Ramparts* and the *Socialist Worker*. I wish also to thank all the individuals without whose help publication would have been interminably delayed. In particular, some of my political colleagues in the International Marxist Group whose encouragement was vital; Ann Scott, the editorial secretary at the offices of *The Black Dwarf*, who spent hours deciphering and typing some of the manuscripts;

9

and Neil Middleton of Peter Owen Ltd, whose resolute nagging ensured that my own contributions were written and submitted to the publisher with dispatch.

Finally, I must add that the choice of all the articles in the pages following was mine and mine alone, and I accept full responsibility for any shortcomings.

Tariq Ali

REGIS DEBRAY

Testimony at His Court Martial
—Camiri, Bolivia

'In reply to the document you have just read, Your Honour, it is precisely the "respect due the law and the authorities" that obliges me to be frank with you. The respect due everyone—civilians and military men, judges and defendants, and prosecuting attorney— cannot be divorced from the truth. So the best proof of respect that I can give you, gentlemen, is to tell you face to face, and here and now, without mincing words, the truth about badly presented facts, the truth about the charges placed against me, the truth about what I think of this trial. It is better so, before your verdict, and not behind your backs in an oblique or covert manner. Otherwise, there would be not respect but servility and opportunism. Let me add something: if I am to be condemned to thirty years in prison, as the prosecuting attorney has asked, I believe it would not be showing "arrogance"—a charge levelled against me several times here—to ask the military tribunal to hear me for thirty minutes, at least once.

'To begin with, I want to express my surprise at the intervention or interruption of the judge advocate yesterday. He interrupted the defence attorney yesterday because he had strayed from the charge, though it seems to me that he had not entered into the political sphere. But I did not ask then why the judge had not interrupted the prosecuting attorney during his first address in the first hearing when he read, even prior to the opening of the formalities, a political congressional discourse, whose content was pretendedly ideological, attacking so-called "red imperialism" (an expression that does not appear in the Penal Code) and Fidel Castro (whose name does not once appear in the indictment), and putting forth the "policy of peace and progress" of the present administration (not mentioned, and rightly so, in the charge). He also levied a strong verbal attack at me without relation to the facts—the facts to which I have been asked to limit myself—calling me an assassin, a hired bandit, a Cuban-paid mercenary, etc., and don't tell me that the prosecuting attorney represents the State and the established law, and that he was only carrying out his duty to censure all that is illegal. Because it is one thing to represent the State, and another to praise a policy; it is one thing to defend the law, and another to attack a political and social régime such as socialism. Moreover, it is one thing to censure a crime, and another to insult an individual. But the prosecuting attorney is not to be reproached. He was absolutely right in settling things in their place right from the start : the struggle of classes, ideas, interests. In other words, the struggle between two kinds of violence : reactionary violence and revolutionary violence. And that surely is the reason, for we should not assume that there is any partiality or complicity on his part, that the judge advocate did not interrupt the prosecuting attorney and is not about to interrupt me either. My defence attorney has not responded to these attacks out of professional integrity and the wish to abide by legal procedure, and he was correct. He has limited himself to destroying the charges bit by bit, and he has done his job perfectly. But when one has been referred to, one generally has the right of reply. And with even greater right when one has been insulted, and more than once, I do not, nor did I, ask for the court's indulgence, but for equity. And it is the court itself that must decide whether or not there is to be equity in this trial at Camiri.

'Yet, I do not have the least intention of countering insult with insult, rhetoric with rhetoric, evasion with evasion; I will respond with a clear and simple exposition of the facts. How can a man not wish to shout out his indignation when he has had to listen, for more than a month, seated and mute, literally as if he were absent from the debate, to a carefully co-ordinated deluge of slander, insinuations, lies ! Not to speak of what I have had to read in these lampoons called—one wonders why—newspapers ! But here I will try to silence all this indignation, this accumulated bitterness, and refer calmly to the facts.

'I therefore "deem it useful to my defence" to help the court develop a clear and precise concept of what the guerrilla action amounted to on the dates corresponding to the military actions that led to this trial.

'I "deem it useful to my defence", in the second place, although the court does not consider itself responsible for all the irregularities committed before or simultaneous with this legal action, to help the court become fully aware of a machination that, even if it will not alter its decision, has indeed altered the record and has had an influence on the debates. I refer to the secret and publicity-seeking plot hatched against me, from the first days of my arrest, by the Central Intelligence Agency of the United States of America.

'I also "deem it useful to my defence" to examine bit by bit the evidence accumulated in this trial, as it is really worth while. After the plea of my defence attorney, I have only a few details to add and some remarks on the methods of accusation.

'And all this calmly. Because we have come to a point when this guerrilla action, or, rather, this first stage of the Bolivian guerrilla revolution marked by the death of Che [Guevara], has already passed into history; to a point at which almost everything can be cleared up, from beginning to end, and without concerning ourselves with whether or not such an element does or does not constitute a crime, whether or not it substantiates the charge (luckily, history has criteria other than penal codes by which to judge what is and what is not just). And, bearing this in mind, and not to be rid of charges that strain one's credulity but to clear up a historic truth that has been distorted here, we called two witnesses, in the record as witnesses for the defence, although this aspect of their testimony did not matter to us. We only wanted them to state what they knew. And since this history was written on the spot by both the guerrillas and the regular army, we have called "Camba", the only guerrilla worthy of the name captured so far by the army, a comrade in ideals, even if, being a prisoner, he is still not aware of what is happening and has happened here. The rest of the witnesses who were guerrillas are essentially deserters, vulgar deserters, some of whom have not even been present at these sessions, as they are already in the army. . . .

'And we have called on an adversary of the guerrillas, an honest, brave man, honest and brave enough to recognize the honesty and bravery of the guerrillas : army major Sanchez. Evidently, it is still too soon for the truth to come out unblemished. There are still pressures, passions, inhibitions, compromises. I would, for example, have liked Major Sanchez to explain whether he feels that ambush is assassination or an act of war; how many ambushes he prepared against the guerrillas; who the foreigners were who participated in the interrogation of the guerrilla prisoners—especially of Vazquez, Bustos and myself—and where they come from; what the interrogation dealt with, etc. But it was not possible.

'And all this, I repeat, not in order to apologize for but honestly to reconstruct the events around which this trial revolves. And, by so doing, we have also shown our respect for the noble memory of Che—Che, who never once sacrificed truth for convenience or personal benefit. Che, who vainly, and on various occasions, tried to get the guerrilla newspapers to the Bolivian people and to others. At first, the newspapers only carried reports on the war, most detailed reports on all that happened, both good and bad, the exact losses on both sides, the victories and the setbacks, without changing anything. And these reports bore the following title : "Revolutionary Truth Stands Against Reactionary Deception." These papers were delivered to us : two apiece to Roth, Bustos and myself, before we left for Muyupampa, and they were confiscated from us there, or, more exactly, from Roth, to whom we had given our four, which he had in his pockets; they were not taken from me, as one witness, Lieutenant Ruiz, has mistakenly testified. But, as this entire trial is apparently directed against me personally, it is no wonder that there are so many inaccuracies in the testimony. These details are not of major importance. What is important in this case, what is of enormous importance is the following : the fact that they have not presented here even a fraction of the documentation seized at Nancahuazu owing to the treachery of an ex-guerrilla called "Chingolo", who was expelled from the guerrilla forces on March 27th by Ramon and is today serving in the army. This documentation ought to include, among other things, a dozen guerrilla field diaries, a list of personnel, notebooks, books, passports, dozens of rolls of film and a manuscript by Che on political economy and Latin America—his last complete work. All of this was taken to Washington for inspection by Mr Dean Rusk, but it has not been brought here for your inspection. But the most painful thing is that Che's diary has, so far, been kept from this court.

'But, of course, it is not a matter of reducing this historic, moving, exemplary document to the simple role of a piece of evidence in such insignificant proceedings as these. Yet it is, after all, there rather than in any other document that we find written the whole history of the guerrillas from beginning to end. It is the only place where you will find the truth of all that was the subject of lengthy discussion here—whether we were combatants or observers, whether or not I was a spy, a liaison, a supplier of maps, a political commissar. There you will find the role of each of us, our individual participation. It is dreadful to think that the court will decide on all this, will issue a verdict, without having asked to see this document which would clear up all its doubts, without exception, and probably other things as well. But precisely here lies the difficulty, the reason why it could not be read. Everything would have been clarified : the accusation would have been completely quashed; the exact importance of each one of us would have been shown. In my case, it would have been clear that I did not have 10 per cent or 1 per cent of the importance they wished to attribute to me officially for national and international political reasons. It would have destroyed, furthermore, all the mechanisms of publicity and propaganda set against me. It would have revealed, for example, that in a period of eleven months Che had not even referred twice to *Revolution in the Revolution*, which has very little for the "arrangement and regulation of the guerrillas" but sufficient enough due to the true value of this pamphlet, which for Che was just another book among the hundreds of books that he had in camp. The court would have discovered that my two previous trips to Bolivia had no connection with the outbreak of the guerrilla struggle this year. But the usual method has been employed, the usual poison. Great "revelations" have been announced, all of them related exclusively to Debray; one or two lies have been "slipped" into the press; an atmosphere of expectation has been created; the machinery of deceit automatically goes into action. And what has come of it? Nothing.

'Yet this has not prevented a civilian lawyer from taking it for granted, with imperturbable calm, that I brought money to Che

Guevara on arriving at his camp. The evidence, says this gentleman, is that it was published in the press. This way, it is daily proved in Bolivia that the sun travels around the earth. There is just one small detail, one that would not much interest this gentleman : and that is, the allegation is false. I never supplied money to Che, who was not a man to mistake names.

'The prosecuting attorney mentioned another phrase of the diary in connection with an alleged mission of mine to make contact with the Communist Party of Bolivia on behalf of Fidel Castro. Although no evidence was presented, this came in handy. I can tell you that I am very skeptical of such a notation, especially written that way. Because, even if I do have good friends in the CPB, I never met with any CPB leaders in Bolivia to discuss any political problem, simply because I am in no way authorized to represent anyone but myself before a political party. Those who try to confuse public opinion and distort the facts with such methods are committing a mistake. They are committing a mistake, because there must be documents which set forth the origin, the beginning of the Bolivian guerrilla struggle, with dates, facts, names—documents that no one can confiscate and that will, doubtless, be made public at the proper moment.

'It does not matter to me whether or not the final verdict pleases the prosecuting attorney; I am concerned about whether or not the verdict is based on truth, on what I am and what I have done, and not based on mutilated documents, perjured witnesses (there are five here, Your Honour—three soldiers and two ex-guerrillas) or sleight-of-hand, such as the evidence presented so far. And I ask even more strongly that the army, the Government, have in their possession all the means to make the simple truth known. I do not request, nor have I ever requested, as the prosecuting attorney has claimed, any kind of immunity owing to my profession as a writer, an intellectual. I am not protesting against being given the maximum penalty, even if it were a question of capital punishment. I am protesting against the grounds for such a sentence. The heart of the matter is not the sentence about to be given, which is of no importance, but the "whereases". In the life-and-death struggle· being waged by United States imperialism and its hirelings against socialism and revolution, as a lawyer reminded us here, it is generally admitted that those who have chosen the path of revolution sooner or later expose themselves to prison or to violent death. I see nothing strange in this, no reason for wonder. The prosecuting attorney repeated several times that it was better to serve thirty years in prison than die in combat. I feel just the opposite. But, in any case, I cannot allow a political sentence for an ideological crime to be passed off as a sentence for a common crime. I cannot allow them to attribute to me a role in a guerrilla organization which I never held, that I be tried as an assassin, a thief; that is what the charge says. I cannot allow them to equate a declaration of joint political and moral responsibility with a confession of guilt. Guilty of what? And on what grounds? Political? Granted. Criminal? Inadmissible. Let them tell me : "We are condemning you because you are a Marxist-Leninist, because you wrote *Revolution in the Revolution*, a book that was once read to some guerrillas in your absence; we are condemning you because you are a confessed admirer of Fidel Castro and you came here to speak with Che without first requesting permission from the authorities, because you did not give us advance notice, because the guerrillas gave you the nickname 'Danton' and you did guard duty two or three times in the guerrilla camp, just like any other visitor."

'That's fine; I have nothing to say. I'm well aware there is still a class struggle, I'm well aware there are Yankee embassies and of their battalions of agents and propagandists, I'm well aware the revolution is still to be made. But when I am told, "We are condemning you because you came to this country twice to spy on us, because you delivered maps and money to Che, because you were on the general staff of the guerrillas, because you planned the military operations, because you gave classes to the guerrillas, because you were a political commissar, a master mind of subversion, and you participated in ambush attacks", then I say no, I protest; because all of this is a series of stories, of absolutely unproven lies, which will never be proven. I will protest my arrest ceaselessly and in every way possible. My attitude should not surprise you. Even if I declare a thousand times that I regret not being guilty the way the prosecuting attorney would like me to be, that I regret not having died beside Che, this does not give you any legal right to sentence me, since penalties are provided for deeds, not intentions. The campaign of slander launched against me by all of Latin American reaction, from General Stroessner to Lleras Camargo, including Luis Conte Agüero and the publicists in La Paz, has involved some very astute tactics, for some time, astute legal-political tactics. When I say, "It so happens that I have not committed any of the crimes that I am accused of, either directly or indirectly; I am absolutely innocent of the charges made here", this is the reply I get : "Then you disown your political ideas, you are incapable of upholding them, you wash your hands of the bloodshed caused by your book." And when I say, "I affirm my joint political and moral responsibility for the actions of my comrades, which are the reason for this trial", then I hear happy cries from the yellow press : "At last the bandit confesses his guilt. . . !" But once again I say, guilty of what?

'It seems that these gentlemen will never be completely satisfied, will never stop barking and spitting venom, until they hear me confess that I was part of the guerrilla leadership, that I picked and reconnoitred the zone of operations, controlled all preparations, planned the ambushes and served as a political commissar and adviser to Che, and that my pamphlet was used as a guerrilla manual, etc. Then, if I admit that such inventions are true, I will be called honest or courageous, consistent and responsible. They simply forget that we must respect the facts and know them before we speak; that the facts are not so malleable. I cannot invent stories just to satisfy their anxiety. They are trying to trap me in this dilemma : either they take advantage of my political commitments to find me guilty of criminal charges, even at the cost of inventions, or they take advantage of my innocence of criminal charges to make it appear that I had no strong political commitment or could not adhere to it.

'Gentlemen, it is not so easy! Here in this room it is a question not of politics—they say—but of applying the Penal Code, of applying the maximum sentence for murder, theft and rebellion to a man who had no participation whatsoever either in person, as an instigator, or indirectly, in the military actions that they want to judge, even though he is in complete agreement with them.

'What do I understand by joint responsibility? As a revolutionary (to the extent to which I can be called one), I feel and I declare myself jointly responsible for all the "crimes" committed by all revolutionaries everywhere in the world, from the printing of fliers to attacks on banks to obtain funds, from illegal meetings to the execution of torturers. For as long as I am available and a leader sends for me, anywhere, and tells me, "We need you. We need you because in our opinion you are the only one who can carry out such a mission; you can do it better than others, and by doing it you help our common cause", then I am ready to do my duty.

'I do not find it at all strange that you want to condemn me for this attitude, this readiness. The *raison d'être* of political trials is to condemn such aspirations, such readiness.

'If, when I asked Che at the beginning of April to allow me to join his group, definitively and immediately, he had answered, "You are physically fit; you have the ability; you are used to warfare, to life in the country; your mission as a journalist can be carried out by someone else later; it is not urgent; stay here with us", I would gladly have remained, as a combatant, as a guerrilla, ready to fight anywhere and as often as necessary. What greater dream for a militant than to be under Che's orders! Unfortunately, I fell sick at the time as a result of malnutrition, as I mentioned in my declaration, and Che did not have much confidence in my physical fitness. I say "unfortunately" because I would never have left the guerrillas and I would not be sitting here, speaking, exposed to all this ridiculous publicity, to imperialist propaganda, to the hatred of the Yankees, and to the particularly active and expansive animosity of their guests of honour, the colony of Cuban exiles. But it so happens that I entered and left the guerrilla camp as a simple visitor; I did share in the daily life of the camp for longer than I expected, because that is where we lived.

'Why, then, do I say that I am jointly responsible for the war actions of my comrades? Because, far from condemning them, I endorse them as necessary and legitimate. Also, because I would have participated in the preparation of these actions and I would have carried them out if Ramon had so ordered or if I had been physically fit. In short, the very fact that I am staying in the revolutionary ranks and that I continue to be convinced that armed struggle is the key to the liberation struggle, particularly in Bolivia, proves that I do not repent of these so-called crimes and that I am prepared to continue committing them. I ratify them, and, adhering to the moral and political concepts which have inspired them, I also inevitably accept whatever consequences may arise from my actions.

'Does that mean that at any moment I may cease to be a "visitor" and become a "guerrilla fighter"? As to this point, which the lawyers and prosecuting attorney have discussed so much, the facts are as follows. At the time of our first meeting with Che no battles had yet taken place, no ambushes, nor were they expected to occur so soon. In spite of that, he immediately established the fact that I was there in the capacity of a visitor. Yes, we discussed the possibility of my joining the guerrillas. But, in addition to my journalistic work, he wanted me to take care of a couple of things on the outside, and, since I myself wanted to settle some personal problems that were worrying me considerably, it was mutually agreed that I should leave the camp immediately. However, we also agreed that after that I would return to Bolivia, and that this time I would come as a guerrilla fighter, to stay.

'Suddenly the situation became complicated. Communications with the outside world had already become difficult. Out of the four visitors present at the camp, Che decided that Bustos and I should be the first to leave, through the town of Gutierrez. A more careful evacuation plan was drawn up for China and Tania, as they had more revolutionary importance. When, after the unsuccessful attempt to leave by way of Gutierrez, I talked to him again about joining the guerrillas, Che, referring to my lack of experience in living in the wilds, answered that for him ten city intellectuals were worth less as guerrilla fighters than one farmer from the area. This convinced me that I would be much more useful on the outside than inside, especially during those moments of isolation, and I reaffirmed my decision to leave the guerrillas the way I had joined them, simply as a visitor.

'However, he did not want to force us to run the risk of a more or less improvised departure. And if you want even more proof that we were not subjected to the rigid discipline of the actual combatants, allow me to point out that, although he had given me his personal opinion several times to the effect that it would be wise to leave the zone quickly. Che let us choose, let us make up our own minds as to whether we wanted to stay a while longer with the guerrillas or leave by one route or another, to follow one plan or another. They were not orders. He had given us his opinion once, and we were free to follow his advice or not. We had interfered enough and to no avail with the guerrillas' movements. There were too many sick men among the guerrillas. So, as far as I was concerned, I insisted on running the risk of departure, once and for all and as soon as possible. Especially since we had never imagined, even in the eventuality that we should be arrested during the trip, that we would receive such treatment, and would be the cause of so much uproar and such a trial. At that time, we thought that the sooner we left the sooner we would be able to return, but this time not as visitors. But why talk about it? What might have been and was not, and, alas, now never will be, does not come under the jurisdiction of this court.

'Why then should a non-combatant declare himself jointly responsible for acts committed by revolutionary combatants? Allow me to make a comparison.

'Miners' blood was shed on Midsummer's Eve. In the middle of the night the army launched a sneak attack on the mines. According to official figures, the morning found the floor of the mine littered with twenty-seven corpses and three times as many wounded. There are twenty-seven families in mourning, too, Mr President, but they cannot cry out for their dead, cannot cry out for vengeance, nor can they appear at any trial as civilians or put up posters in the streets. Twenty-seven families in mute mourning. All those wearing military uniform are, to my way of thinking, equally responsible for the crimes committed that night. Even if you did not conceive, plan or carry out this repression, as I see it, gentlemen of this court, you are equally responsible for them from a moral as well as a political point of view.

'First, because you do not condemn these acts; you approve of them, you say, as a necessary evil for preventing an even worse evil to the constitutional order : generalized subversion. In Nancahuazu and Iripiti we see necessary evils preventing an even worse evil to the people, that of generalized oppression.

'And because, as a matter of discipline, you would have agreed to take part in them if you had been ordered to do so.

'In short, because you have not cast off the military uniform after Midsummer's Eve. Except for the mentally sick and the fascists, no one likes men to have to make history by killing. But if you want to talk about crimes, where are the innocent ones? All of us here —judges as well as defendants—are accomplices to crimes. You do not represent peace and happiness, while we represent violence and pain. Each one has to decide which side he is on—on the side of military violence or guerrilla violence, on the side of violence that represses or violence that liberates. Crimes in the face of crimes. Which ones do we choose to be jointly responsible for, accomplices or accessories to? You chose certain ones, I chose others—period.

'But let's look at the facts. Let's see whether or not my comrades committed murders, whether or not my comrades are criminals. In his first appearance, the prosecuting attorney asked the court to set "an exemplary precedent". That is, in view of the fact that the death sentence could not be restored in time, despite the fact that General Barrientos had asked Congress for it, the prosecuting attorney called for the maximum sentence in effect now : thirty years. Since this sentence is only passed in the case of murder, parricide or treason, and since I have not betrayed my country or killed my parents, a double accusation had to be dreamed up, Mr President.

'The first step was to label the March 23rd and April 10th ambushes as "murder". It was then necessary to prove that on March 23rd the army troops did not know of the existence of the guerrillas and were caught unawares, "with their picks and shovels", carrying out routine missions in the area. That's why the prosecuting attorney calls "the assailants" not guerrillas but "bandits".

'Second, it was necessary to prove that I had participated in these "murders", if not directly at least indirectly, by "induction", as an essential part of the guerrillas' military set-up.

'Let's take the first point, the ambushes.

'On March 11th at 7 a.m. in the guerrillas' base camp, when no one had yet thought about military operations, two men from Moises Guevara's group, assigned the mission of going to hunt game, picked up their carbines and went down to the river, but, instead of turning right, to the east, where the hunting grounds lay, they headed west, towards Camiri. They were the first deserters, present here as defendants. The farce has gone so far as to include them among the defendants, which has them somewhat displeased, I understand.

'On March 14th they were arrested in the area before they were able to reach La Paz, where—according to their written statements —they wanted to go "to turn in their report".

'The same day they made highly detailed statements, since one of them turned out to have long-standing ties with the DIC and "Political Control". He says, textually, in his statement after being arraigned, that he "had joined the guerrillas to carry out an intelligence mission, thinking he would gain some benefit from his informing". His written statements of March 14th and 15th form part of the record, beginning with page 30. As they could not be read publicly, I beg you, gentlemen of the court, to read them carefully. There you will find an exact rundown on the guerrilla organization : the fighters there in the base camp at that time (twenty men), the fighters engaged in exploring Vallegrande with Che (thirty men), the nationalities of the guerrillas, names, plans, the position of the camp, their trails, the existence of radio transmitters, etc. There you will not only read of the presence of Che, there under the *nom de guerre* of Ramon, but you will also discover when and how he got to Bolivia, using what disguise, all about his pursuits, his belongings, how they were waiting for him to show up at the base camp at any moment, etc.

'Antonio, the chief of the camp at that time, had unreservedly treated them as comrades. He even showed them the whole collection of photographs—which were still confidential—that had been taken of Che and those who had been with him ever since November. So, without waiting for him to return to the camp, they left. They admitted that they had immediately served the army as guides by land and from the air, and that later, before March 23rd, they were sent over to General Headquarters in La Paz to complete their report. In case there is any doubt about this, Choque-Choque, who also belonged to the Moises Guevara group, was taken prisoner on the 17th without offering any resistance. He confirmed what his comrades had said and immediately joined the troops as a guide, showing them the way to the camp and pointing out details about the defence system. At this point Major Sanchez explained how Choque-Choque had come at the head of the troops which had seized the camp early in April.

'The third source of information giving the army, before Nancahuazu, a complete picture of the guerrilla situation was a guide named Vargas, a uniformed civilian who was to meet his death in the ambush of the 23rd while guiding the military column to the camp. This individual, who lived in Vallegrande, had been rashly visited by Marcos, head of the guerrilla vanguard, and his troops. They came to him early in March, pretending to be foreign geologists, and tried to buy food from him, since the food supplies of the guerrillas who were exploring that zone with Che were very low. Vargas was suspicious and followed them closely from Villegrande to Nancahuazu. Thereupon he went to report his suspicions to the Camiri 4th Division Headquarters.

'On the basis of the additional series of reports made by Algaranaz, plus the sudden appearance of Marcos and the vanguard, the army, naturally, before Marcos's peons, mobilized and took the offensive. On March 16th the army seized the house of Coco Peredo ("the house with the tin roof"), and a soldier was killed in the operation. In the following days the army, which had already located the camp, sent patrols farther and farther out. Reconnaissance planes flew over the zone all day long. The guerrillas found themselves not only blockaded, with supplies running low—since the farm and the road to Camiri had been cut off —but also taken by surprise while not sufficiently trained, and scattered, since Che and his men, who had planned their arrival at the Nancahuazu camp for March 1st, were delayed twenty days. Messengers were sent to him to warn him of the unforeseen circumstances.

'Meanwhile, Marcos, who, with the help of Antonio, had taken over the base camp, decided, due to the lack of sufficient forces to hold out against the growing pressure of the army, to withdraw and move farther back. And on the 20th, when Che finally arrived, he found the guerrillas retreating in the face of an army offensive. He saw in this hasty retreat signs of defeatism, ousted Marcos from his post, made everyone return to the base camp and decided to defend it against any army attack. Thus, with the aim of cutting off the advance, he sent a group of six men to take a position at a point some three hours from the camp in the Nancahuazu ravine. And the ambush took place on the 23rd.

'What happened on those days, before the 23rd, had a decisive and fatal influence on all the activities of the guerrillas later. But I gave this brief account only to show you how the prosecutor's thesis, even basing itself on false testimony, does not stand up under examination. The army was not at Nancahuazu on a "routine mission", much less with "the purpose of opening up a road". It did not have, precisely, "picks, shovels and machetes", as Sergeant-

Major Plata said. It had come with 30-calibre machine-guns, .60-mm mortars, radio transceivers and air support, and it knew where it was going; it was going to seize the base camp in a combined manoeuvre with another military column that was advancing from the other side, from Gutierrez. It was a classic encirclement. The air force was ordered to begin bombing the camp at 12 a.m. on the 23rd. At any rate, even if public opinion was not yet aware of it by that date (even though the press, strangely enough, had been publishing rumours about the guerrillas since early in March), for the two opposing sides hostilities had already begun. They had begun for the guerrillas precisely on March 11th, date of the first desertions, which placed the camp in a state of alert; they had begun for the army a few days later, with the seizing of Peredo's farm.

'Moreover, on the 23rd the army was on the offensive and the guerrillas on the defensive. If tactically the army was caught off-guard by the ambush, strategically the ones who were surprised were the guerrillas, who did not take the initiative in the fight, but, rather, evaded it at first. For all of these reasons, that ambush was not murder, but rather an act of war, tactically and premeditatedly declared by both sides.

'Was the ambush cruel? Undoubtedly, as any ambush is. It is a combat method that has existed ever since the weak have fought the strong. It is used in all people's wars in every period of history and is still employed in regular warfare. Were innocent officers and men killed? Certainly. Were the Bolivian soldiers who fell at Altos de la Paz in 1952, struck down by the miners' bullets, personally responsible for latifundia, for Rosca's extortion, for starvation wages? Were the Alto Peruvians who, in defence of the Spanish Crown, fell under the bullets of the Lanza brothers, the Padilla group and the Azurduy group responsible for monarchical absolutism, for the *ponguenjo*, for the Spanish monopoly over trade? Obviously not. These victims were also victims of the prevailing régime of oppression, whose blindly loyal instruments they were.

'In all these periods of history, the men in uniform were the first victims of the exploitation and repression they defended, not realizing, in the majority of cases, what they represented. They were the victims of their legal duty, which became invalid, senseless, empty. This fact permits us to respect and to sympathize with their families, but it does not permit us to allow the social régime that uses them to maintain itself in power to make demagogic propaganda with them. Revolutionary war is not a question of individuals facing individuals—everyone has a family, parents, sons, loved ones, a childhood. They are but mere representatives of two irreconcilable orders. These acts of war are the fruit of social, economic and moral antagonisms existing independently of the will of the actors and preceding them. No one has created these antagonisms, and no one can take them away, but they should indeed be surmounted and settled. Naturally, the tragedy is that we do not kill objects, numbers, abstract or interchangeable instruments, but, precisely, on both sides, irreplaceable individuals, essentially innocent, unique for those who have loved, bred, esteemed them. This is the tragedy of history, of any history of any revolution. It is not individuals that are placed face to face in these battles, but class interests and ideas; but those who fall in them, those who die, are persons, are men. We cannot avoid this contradiction, escape from this pain.

'If the ambush in itself and by itself is murder, then the Yankees in the Canal Zone, at Fort Brigg, are past masters of this art, since the first thing they teach the Latin American military and the Bolivians, in their jungle course, is to set up ambushes against the guerrillas, the tactics and theory of ambushes. If the ambush in itself is murder because the fight is not on an equal footing, because the risks are not the same, then there are many assassins in the Bolivian Army, which has set up more than one ambush. Nancahuazu and Iripiti were not ambushes of extermination : the proof of this is the number of prisoners who could have been liquidated. They were intended to seize weapons with which to arm the farmers later and prevent access to the base camp. What was truly an ambush of extermination, a ruthless ambush, was, for example, the one the army planned against a guerrilla rearguard in Vado del Yeso. There, according to the testimony of Major Vargas who directed and prepared the operation, they waited until the guerrillas were crossing the river and then opened fire on them from both sides of the river, from behind, from the front and from the flank. Out of eleven guerrilla fighters, there remained only one prisoner. There, the objective was to kill, to kill anyway, and nothing more. There, without being able to defend themselves, except for one or another blind volley, Joaquin, Tania, Alejandro, El Negro, Moises Guevara, Braulio, Pablo and others fell. Should

I say that this was murder? No. It was an ambush, oddly cruel, but it was not murder.

'The army took skilful advantage of a tremendous mistake on the part of the guerrillas, or of good luck or better knowledge of the terrain, or the places where the Rio Grande could be forded, just as the guerrillas, a few months before, at Nancahuazu and Iripiti, had taken advantage of the army's errors. This is just as true in guerrilla fighting as in any other kind of warfare. If Vado del Yeso was not a murder or an act of cowardice, how can Nancahuazu be termed one? Or perhaps there are two standards, two ways of judging things : one for the army and another for the guerrillas? Perhaps it will be argued that the guerrillas started this, and that the army is not to blame if it has had to resort to the same methods : that the guerrillas are responsible for this whole series of ambushes, since they are the ones who initiated such tactics. A great deal can be said on this matter. What is true is that the ex-miners who took part in the ambush at Nancahuazu had the feeling, had the certainty, that they were continuing a fight, a very old fight against the army, a very old enemy, and, even if they used new methods, that this was not a fight they had started at all, for it began a long time ago, there at Catavi, around 1946— even before.

'However, the truth is that, instead of frankly and directly condemning a cause, a revolutionary idea, condemnation, hypocritically, has been formally directed against a combat method, against tactics of warfare, without taking into account that this method— the use of the ambush—is universally employed, and is equally employed by army forces against guerrillas, by the very forces that call such methods murder when used against them, and heroic combat when army forces use such methods against revolutionary guerrilla forces. Moreover, Your Honour, one must be frank. The March 23rd operation was badly carried out on the part of the army, with a complete lack of responsibility, and the guerrillas are not to blame for that. What was left unsaid was that those soldiers and officers were sent out to risk their lives—and those are the words of Captain Silva himself during his testimony—without taking the most elementary precautions. According to what guerrilla combatants have told me, the troops gathered and deployed themselves on a beach facing the guerrillas, without even spreading out. Everyone knows—it is included in any military manual—that upon entering a danger area every member of a marching column must keep fifty metres behind the man in front of him. Those troops had gone there to take a guerrilla camp. How could they have acted that way, with that lack of forethought, since they knew what kind of guerrillas they were dealing with, knew what sort of guerrilla organization they were faced with, and also knew that Che Guevara was in the area? However, this is another problem that I will not attempt to go into.

'I want to emphasize something which is obvious to me, that in this naturally cruel struggle, despite all the difficulties involved, the guerrillas fought from a position of principles, never for a moment abandoning the greatest respect for human beings, the greatest sense of humanity. All the wounded were cared for with the best facilities available; prisoners were cared for, fed. Blankets were provided to protect them from the night cold. It has been said that the dead and the prisoners, or some of them, were stripped of their personal effects. Their boots, yes, because in the jungle boots are a vital necessity and the guerrillas had no shoemaker. Their uniforms, yes, because the guerrillas have no one to make uniforms nor cloth to make them out of, and the army has these things. However, prisoners were given civilian clothing. None of the dead, according to what the guerrillas told me, were left without clothing. It is true that they were not buried immediately, and descriptions have been given here several times of what the bodies in a state of decomposition looked like, eaten up by buzzards and worms, in what condition they were found later. But whose fault was that?

'Che's first decision when Coco Peredo went to the camp to make his first report on the morning of the 23rd was to send out doctors immediately, and he gave the army a forty-eight-hour truce so they could come and collect their dead, since El Pincal, where the troops were concentrated, was very close to the scene of combat. That explains why the guerrillas did not bury the dead. That was the sole reason. And it was only much later that the guerrillas realized that no one had come to take away the bodies, but by then it was too late. None of the prisoners, officers or soldiers, were abused, physically or morally. Major Sanchez has stated here that at Iripiti the doctors delayed for an hour before taking care of the wounded, and he supposed that medical attention was provided for the guerrillas first and for the army troops later. However, except for Rubio, who was wounded in the head and died a few minutes later, the guerrilla forces suffered no wounded at Iripiti. Even if they had, there were definite orders to take care of the most seriously wounded first without considering whether they were guerrillas or soldiers. No, what happened was that the camp where the doctors were, was half an hour away from the place where the ambush took place. And this—along with the time needed to send for them—explains why an hour elapsed before they arrived. Nothing else.

'By then we were running short of medicine, especially glucose. When one doctor, before starting out, asked Che if it were not preferable to save part of the liquid glucose available for the use of the guerrillas, since there was no way to replenish the supply, Che answered that this could not even be taken into consideration and, if necessary, the supplies on hand should be all used up in order to save their lives, that, whatever the cost, the enemy wounded must be treated, even when they were in a hopeless condition. As for the accusations concerning theft and looting, I believe that it is not necessary to go further into the matter : it is well known that, aside from the weapons captured, nothing was stolen from the prisoners. Not a single piece of meat, not one potato, not a single kernel of corn was ever taken or confiscated from a farmer without payment, at a price set by the farmer himself. And when the owner of a farm was absent, an amount of money equivalent to the value of the products appropriated was left with a peon.

'What does the prosecuting attorney base himself on when he accuses the guerrillas of being bandits and common criminals? The prosecuting attorney has stated from the very first day of the trial that such bandits cannot be compared with the guerrillas of the independence of Alto Peru, with the great founders of the nation, the Camargos, the Warnes, the Padillas, the Lanzas. The prosecuting attorney has said they are not guerrillas, because they fight like cowards, hidden in the jungles, employing ambush tactics, in contrast with "our miners" who are really courageous because they fight in the open countryside, face to face. And is it not true that the guerrillas of the independence struggle fought in the jungles, in the mountains and gorges of Inquisivi, Coroico and Vallegrande? And what did they do if not use tactics of ambush, death-dealing bloody ambush of Spanish forces, cornering them in the mountain passes, burying them under stones and rocks rolled down from the mountain tops? And did they by chance care for the wounded? And I ask myself what the prosecuting attorney admires most in the miners of the plateaus, if it is their courage, their will to combat practically unarmed on open, flat terrain, giving previous warning, or is it not rather the ease with which the army usually liquidates them?

'These are not guerrillas, the prosecuting attorney stated later, because they do not fight under any flag. They have made no declaration of war. It is quite possible that, since they were taken by surprise by a sudden army attack, the guerrillas did not have time to send a declaration to the outside world, in the form of leaflets or communiqués, for example. It is possible that this was a mistake. At least that is my personal opinion. But this does not concern the court. The important thing is that the guerrillas did have a flag, the highest and noblest in all Latin America, and that flag is the name of Che. The army knew this before going into action, and everything possible was done to hide the fact, to hold back, for example, guerrilla communiqués and Army of National Liberation war dispatches. Yet they later seem surprised because the flag has not appeared. But, above all, the prosecuting attorney states, they cannot be compared with the guerrilla fighters for independence because they are foreigners.

'It is true there were foreigners among them, but naturally a minority. The vast majority were Bolivians, but there were Peruvians, Cubans and one Argentinian. Is this by any chance something new in the history of Bolivia? Is this by any chance in contradiction with the profoundly national and patriotic nature of this liberation struggle? We need not cite the examples here of Bolivar, Sucre, Santa Cruz, Belgrano and the four reinforcement armies from Argentina; of the Venezuelans, Chileans and Argentinians who founded Bolivia and all of Latin America. We are speaking only of guerrillas who fought for independence—and not the top leaders of the regular armies. We are speaking of the Padillas, the Warnes, the Lanzas. I have here in front of me a book published by the San Francisco Xavier University of Sucre, the *Diary of a Soldier of Alto Peru Independence*, written about 1820 by a guerrilla who fought in the Sicasica and Ayopaya Valleys, at the time of

Bolivia's birth as a nation. He was, as a matter of fact, one of the "factions"—that is, of the guerrillas commanded by Jose Manuel Lanza. And the following is taken from the prologue :

' "Most members of the faction are from the valleys—that is, they are Indians or *mestizos*. But the faction also includes a host of unseasoned armed men from many places, and of all kinds, unusual groups grafted on to the main stem. Of course in the Alto Peru faction there are many from other parts of the country : Orurenos, Cochabaminos, Pacenos, and even Crucenos. . . . There are also soldiers from other parts of the Americas in the faction : some Bonaerenses (inhabitants of Buenos Aires), Tucumanos and Paraguayans, leftovers from the Rondeau's Argentine expedition. Others present in the faction include Peruvians from Cuzco, and there are also Negroes. And even Englishmen—who arrived in the valley God knows how or when—are included in the Indian-*mestizo* force fighting against Spain in the southernmost part of the Alto Peru mountain area." (Gunner Mendoza L., p. 38).

'It is not the job of a Frenchman to teach a Bolivian military prosecuting attorney the history of his country. But since so much reference has been made to that history, gentlemen, here are the facts of history. Thus, Bolivia was liberated from the Spanish by men who came from every corner of Latin America to help found Bolivia and all of Latin America. And similarly the same fraternal union of Latin Americans, tested in combat and the life of the battle campaign itself, will liberate Bolivia from Yankee imperialism. A socialist Bolivia will be founded, and the whole continent whose centre is Bolivia will do the same.

'For Che the true difference, the true frontier, is not the one which separates a Bolivian from a Peruvian, a Peruvian from an Argentinian, an Argentinian from a Cuban. It is the one which separates Latin Americans from Yankees. That is why Bolivians, Peruvians, Cubans and Argentinians are all brothers in the struggle, and where one nationality is fighting, the others should also be fighting, because they have everything in common, the same history, the same language, the same patriots, the same destiny, and even the same master, the same exploiter, the same enemy which treats them all alike : Yankee imperialism. "In South America," said Bolivar, "the fight is for every man, no matter where he may be." When in 1821 Bolivar offered Pueyrredon, Chief Director of the Rio de la Plata Provinces, brotherhood and the direct aid of Venezuelans, he sent the following message : "All the republics fighting against Spain are united by one implicit and actual accord, by the identical nature of our cause, principles and interests; thus it seems our action should be the same united action."

'And this implicit accord became a flesh-and-blood reality in the army that went to liberate Bajo and Alto Peru, to create Bolivia, that army which the Liberator reviewed shortly before June, in Pasco, "where there were gathered together men from Caracas, Panama, Quito, Lima, Chile and Buenos Aires : men who had fought at Maipu in Chile, at San Lorenzo on the coast of Panama, at Carabobo in Venezuela and at Pichincha at the foot of the Chimborazo". Che, Bolivar's historical heir, did not have time to amass that army in the jungles of south-east Bolivia, but that was the idea. It is difficult, it seems utopian, but it is invincible, and will win. In his letter of 1815 from Jamaica, Bolivar launched the idea of an integrated Latin America, far removed from criminal individualisms, and the idea of integral Americans was born as well. A century and a half ago, this was a premature vision. And today it still seems premature to some, and that is why Che died; but his death was not in vain. Che will not have "sowed in shifting sands". He took up the tradition of liberation, the most patriotic, the most Bolivian, the most Latin American of traditions.

'Others have taken up chauvinism, in the spirit of individualist rancour, which has no roots in any part at all of the history of independence. When a tiger is marauding in a neighbourhood, and a lamb, just one of the flock, wants to keep its neighbour away by saying, "You are not from here. This part of the pasture does not belong to you, you have to stay in your country, which is on the other side of the river", this lamb, instead of getting all the others to unite against their principal enemy, betrays those of its own class, places their lives in danger as well as its own. It certainly must have made a deal to ally itself with the tiger, but it is wrong if it thinks that it can so escape the tiger's claws. No treaty of alliance can be valid between a carnivorous nation and one that can be eaten; in such a choice morsel as Bolivia, chauvinism, reactionary nationalism, is nothing more than a sentimental façade for the cold bricks of a sell-out treaty.

'I know, here we must limit ourselves to the facts, as you, Mr President, have repeatedly pointed out to me. The entire world recognizes the fact that guerrilla fighters commanded by Che are the heirs of the guerrillas of the first wars of independence of Bolivia's first patriots. If I have referred to present happenings and certain events in the past it is because even in this room, in this trial, in the presence of the widows of those soldiers who have been killed, it is not possible to distort this truth without distorting history itself. And now let us take up the second of the false charges against me, and note the fashion in which the prosecuting attorney tried to show that I was a high-ranking guerrilla leader. I shall be brief, because my defence attorney has already made the necessary statements in answer to the evidence presented by the prosecuting attorney. I simply wish to add a few words on certain points and to unmask the methods used by the prosecution.

'Ever since the opening of the charges and rebuttals, we have been subjected to a series of "revelations", very well spaced—one sensational revelation per day—and designed to confuse the issue completely. I say "revelations" because the documents or evidence exhibited were always presented by the prosecuting attorney "at the last moment", taken from who knows where, without giving the defence the opportunity of examining them or even learning of their existence. And I call these "confusing revelations" because it gives us something to ponder over, since, when my defence attorney could get near enough the exhibited evidence after the debate ended, he realized each and every time that the so-called evidence was a fraud. However, taking advantage of the professional modesty of the defence attorney, and his complete ignorance of what was being presented—as well as the enforced silence of the accused—the prosecuting attorney had a free hand to employ certain methods, sensationally juggling the facts with the national and official press acting as cynical accomplices.

'First revelation : two photographs in which I can be seen with a gun. One photo in the company of Che, the other alone. Newspaper headlines : "Debray photographed with weapons!" There is one important detail missing. That is, that there are no guns in the photographs; these are two pictures taken from a total of some thousand seized in a storeroom. But what does that matter? The effect has been achieved. Of course I recall very well when they were taken. They were taken at the base camp, and I had neither a holster nor a gun. I only carried a rifle when I did guard duty or went on hunting trips.

'Second revelation : my clandestine entry into the country. This was proven, newspaper headlines claimed. The weak point in this tale was that the prosecuting attorney had my passport in his possession and it had been stamped correctly. Then he dreams up the clever ruse of treacherous clandestineness. My "clandestine status" in Bolivia has been so immoral and so subtle and cowardly that I have not once departed from the most strictly legal procedure. I made contact with an unknown Bolivian who knew the password, the prosecuting attorney claimed, not recognizing that this would only prove that I needed a middleman to get to the guerrillas, because I couldn't go by myself, as no journalist can. And of course he has neglected to mention that I have been staying in hotels, travelling under my own name, with my passport, and that this has all been recorded.

'Another disclosure : I have lied on my declaration form, since I had entered Bolivia illegally from Peru in 1964. This was published in the press as an undeniable fact. But the trouble is that my passport shows the contrary. But what does that matter? It will then be said that I wished to cover up my expulsion from Peru in March 1964 by losing my passport in Chile and obtaining a new one. The trouble is that I lost my passport before that time, in Ecuador, in January 1964, and that is why I was deported from Peru, simply because I had no passport, only a safe-conduct issued by the French Embassy in Quito. But what did this matter to the prosecuting attorney and the press? What counts is to get a sensational headline.

'Another blow : my "guerrilla" notebook was "confiscated in Muyupampa". You can read there, according to the prosecuting attorney, in addition to things about my obsession for blood and capital punishment, that "Ramon gave me a mission to be carried out in Mexico"; that the Government press and the civil party were to repeat, very noisily. It was bad enough that this phrase is purely an invention, as you all realize. But, even worse, this notebook was written after my arrest, in my cell : what is written there are the circumstances of my arrest and the preparation for my execution. To top everything off, this notebook, of a strictly personal nature, was taken from me at gunpoint in Camiri by Major Echeverria, who later told me it had been lost. But it suddenly appeared in the hands of the prosecuting attorney. Such are the methods of the prosecution : seizure and alteration of personal papers.

'Another sensation : the diary of a physician, a guerrilla doctor, who was unknown to the prosecution. At first the document was read, skipping pages, phrases and words which contradicted the thesis the prosecution was trying to develop. Headline in the official press : "Che Brought in Debray and Bustos as Combatants." The diary says nothing of the kind; the doctor's diary simply expresses a personal opinion, since the doctor did not take part in leadership meetings, where our possible joining was discussed. But what does that matter? If one really wished to clarify this point, it would be sufficient to check the personnel registry, brought up to date by Rolando and now in the hands of the army, but this would have a negative publicity effect.

'A new revelation was a copy of *Revolution in the Revolution*, which was dramatically handed to the court after being found in the knapsack belonging to "Joaquin the Cuban", who fell at Vado del Yeso, proof that this book served as a breviary for the guerrilla. It could well be that Joaquin had it, because he had not read it before, and if it could help him in anything—this magnificent revolutionary—and instruct or divert him, I am happy. They forgot to tell the tribunal that every guerrilla had, as a general rule, three or four books in his knapsack, because a revolutionary can't leave off studying even for a single day. But why was *Revolution in the Revolution*, and not any of dozens of other books confiscated from fallen guerrillas, shown? They also forgot to tell the tribunal that the other copy of this booklet which Che Guevara read and wrote comments in one day in April, was simply found in the store in Nancahuazu, where Che left it with a hundred other books : novels, poems, short stories, reports and books on mathematics that he read in the camps.

'But the best thing, the most amazing thing, was the revelation of the maps. There we reach great theatrical art. It is, then, like the headline on page one of a large, supposedly Bolivian newspaper :

"Debray's Situation Seriously Compromised." And to what extent! First a sales slip for some commercial maps which I bought quite some time ago was presented, for purposes and under circumstances which appear in my declaration. Then the prosecuting attorney put a quantity of fifty maps found at Nancahuazu on the tribunal table, and felt satisfied. The demonstration was over; the official newspapers which form public opinion didn't ask for anything more. I bought maps, and the guerrillas had maps of the country. Conclusion, I had provided the guerrillas with their maps. The only thing is that, upon examination, it turns out that they aren't the same maps—neither in quantity, nor type of map, nor regions. . . . But what does that matter? The important thing is that both cases involve maps. Publicity doesn't need anything else.

'Why speak of a ridiculous report made by the police of Teoponte on the basis of rumours, three-fourths of which were invented? Why speak of false witnesses, who even contradict themselves?

'And as none of this "evidence" is convincing, and as it is widely known that I have not participated in any military action—not even in its preparation—that nor have I been a political commissar or anything like it, and that I never gave courses to any of the guerrillas, there only remains my work *Revolution in the Revolution*, which proves me, according to the prosecuting attorney, to be the "intellectual author" of the so-called murders of March 23rd and April 10th. That is the only resource they have left to justify— along with murderous nature—their request for the maximum punishment.

'I inform the tribunal that I would make myself perfectly ridiculous if I were seriously to accept, even for a moment, its flattering imputation that I have master-minded the guerrilla movement. Therefore, I do not want to answer that charge here personally. My defence attorney, in his summing-up, has perfectly demonstrated, by a simple analysis of this book and a simple relation of events and dates, how inane this accusation is. I will limit myself to the last part of the reasoning of Dr Novillo in his examination of this "evidence"—that is, *Revolution in the Revolution*, part of which he was prevented from reading by various interruptions by the judge advocate and by the public. It reads as follows :

' "c. Common meaning :

' "(1) In its chapter 'The Principal Lesson of the Present' the book in question culminates its description with the rejection of the system of political commissars, a system which, according to the author, 'does not seem to correspond to Latin American reality'. However, he does not know that the system of political commissars is the system used by the Bolivian guerrillas, as in the case of Inti and Coco Peredo, both of them political commissars and sub-chiefs. How is this to be explained if the book by Debray served as the code for the guerrillas?

' "(2) In the works by the sole and highest political and military leader of the guerrillas—works known throughout the world, which constitute true guerrilla manuals, complete with outlines, drawings, military details and technical instructions—such as *Guerrilla Warfare* and *Guerrilla Warfare: A Method* by Che Guevara, all the directives and norms followed by the guerrillas are found already shaped, so the work by the novice Debray would clearly be of little or no use in their organization.

' "(3) It is illogical and even ridiculous to think that a man such as Che Guevara and the experienced guerrillas who accompanied him would need the theoretical work of a twenty-six-year-old university man without any authority and of no military competence. The book was so unnecessary for the planning of their operations that they relegated it to their stores, along with a hundred other books, in spite of the fact that Che always had books with him in his knapsack."

'I want to apologize to the tribunal for having had to review all that has taken place in this trial in this way; for having had to get down to these details, to these petty items, to these common-sense considerations that, perhaps, do not interest you greatly—nor do they me. Both you and we know that none of this gets to the bottom of the matter. But since one ought, as the judge advocate has stipulated, to limit oneself to penal matters, the trial is reduced to this, the charges and rebuttals are reduced to this, and one ought to speak only of this. I have done so only to show you, gentlemen, how the charge has been pushed along from beginning to end : proceeding not from evidence to accusations, but from accusations to evidence —that is, from pre-established accusations to the search for evidence to back them up—and, on their not being able to find the necessary evidence, they have invented, constructed or altered it to fit their needs. The prosecuting attorney had no other way out. And this is why he sets his demand on the first day, even before the examination of evidence.

'Such a procedure is not accidental. At the beginning I spoke of a political—as well as police—machination, where the CIA played an outstanding role. Whether the CIA wants it or not—and certainly despite it—this process derives precisely from that organization. The "Debray case" was artificially created from the very day of my arrest. First, for truly political reasons, the Government has used me as a mere political instrument of agitation and propaganda. I offered the Government several advantages : I was a foreigner, a fact which permitted the Government to confront me with Bolivian nationalism; I was a Marxist-Leninist; I had written on revolutionary subjects; I was a friend of Cuba and her leaders, a fact that permitted the Government to speak of an alleged intervention by the Cuban Revolution, even though not a single item in my statements shows any relationship with Cuba except from the point of view of political friendship and ideological conviction. This also gave the Government the opportunity not to speak about other persons, thus focusing public attention entirely on me.

'And now comes the second pillar of the machination : the CIA. Since I had refused all his proposals and deals, the CIA representative—after making a full report to the Bolivian Government— gave the Government free rein to concentrate all its propaganda upon me, investing me with an importance, a significance they knew perfectly well was completely false. You may ask yourselves why, in defiance of all constitutional and humanitarian norms, I have been kept incommunicado for more than two months. Could it be because I've been subjected to many interrogations? No, very few of them. The first interrogations took place in Choreti—there's no mention in the record of many unpleasant meetings with CIA hired killers, excited officers who are much more experienced in punching and kicking than in questioning—and were conducted by an agent of the CIA, a Panamanian or Puerto Rican bearing the alleged name "Dr Gonzalez", an educated, shrewd man; once in the presence of Colonel Arana; on another occasion, in that of Major Quintanilla; and on still another occasion, in that of Major Sanchez. Never did this Dr Gonzalez pretend to believe that I was a guerrilla, much less a guerrilla leader. Since he was well acquainted with my record, with the way I had been arrested and the way in which guerrillas act, this gentleman came to the conclusion that I was directly involved in a confidential political mission abroad. The entire interrogation centred not upon the guerrillas but rather upon data, organizations and names—from France, Italy and Cuba—allegedly related to what he called "international communist espionage".

'They also showed great curiosity about Che. At that time I told them that I, too, shared their curiosity, that I—like any other journalist—had harboured the hope of locating him, but that I had been mistaken; that the major leader was Inti, etc. . . . They knew this wasn't true, but they lacked both eyewitnesses and detailed material evidence to prove it. That was all, until the same men, accompanied this time by Major Saucedo, Chief of the Second Section of the 8th Division, and always headed by the mysterious and powerful Gonzalez, showed up three weeks later at "Manchego".

'This time they were the bearers of fine eyewitness accounts and detailed statements, and I had to admit that I had succeeded in having a press conference with Che. I gave them a detailed description of that interview. Gonzalez, guided by a report written in English, asked me an endless number of questions about my *curriculum vitae* from my childhood to the present day. The interrogation lasted the whole day, but he was never able to verify the alleged clandestine liaisons, that alleged confidential mission which, according to him, was the cause of my presence here. He offered me protection and silence in the name of the Bolivian Government—even though he was not a Bolivian—if I should decide to co-operate with them. At the end he proposed that I make a public statement recanting "my acts and my ideas" and denouncing Cuba, communism, etc., in exchange for my prompt and discreet release. You can see how, for the CIA, there is no limit to unscrupulousness; no limit to its contempt for man. You can also see that in my case what it has been pursuing, from the very beginning, is not justice but propaganda.

'And here I wish to pay homage to the memory of Vazquez. On May 12th, 1967, I was told that he was kept under guard "like a religious relic", subject to every security measure, since a false priest,

39

a man disguised as a priest—they said—had come to kidnap him from the hospital. This makes the story of the escape—of which there is no serious proof—quite incredible. Of course, there is no proof of his murder; at least I don't know of any, and I must say, honestly, that to me, Vazquez's fate still remains a mystery.

'What is certainly not a mystery is the deceitful, cunning, perfidious way Vazquez was forced to confess by taking advantage of his physical weakness as he lay on a hospital bed. Vazquez was approached by a Panamanian who claimed to be a journalist of the Communist Party and a possible contact man with the outside. Thus deceived, Vazquez had no qualms about saying confidential things, which the man recorded. Later, Vazquez had to confirm and amplify these to the police. And, without a doubt, those who interrogated him, the same men who interrogated Bustos, myself and many others, must be in a position to clear up what really happened to Vazquez. I only want to make it clear to the court that Vazquez's statements—very important ones, as he had been present from the very time of Che's arrival—where he stresses that my status was that of a visitor, do not appear in the record, and that the unsigned loose leaf, which is there to substitute for the statements, does not fool anybody.

'After that May 12th the Bolivian and foreign investigators did return, but they never spoke to me again. There were no more interrogations, at least for me, until the end of my incommunicado period, a month and a half later, in Camiri. Why was I kept incommunicado for so long a time? Why didn't the United States bishop, Kennedy, show up before? Simply because more time was needed to set up this tremendous publicity and propaganda machinery against me, while simultaneously turning me into an important figure, a prominent figure, a first-class "criminal", a bloodthirsty adventurer who was also a master of "sensational revelations". The whole thing would be really comical had it not been so well arranged and, furthermore, arranged behind my back. When I heard about it in July I thought I was dreaming, and for several days I failed to grasp the full meaning implicit in the whole "show". And surely you could not help but be deeply impressed by that display of slander, lies and official as well as private attacks concentrated upon my person. What I am about to tell you may help you understand the reason for all that.

'At the beginning of July, one or two days after I appeared at the inquest before Judge Flores, several Cubans from the CIA arrived at Camiri to interrogate the prisoners once more. They introduced themselves as men sent by Dr Gonzalez or as substitutes for Dr Gonzalez. The one assigned to me has one great virtue : he is frank, and he spoke without beating about the bush. He asked questions about my address book—luckily a harmless book—which was taken from me in Muyupampa, and about other documents such as a credential from Mr Maspero, a card from the editor of *Sucesos* and some official French papers. This may explain why those documents could not be presented here. This man kept them in his brief-case and had to take them to Washington or some other place. This Cuban also spoke to me about Cuba, of certain statements made by Venezuelan prisoners, but what's important here is the man's evident frankness. Towards the end he said : "Everything depends upon our reports. Your fate is in your hands. We know very well that you're not a guerrilla chief, but you must have been entrusted with some clandestine mission which we are interested in learning about. If you co-operate with us, if you answer my questions truthfully, without trying to fool us, I assure you that all this machinery set up against you will be made to disappear very soon. We can destroy it in a few days, just as we built it up. Attention will be no longer focused upon you, and people will talk about you as they do about anyone else. No more speeches, no more press campaigns, no more posters in the streets, no more demonstrations."

'Mr President, as this man spoke to me, a few dozen people out there beneath my window were calling for my head.

'It appears that when this man left he wasn't completely satisfied with the result of the interview, so the little machine went on working faster than ever before. By all possible means, my name was systematically linked to that of Che, very cunningly making it appear that it was thanks to my "information" that his presence here was revealed, even though it was well known that he had been here since the middle of March. My name was linked to Fidel Castro's—as you have all seen on the posters that cover the walls of this building—as if there could be any possible comparison made between two historic leaders, two of America's leaders, and an ordinary journalist, a simple student of my age and nationality.

From Miami, from Washington, there came pamphlets, serial style, published by the great local press here depicting me as one who had drunk blood since childhood; or in Havana, breakfasting while a mass-execution was being held, and later as captured in the woods as I hid, trembling with fear, behind a tree. When infamy breaks loose there's no end to it, there's no limit to its inventiveness. Cruelty here, in Camiri, took very subtle forms : periods of unexplained "incommunicado" status, complete isolation in my cell, while other prisoners were together. It reached the point where I was forced to wear this striped uniform of a common prisoner, number 001, a uniform that had never been used before in Bolivia, not even for the common prisoners. A uniform that none of my fellow prisoners here, that none of the army prisoners had to wear. All this is a natural outcome of animosity, of a desire for revenge and of political frustration.

'And, to top the honour, you know how first all the publicity was oriented, aimed at me, and how later they said that I myself had looked for this publicity, as though I myself had chosen to be incommunicado for two months, as if I myself had staged this spectacle, as though I did not have to defend myself, to explain, to reveal the truth through the newsman within my reach. Was I supposed to listen silently and agree with this deluge of propaganda and inventions? Why should they call dignity in protest, the simple spirit of resistance, "haughtiness", "arrogance", "a desire to provoke them"? What do these gentlemen want? Collaboration, complicity, silence on all these proposals, these despicable offers, this plot? In the future I will be only as arrogant as they are insulting.

'Truthfully, I would not like to be in the place of those who set up this scene, and who have in their hands all the documents necessary to reveal the truth. The truth will out, even though it proves to be disappointing to the prosecuting attorney, the plaintiff or this tribunal. For some reason, I am losing prestige in General Barrientos's speeches. This "de-escalation" is inevitable. I began as a co-leader, I think, and I later became a political commissar, later intellectual author and combatant, and now the latest news I have been able to read calls me a simple "courier". This indeed is closer to the truth. It is a much better reflection of my exact role. I accept the term, if it is necessary by all means to find some way to include me in the guerrilla roster. It is true, gentlemen, that, in addition to my work, to my journalistic mission, I had some other missions to perform in France. Nothing out of the way. When Bustos and I left the guerrilla encampment Che was waiting for some people from outside—I mean from La Paz, true couriers. Unfortunately, they never arrived. And since no guerrilla could leave the front to carry out a mission in the city, on a strict order from Che, you find here one of the motives for the "failure of the guerrillas" in this political and military strictness so typical of Che, according to which no combatant once incorporated in the mountains could return to the plains. And since they could not go from the plains to the city either, perhaps this terrible misunderstanding arose, with each one waiting for the other to come to him to solve problems of the greatest urgency.

'Let's return to the trial. This political trial, in which the defence was not able to speak of anything except the Penal Code, and the prosecuting attorney was able to speak of everything except the Penal Code and especially of politics, is evidently symbolic. Guerrilla warfare is being tried here, through me. They have asked for thirty years' imprisonment for guerrilla warfare : I doubt very much that guerrilla warfare will tolerate it that long, and it is too bad that the prosecuting attorney does not have another more drastic sentence in his arsenal that would put an end to this problem. But, for the moment, the problem to be solved is something else, and it is very simple, much simpler : how to carry out such a trial with such defendants? If the civil party had a sense of humour, he would have taken some precautions as to his rhetoric before asking for "indemnity for damages and losses" for the military victims, from six defendants whose only common ground is that they do not deserve the name of guerrilla, and who have not, for many different reasons, ever fought against the Bolivian Army : three deserters who really deserve to be decorated for the inestimable service they have rendered the army; a large landholder, enemy number one of the guerrillas in its first zone of operations, one who denounced them to the authorities twice without really knowing exactly what the trouble was; and two liaisons, if you wish definitely to use that term : Bustos and I.

'This wasn't very promising material. Then they found the solution, they just had to think of it : instead of carrying out a trial appropriate to a so-called principal defendant, they have created a defendant to fit the trial they had planned. This way they have lifted me out of the most terse anonymity and raised me to this suspicious and undeserved notoriety. The player making his own rules, just as the prosecution has made up its own evidence. A great honour for one man!

'To attempt to try the Bolivian guerrilla movement through any one man is legally unacceptable, but morally, for this speaker, unimpeachable. But there is more. As the prosecuting attorney said in the beginning, it is Cuba which he wishes to try here through me; he wants to put Cuba on trial. But this I will never allow or accept. The prosecuting attorney called revolutionary Cuba a "centre of criminal insemination". The only "centre of criminal insemination" that I know of is the United States, which has exported its crimes, its bombs, spies, tanks and its warships to Panama, the Dominican Republic, Guatemala and Cuba. There is only one defendant in this room and that is Yankee imperialism and its lackeys. But since one cannot speak here of revolution and counter-revolution—a right which is reserved only for the prosecuting attorney—let me at least, Mr President, answer two concrete charges made by the prosecuting attorney. First he called me a "French-Cuban", a mercenary at the service of Cuba. This is just another adjective to him. To me it is both an honour and a cause for happiness. However, nothing in the world gives the prosecuting attorney the right to take away my nationality. Although it is true that my personal friends have helped me in my work, Cuba has nothing to do with my coming here or my trips through Latin America. My presence in Bolivia is solely the result of my personal decision, made with the agreement of my editor in France and a Mexican magazine. The fact that I worked in the University of Havana, like many Europeans, the fact that I have studied the revolutionary history of Cuba and have great admiration for it and those who made it, does not mean Cuba has any responsibility for my movements and personal initiative. I serve a cause and not a state; I respect that state because it serves that cause and not its selfish state interests simply because they may be confused with that cause. I take full responsibility for my actions. If the prosecuting attorney wishes to place Cuba on trial—and my declaration does not contain a single word about Cuba—may I remind him that there is an organization that specializes in this type of complaint : the Yankee ministry of colonies, also known as the OAS.

'The prosecuting attorney also said that I brought "my master Fidel's orders" to the Bolivian guerrillas. There is no doubt that he means that the Bolivian guerrillas received orders from outside. He knows this is not true. They received orders from no one except the leader they themselves had elected, Ernesto Che Guevara. Now I'm asking him to say what these orders were. Even the CIA had to return to Washington without proving a single one of these alleged orders. How could the CIA discover something that doesn't exist? Fidel does not give, nor is he able to give, orders to anyone, because no man, no matter how great he is, no matter how intelligent he is, no matter how generous he is, can dictate the course of history, avoid the unavoidable or do the impossible. No man can tell other men to sacrifice themselves for the cause of liberation, because men do not give up their comfort, their children, or the light of the sun, men do not die simply to follow another man's order, but rather for their convictions, through an inner choice, a necessarily personal one.

'But there is one even more insulting word in all of this, as insulting to me as it is to Fidel himself; and that is the word "master". The prosecuting attorney confuses master with friend. The master, the only master is the man who becomes rich through the work of the poor, the people of Bolivia, who exploits and humiliates them, loots and represses them, who has invested his dollars in Bolivian soil : Mr Johnson. Cuba has neither dollars nor privileges to offer anybody. She has nothing to offer but her example. The example of sacrifice, courage and austerity. It is up to everyone to choose between the master and the exemplary friend : between Johnson and Fidel.

'I am about to conclude.

'A lawyer for the civil party expressed his fear that the defence, by asking for clemency, might deny the winners the right to judge the losers. But who is asking for clemency? Who dares speak of winners? Who admits defeat? Has Che been defeated because he died? For many years Che risked his life and miraculously escaped death. Many years ago he made the decision to fight in the front lines wherever he was needed, here or anywhere else, and many years ago accepted his having to die at any moment. He used to say that his sacrifice would not mean anything, that it would only be an accident in the course of world revolution, and that afterwards it was up to each one of us to bring a seed out of his blood. There are some men who are even more dangerous when they are dead than when they were alive, even when those who fear them cut the hands off their bodies, cremate the bodies and hide the ashes. For us Che now begins to live, and the revolution continues.

'No, I will never ask for pardon for the losers. I will never address you as the winners. On the contrary, I say that, even though I regret that I am innocent of all the charges against me, I am guilty in your eyes for believing in Che's final and forthcoming victory. I am guilty of wanting to carry out the irreversible commitment made by any man who had the good fortune of seeing Che live, think and fight; the commitment of remaining faithful to him and following his example to the end, to the best of one's ability. I will do my best to be worthy some day of the disproportionate honour you will do me by condemning me for something I did not do, but which I now more than ever wish to do. And calmly, with all my heart, I thank you in advance for this harsh sentence I expect from you.

'I have finished.'

ERNEST MANDEL

The New Vanguard

Any analysis of the student revolt must start from one basic consideration : the university explosion. A new social grouping has emerged from the very vitals of capitalism, from all that it considers its essential 'achievement' : the higher standard of living, the advances in technology and the mass-media, and the requirements of automation. There are six million university students in the United States, two and a half million in Western Europe and over a million in Japan. And it proved impossible to integrate these groupings into the capitalist system as it functions in any of these territories.

The students have not found the necessary material facilities for their studies in the universities. They have not found the kind of education they were looking for. And above all when they leave the universities it is getting harder and harder for them to find the kind of jobs they rightly expected when they started their university education.

A young student writing in *Le Monde* the other day described 'our' society as a 'society of abundance', a society in which 'everyone' is now guaranteed full employment and a steady rise in his standard of living. Evidently, he did not put his glasses on when he read the Western European unemployment statistics. He did not see that in the last two winters there were three million unemployed in Western Europe. He did not see that the number of unemployed in France itself topped a half-million—and this in the midst of a Government-proclaimed economic expansion. He did not notice the large number of young people in this mass of unemployed, to say nothing of the still larger number which the statistics do not include. He did not see that the unemployment rate among the youth in the black ghettoes of the United States exceeds 20 per cent —which explains a lot of things. In brief, what he, as have innumerable devotees of capitalism, failed to see is that this system, far from solving all economic and social problems, has not even remedied the basic evils of nineteenth-century capitalism, while it has added a series of new contradictions that have proved more and more insoluble.

Capitalism confronts the student youth with insoluble contradictions, not only in the university but also in the economy and in bourgeois society, which is in permanent crisis. Some people have talked about the inadequacy of the universities and, like good reformists, called for university reform. Therefore, when the students turned their backs on this reform of the bourgeois university, they were accused of rejecting 'dialogue'. But what the students in revolt rejected was in fact dialogue within the pre-established and supposedly immutable framework of the bourgeois State, of the bourgeois governments in Western Europe and Japan.

The students have been told : 'The budget isn't large enough to guarantee all of you the university buildings, professors and assistants, restaurants, dormitories and, above all, the high quality education you demand right away. You have to be satisfied with gradually changing the existing situation, which we all agree is unsatisfactory.' And when the students are told this, they are a thousand times right to answer : 'Stop this nonsense about the appropriation for education and the resources of the public bodies. Talk in terms of the economic resources available in this society. Admit that while there isn't enough money for the universities, there is more than enough for advertising and superfluous gadgets. Admit that the reason you can't find the billions needed for a university system fit for the twentieth century is because you're squandering billions for your "*force de frappe*" (France's nuclear striking force). Admit that you are stifling immense productive, technological, cultural and intellectual forces because you prefer to create destructive forces.'

In this sense, and rightly, the students reject 'dialogue' and reject 'university reform' in the context of bourgeois society. For, they have understood the nature of this society. And this awareness, together with their special situation in society, has made them the weakest link in the neo-capitalist chain today, the first to crack throughout the Western world.

What the student revolt represents on a much broader social and historic scale is the colossal transformation of the productive forces which Marx foresaw in his *Grundrisse* (Outlines of a Critique of Political Economy) : the reintegration of intellectual labour into productive labour, men's intellectual capacities becoming the prime productive force in society.

This is still embryonic and is unrealizable within the framework of capitalist society, but it is already powerfully announcing itself. In speaking of a third industrial revolution, of a scientific revolution, many Marxist sociologists have not always drawn the obvious conclusion about the place of intellectual workers in society. They do not understand that as a result of profound changes in intellectual employment the majority of university graduates will no longer be bosses, or professionals, or even direct agents of the bosses with strictly supervisory functions, but white-collar employees of the State or industry, and thus part of the great mass of salaried workers. They do not understand the specific character of the student *milieu* as a special social stratum, with which students from bourgeois backgrounds often assimilate, breaking their ties with their family environment without yet being integrated into the social environment of their professions-to-be. There is an unwillingness to understand, or accept, a fundamental fact—that man's chief productive force will be his creative intellectual power. This intellectual power is only potentially productive today because capitalist society beats it down and stamps it out as pitilessly as it beats down the personality and creative impulse of the manual workers.

There is then at the base of the student revolt a high consciousness of a new dimension which has been added to the classical alienation of labour produced by capitalist society, produced by all societies based upon buying and selling.

We can say that this intellectual labour power is doubly revolutionary and productive today. It is so because it is conscious of the enormous wealth it promises, which could lead us rapidly to a classless society, to abundance. It is so because it is conscious of all the contradictions, injustices and barbarities of contemporary capitalism, and because the results of its becoming conscious are in themselves profoundly revolutionary. The development of this consciousness occurred first of all among the students, for a very simple reason : because the traditional organizations of the workers' movement are profoundly bureaucratized and long since co-opted into bourgeois society. When the workers' movement does not erect multiple barriers against the penetration of bourgeois ideology into the working class, most of the workers succumb, at least in 'normal' conditions, to the preponderant influence of bourgeois ideas—as Marx and Lenin never failed to repeat.

However, when among students who are a larger minority, they can free themselves by individual thought from the constant manipulation and mental conditioning of the great public-opinion moulding instruments in the service of bourgeois society and capitalism. This is precisely because students are in a more privileged social and intellectual situation than the workers.

It is an unquestionable fact that the revolt against the dirty imperialist war in Vietnam arose from the students and youth in the United States. It was these American students and young people who set in motion a powerful movement against this war, eventually drawing in masses of adult black workers and now beginning to affect the white workers also.

Essentially the same process has been set in motion in Western Europe and Japan. From among these students and young people emerged the most powerful mass-mobilization against the war in Vietnam, which at its outset went beyond the absolutely opportunist and capitulationist phase of movements 'for peace in Vietnam' or 'for negotiations'. We have seen young revolutionaries by tens of thousands go into the streets of Paris, Berlin, London, Copenhagen, Rome, Amsterdam and Brussels to launch the only valid slogan—the slogan of full and complete solidarity with the Vietnamese people, the slogan of victory for the Vietnamese revolution.

In its twofold revolt against the bourgeois university and the imperialist war, the student vanguard has become conscious of the necessity of rising up against bourgeois society in its entirety. Now, it is drawing logical revolutionary socialist conclusions from its anti-capitalist consciousness; it is preparing itself for a socialist revolution. For, without a proletarian socialist revolution, there will be no overthrow of the capitalist system, not in Western Europe, nor anywhere else in the imperialist world.

Another comment must be made on this subject. The 'revolutionary' concept, in the proletarian, Marxist sense of the term, has always implied another idea : 'internationalism'. This internationalism was demonstrated during the period when Che Guevara, an Argentinian, fought for the victory of the Cuban Revolution, then went on to die for the Bolivian Revolution. At a time when even the technocrats are talking about the need for a united Europe, a secretary of the French Communist Party describes our friend Danny Cohn-Bendit as a 'German anarchist'; on the contrary, it is Cohn-Bendit who represents proletarian internationalism, and the CP secretary who personifies *petit-bourgeois* nationalism.

The description that Comrade Bensaid has given us of the way in which the March 22nd movement was organized should remind us all of a striking parallel : the way in which Fidel Castro and Che Guevara began to organize the armed struggle in Cuba. They also began by saying : 'We are going to put aside the tactical differences that divide the various tendencies in the revolutionary movement. Once we agree on the essential thing, on the action to be initiated, on the way to break from the stagnation and backwardness of the traditional movement, on the way to initiate the struggle against imperialism and the oligarchy in Cuba by the armed road, we will little by little create a process that will gradually accelerate by its own internal logic, that will make it possible to classify and reclassify the various tendencies by experience.'

This attitude is essential for all who want to free themselves from the empty verbalism which has done so much harm. After a certain point, the movement can only progress through action, and the absence of action condemns it to permanent division and prolonged sterility.

As other comrades before me have said, an urgent task is the integration of the students into the workers' movement. Yes, the workers' movement must win back the student movement, particularly inasmuch as the students are workers. But this cannot be accomplished by way of the ossified and bureaucratized structures of the traditional workers' organizations. It is within the working class, rising up in spontaneous struggle against the capitalist system,

51

creating its own new leadership, its own committees, that this will take place, through action and in action, in their mutual interest, the supreme interest, of the revolution. It will not take place in the traditional organizations, because of the spirit which today inspires this new, young revolutionary vanguard. And if we fight for this union, if we fight for this alliance and this convergence between the student revolt and the struggle for the proletarian revolution in Western Europe, it is because we know very well that neither by virtue of the place which they hold today in society can the students alone overthrow bourgeois society in the West.

They can and they must play a powerful role as detonator. By playing this role within the working class, above all through the intermediary of the young workers, they can free in the working class itself enormous forces for challenging capitalist society and the bourgeois State.

Today we see on a world scale the rise of anti-imperialist and anti-capitalist forces, an authentic new world revolutionary ascent. The heroic struggle of the Vietnamese people against American imperialism, the Cuban Revolution, the struggle of the courageous guerrillas in Asia, Africa and Latin America, and the struggle of the black masses in the United States for racial and social libera-tion, are all basically one and the same struggle.

And this struggle of the most oppressed masses, of the masses of the countries of the Third World and of the black masses in the United States, is beginning today to receive a significant response in the imperialist countries. This is evidenced by the mass-mobiliz-ation against the dirty war in Vietnam; the mass-mobilization of the student movement; by the mass-mobilization of the young workers in very arduous strikes and demonstrations in Le Mans, Caen, Turin, and in Bremen and Essen against Springer. An integral part of this struggle is the struggle of the student and intellectual vanguard in the so-called socialist countries of Eastern Europe and the USSR. We send particularly warm greetings to the students and workers in the vanguard of this struggle. For, as much as we are on the side of the Soviet Union and the 'socialist camp' in any confrontation with imperialism or the *bourgeoisie*, we support also our comrades Kuron and Modzelewski, and the courageous vanguard of workers and students of Warsaw and Poland in their fight against bureaucracy and for real soviet democracy, which can only be a democracy of councils, a democracy based on workers, students and poor peasant councils as Lenin taught us.

When this world-wide struggle that is already in progress makes it possible to draw in the adult workers against the incomes policy, against the *économie concertée* (union Government agreement to hold down wages), against the revival of unemployment, against job insecurity, against the integration of the unions into the bourgeois State, against the more and more marked drift everywhere in Western Europe towards authoritarian, 'strong states', against NATO and the Atlantic Pact, to achieve a revival of the workers' movement which will develop into workers' struggles challenging the capitalist system itself, then we can transform today's vanguard into a mighty revolutionary party, marching at the head of the masses.

Then, all together, we will be invincible. Then, all together, we will complete the great work begun fifty years ago by the October Revolution, and bring about the victory of the world socialist revolution!

TOM FAWTHROP

Towards an Extra-Parliamentary Opposition

STUDENTS TODAY—WORKERS TOMORROW

Over fifty years after the Russian Revolution and forty-four years
after the first Labour Government in Britain, a vital truth is beginning to stir the conscience of socialists in this country—a conscience
that has always been more effective as a smokescreen than as a
real agency of social change. This truth, for so long buried beneath
the myths of the Cold War and of welfare statism, is simply that
socialism cannot be reached by the path of social democracy.

The year 1968 will be remembered as the period when the
frightened rulers of the USSR sent their troops into Czechoslovakia,
but it will also be remembered as the year of France and as the year
of an international student protest which treated national boundaries with the contempt they deserve. The most effective socialist
response to the Cold War has been led by students who have made
Vietnam and, more recently, Czechoslovakia, the focus of their
revolt. The capitalist press, to its own intense consternation, finds
itself unable to account within the traditional framework of abuse
for this international movement towards socialism. The phrase
'Kremlin conspiracy' today carries no conviction when applied to
the young people of Europe. The independence and spontaneity
of the movement, its total lack of subservience to any manipulative
ideology—Russian or Western capitalist—provoke the politically
illiterate into indignant cries of 'Anarchy'.[1]

But despite the obvious desire of the press to invalidate the movement by giving it labels which would make it unacceptable to most of their readers, even they have been compelled to admit that it was not the representatives of the Right who mobilized protest against the Russian invasion of Czechoslovakia. The first and the most effective protests were led by the same people who have regularly protested against the American invasion of Vietnam. It was interesting to see that these people, who are normally attacked in the press for their behaviour over Vietnam, were suddenly transformed, by the press, in their relationship to the struggle for freedom in the world. It would be hard to find a clearer example of Western double standards. This hypocrisy was seen again in all its self-righteous moralizing in the Labour Government's attack on the USSR : 'Russian imperialism . . . a savage denial of the right to self-determination of the Czech people. . . .' We may contrast this with the failure to castigate American imperialistic domination, which includes in its long list of offences military intervention in Greece, Iran, Guatemala, the Dominican Republic and South Vietnam. This is seen, of course, as 'defence of the Free World'.[2] This double standard is part of the vicious game of power politics which we know as the 'Cold War'. It is a game played at the expense of the working classes of all the countries involved, both Eastern and Western. For it is their standard of living and hope for the future which is being steadily depressed by virtue of their paying for the monstrous armaments budgets of the big powers which play that game.

Propaganda, oppression and manipulation, together with the frequent betrayals of social democracy, have resulted in the virtual paralysis of the masses. It is because of this that the student movement has mushroomed in importance. The developing role of the movement as a major political force is not the result of a monolithic organization. It rests instead upon the natural coalescence of shared aims and ideals within a common framework of international oppression. Students are reacting to similar stimuli everywhere : to the explicit police states of Eastern Europe; to the

---

[1] Of course there are anarchists among the revolutionary groups, just as there are a variety of other radical views represented, but 'anarchy' is, to say the least, an inadequate description of what is being urged.

[2] For a full account of US policies in the Cold War see David Horowitz, *From Yalta to Vietnam*.

thinly disguised but no less coercive police states of the West. It is simply the case that in France, Italy, West Germany and in so many other 'free' countries, civil rights rest on exceedingly frail foundations; these 'civil rights' are seldom able to secure militant students from the same threat of arbitrary arrest faced by their comrades in Poland, East Germany and Hungary.

IDEOLOGY OF THE WESTERN STUDENT MOVEMENT

Although the movement is inspired by men such as Marcuse, Che, Trotsky, Mao and others, it is more than something built upon revolutionary textbooks. The ideology of a live movement can only be understood in the context of the experience and development of its members. The ideology of the old factions and sects on the Left may stand still and ossify; the ideology of the new movement does not and cannot. For it has realized that further progress along the path of socialism means throwing aside the rotting corpse of social democracy, upon which the vultures of Fabianism, careerism and orthodox communism are still sustaining themselves. These three with their necrophiliac passion for a dead social democracy are themselves to be thrown on the rubbish-heap as the last of the 'reformists'.

The failure of the parliamentary Left is not peculiar to the Labour Party, but is to be seen in all the social-democrat parties throughout Europe. Even the watered-down version of socialism espoused by these parties is ditched once they come to office and are compelled to face the harsh 'realities' of economics. To face these 'realities' with plans, pamphlets and goodwill is not enough —international bankers are not well known for their love of the man-in-the-street or for any lasting interest in a more humane social order. The problem is that the movement of working men and women which helped form the social-democrat parties has now lapsed into an apathy born of political frustration and disillusionment, with the result that the whole concept of a Labour movement has become an empty symbol. We have only to consider the role of Transport House in Britain in suppressing the spontaneous activity of large numbers of people within the Labour Party— particularly the Young Socialists—and in replacing that spontaneity with a dead electoral machine, to recognize the symbol for what it is. Once the machine had served its purpose, Parliament and the Cabinet were essentially on their own. They began to glory in a fictitious autonomy which was, in fact, completely dependent upon the political attitudes of those who occupied the 'commanding heights' of the economy. Time and again, both in Britain and on the Continent, the moderate policies of ostensibly reforming governments have been frustrated by powers not accounted for in our constitutional analyses. Thus we see that the moderate reforms of labourism such as full employment, an adequate health service completely financed by Government spending, full education (granting, for a moment, the traditional meaning of that word), are all being abandoned as a result of the needs of Western capitalist economic hegemony. As more and more reformist governments founder, so we see a growth in the apathy and despair of the electorates of Western Europe. We have learnt the lesson of social democracy : reforms are only acceptable if and when they do not damage the essential interests of capitalist economies.[3] Such interests have little to do with either the needs of the people on the one hand or the human and material resources available on the other.

No reformist government can go far without massive popular support of the kind once enjoyed by the Labour movement in Great Britain. But it is now too late for the social-democrat parties of Europe, including the Labour Party, to change their élitist ways. They have all been drawn into the web of consensus government and are effectively isolated from their bases of mass-support. The oligarchic careerists at the top of these parties have effectively trapped the idealists at the bottom. As a result of this encapsulation the whole notion of socialism has been distorted by the Cold War, bureaucratization and by both Eastern and Western failure. Thus it is that the real voice of socialism is all but inaudible to the vast majority of the working population. It is because of all this that in the future progressive social reform in Europe will be increasingly identified with revolutionary change, for such change will depend

---

[3] Economic and political power must be largely equated, since it is impossible to wield the former without deeply affecting the latter. It is only economists or those with a particular axe to grind who insist that there is no vital connection between the two.

57

more and more upon the power of the 'masses' countervailing against the weight of dead political establishments.

It is here that the connection with the student movement is made, for its ideology is to be found in the language of socialism, of Karl Marx. This is not the depersonalized and denatured Marx worshipped by some, nor the doctrinaire Marx fashioned by others : the movement is talking the language of the Marx who recognized the creative power of man and who saw how this creativity was and is suppressed by the forces of an oppressive environment. It is a language in which history may be seen in terms of the 'anonymous' masses, the collective force of mankind, who will always be the essential basis for human liberation from all forms of tyranny. It is these 'anonymous' masses, the ordinary people, who are the backbone of the resistance in Czechoslovakia and Vietnam today. The critics of Marxism usually miss the point, for what they are thinking of and, against all the evidence, insist upon calling 'Marxism', is the rigid defence of nineteenth-century formulations common on the traditional 'Left' and which is actually the very negation of the spirit of Marxism. Marxism as an analytical method and as a political perspective on a changing world continues to guide and inspire man in his perpetual struggle against oppression. A Marxist account of things gives the ideological content to struggles of every kind, from that of the fight against feudalism, landlordism and neo-colonialism in the backward countries to the battle against the most sophisticated forms of oppression and alienation to be encountered in the industrial society of modern monopoly capital.

We talk of different Marx's and of differing Marxisms, quite aside from the corrupt and incorrect forms to be encountered among so many revisionists. To do so is merely to reflect the vast intellectual stature of the founder of modern socialism : he was able to organize a chaotic mass of human phenomena and bring into a single and all-embracing sociology of revolution the insights of many disciplines. His particular blend of philosophy, history, economics, social psychology and politics is so remarkable an achievement that most of us are only able to come to grips with fragments of it. It is this fragmentation which accounts for so much of the obvious distortion of his work and ideas. Thus in place of an advancing revolutionary methodology we find a creed, an 'ecclesiastical' dogma, a 'Church'—for instance, the Kremlin and the orthodoxy of Muscovite communism. The line of descent, which begins with the foundation of the Cheka in 1918, is that line of distortion which finally degenerated into the falsifications of Stalinism.

One of the great ironies of history is the way in which Marxism was 'inevitably' stood on its head.[4] Thus it has become impossible for doctrinaire Marxists to allow for any socialist account of revolutionary activity outside a highly industrialized community. Poor and backward countries fighting for their freedom from capitalist hegemonic control cannot, in the view of the 'orthodox', produce socialist revolutions. It is in this sense that by the time of Stalin the dialectic had turned full circle.

Whatever the grotesque perversions of the basic principles of Marxism,[5] it is clear that the overriding concern of Marx is what has been taken over by the students, the concern for revolutionary FREEDOM.

FREEDOM

From the Berlin Wall to the paddy fields of Vietnam the 'democracies' of men such as Ulbricht and Johnson are imposed upon their victims by the gun. These barbarous régimes, engaged in the systematic destruction of human life, justify their actions in the name of freedom. If there is one overwhelming political fact to be proclaimed, it is that the communist world is not communist and that the free world is not free.

Freedom is not the subjective experience of the powerless individual who celebrates the survival of Parliament or Congress once in every five years. Nor is freedom a matter of abundant supermarkets, bingo-halls and casinos. We have to realize that the concept of freedom in our society is permeated by monetary values;

---

[4] One of the many disastrous distortions of Marx's own position has been the tendency on the part of some Marxists and some Marxian critics to turn him into an economic determinist. To do this is, of course, simpler than coming to terms with the extreme subtlety of his analysis.

[5] These are spelt out in their most accessible form in Karl Marx and Friedrich Engels, *Manifesto of the Communist Party*.

it is just another commodity available to those who have the money to buy it. Unfortunately, most workers cannot afford a first-class packet of freedom which should include economic security, travel abroad, guaranteed promotion, opportunity to choose and change one's job, etc. For the majority a second-class packet is the most that can be expected—a packet which gives them the 'freedom' of expression, the right to oppose the capitalist system and the right to strike. But freedom of expression must not be exercised in working hours; opposition is fine, so long as it is confined to Speakers' Corner; and the workers are free to strike provided they get the agreement of the employers, the Government, the Prices and Incomes Board and the TUC first. The second-class packet of freedom offered to the citizens of the countries controlled by Soviet bureaucracies also contains such 'freedoms' as a controlled press and the periodic celebration of a dictatorship.

What is meant by freedom in the language of socialism is that condition in which men own and control the resources of their own society; that condition in which those resources are used for the greatest benefit of the majority. This control can never be an abstract relationship between men and the means of production, but a concrete and democratic relationship between power and resources on the one hand and men on the other. Such a relationship is one in which there is collective democratic control over all the managerial functions of the society. Unless freedom is understood clearly as the actual and concrete power of action by an individual in relationship to his social environment, then it becomes the empty phrase of propaganda. Freedom as is pursued now by the old-established societies of the world makes a mockery of man who, in these societies, has become the mere tool of his own creations and is overshadowed by the technological world of his own making.

However, this technological world in which we live is not simply a neutral formulation consequent upon industrial development : it is a specifically political formulation, with values and directions given it by the socio-economic system called capitalism. This system, with its own needs and priorities, is not in any way fundamentally changed by the development of technology; rather, it gives direction to the forms technological development shall take. We have also to see that technology does not alter the basis of capitalism, and that this kind of society is not affected by a greater degree of central planning, by the provision of fringe welfare benefits, nor even by the introduction of State control of some industries. All these things are a normal part of the growth of monopoly capitalism. Clearly the age of corporate or oligopoly capitalism satisfies the bureaucratic socialists of labourism. These anyway were never able to conceive of socialism as the self-determination of millions struggling against the twin threats of fascism and corporate capital in order to establish the kind of society Marx saw as the destiny of all men.

Freedom is both an individual and a social concept. Individual freedom is, in a sense, negative (the protection of civil and personal liberties), and is dependent on the idea of social freedom. Social liberty concerns the positive way in which individuals can determine their own future by political action within the framework of a classless society. In a society dominated by a class structure, civil liberties and personal freedom have always meant much less to those in the 'lower' classes than to those in the 'upper'. Such liberties tend to flourish only in quiescent times, when people are apathetically accepting the social injustices of their class society. They are seen not to be liberties once the majority is mobilized against the structures of power, the best recent example of which is to be seen in the May 1968 revolution in Paris.

STUDENT POWER AND WORKERS' CONTROL

Broadly speaking, the points we have been considering are what form the ideological background to the student movement. Revolutionary socialism is the political movement of those who are struggling to create an alternative form of industrial society. One which does not take for granted the permanent division of humanity between the rulers and the ruled; one which does not insist upon the rigid separation of those who use their brains from those who use their hands. These are the divisions which keep men subject to their capitalist masters—and so long as students and workers are kept apart, the ruling classes have little to fear. The worst they will suffer will be the consequences of an occasional demonstration or the inconvenience of a few strikes.

'Student Power' is the collective expression given to the resistance of students to all the ideological pressures of capitalism;

pressures which permeate the entire capitalist system. It is a natural expression of Marxism in the twentieth century and has come about because students are beginning to recognize the extent to which all institutions of higher learning are being incorporated into and becoming subservient to the system and needs of monopoly capital. The immediate target of student revolution is the educational structure, precisely because, as with technology, it has become an instrument of the capitalist state. We can see this in a number of ways :

(1) The capitalist educative system is one primarily for an élite and reflects the different educational opportunities available to the different classes within the society.

(2) These differences are all too obvious in the institutions of tertiary education, where we see a binary structure setting up different classes of students. Hence the difference between universities, colleges of technology, etc.

(3) Capitalist ideology, with its values and assumptions sustaining the myth of the affluent society, is concentrated in the universities and colleges of higher education.

(4) The authoritarian and hierarchical nature of primary and secondary education is perpetuated in universities and colleges, although its manifestations are different. The lack of democracy in higher education is evident in the way that the power to determine the ideological patterns of the courses rests solely in the hands of the authorities.

(5) Both (3) and (4) tend to condition students into acceptance of the capitalist norms. That is, students come to accept the university hierarchy and to accept the training for and allocation to the higher echelons of capitalist society.

Thus student power is concerned to achieve collective action that will substitute democratic for capitalistic education, democratic education as opposed to the education of a select few from whom the governing classes are drawn. In a way there are great contradictions in the existing educative system, for it includes at once the values of liberal education and the demands of capitalist society. But these liberal values are the values of the past—the 'well-rounded personality' of the liberal dream is what has produced capitalism.

Socialists must transform that dream and relate it to a wider struggle, one which is taking place in all sectors of society. It is the struggle for a new social order based upon the workers' democratic control of industry.

The basis of any student/worker alliance will be their common aims and objectives in taking control of their respective working situations. Socialism without workers' control is no more than a vast state bureaucracy, in which the nature of human relationships remains substantially unchanged. Perhaps, if the Czechs succeed in getting rid of Russian control, we may see the beginnings of a genuine socialist society. But even so, Czech communism is still far removed from Marx and the total freedom and democracy demanded by revolutionary socialism. The dictatorship of the pro-letariat has often been misinterpreted, but for Marx the notion was akin to that of the Paris Commune :

> The Commune was formed . . . by universal suffrage in the various wards of Paris, who were revocable at any time. The majority of its members were naturally working class . . . the police, which until then had been the government, was at once stripped of all its political attributes, and turned into the *responsible* and at all times revocable instrument of the Commune. So were the officials of all the other branches of the administration. From the members of the Commune downwards, public service had to be done at workmen's wages. The privileges and the representation allowances of the high dignitaries of state disappeared along with the dignitaries themselves. . . . Having once got rid of the standing army and police.[6]

This was the first attempt at the practice of Marxism, in Paris in 1871; this was the first soviet in operation. Since that time these revolutionary institutions have spontaneously sprung up to challenge the old order in more than half a dozen countries. In Russia in 1905 and 1917, in Germany, Hungary and Bulgaria, during the Spanish Civil War and even in the Hungarian Revolution in 1956. The way in which revolutionary history constantly repeats itself, the dogged determination with which the workers establish soviets whenever a situation of socio-economic crisis gives them the oppor-

[6] V. I. Lenin, *The State and Revolution.*

tunity, provides a graphic demonstration of the essentially spontaneous basis of every revolution. The soviet is the basic political organ
of any future socialist government. Representative 'democracy', in
which all decision-making is handed over to a governing élite every
few years, is the natural political form of capitalism, but a new
society built upon a non-élitist basis needs new political institutions.
Such new institutions would mean :

(1) That all decision-making of basic social consequence be
carried on by public groupings.

(2) That politics is seen positively; that is, as the art of creating
collectively an acceptable pattern of social relationships.

(3) That politics has the function of bringing people out of isolation and into the community, thus making it a necessary part
of finding meaning in personal life.[7]

Soviets can function properly because their members have a
genuine control over decision-making. It is these groupings which
can also, through mandated delegates, exercise control over the
wider social groupings. It is thus that government becomes the
concern and *practice* of all, and not simply the privilege or voca-
tion of a few. In short, politics is about the quality of life of every
citizen.[8]

FROM UTOPIA TO REALITY

When observed from the comfortable, settled and complacent view-
point of middle-class life, the idea of workers' control and self-
government seems to be a utopian dream. The middle class do not
feel the need, during periods of social calm, to break out of the
ideological fetters of the old order; thus they assume automatically
that while workers' self-government is a 'nice idea', in reality it
could not work. Provided that the consumer goods continue to
flow in their direction, they are content to ignore the fact that their
settled order is the product of an underpaid, overworked and

[7] Cf. Paul Jacobs and Saul Landau, *The New Radicals*.
[8] The self-governing function of the soviets in Russia was destroyed in
the course of the civil war in 1918 and never restored.

largely socially excluded, working class. As long as the settled order continues for the middle class, they will always opt for private solutions to social problems.

However, it is largely political myopia that prevents us from seeing the infinite potentialities of the future. Of course, if we analyse the political attitudes of workers today and, on the basis of these attitudes, predict a future revolution, we are merely being unrealistic. But for those of us who are revolutionaries this is beside the point; unlike any other political group, we should be aware of the eternal reality of change. Continuous change in attitudes, in political responses, changes in the economy, changes in the political perspective and structure, changes in the degree to which the nature of capitalist social control becomes overt, above all changes in the whole theory of revolution in modern industrial society, are all part of the day-to-day reality of what is to be assessed when considering revolutionary potential. Change transforms yesterday's dream into today's reality—the impossible suddenly becomes the possible. This we have seen in the events in France during May 1968. Who, even in mid-April, could have predicted that in a month's time nine million workers would occupy their factories and demand workers' management (*autogestion*) of industry? Even in Britain we have seen enormous changes within the last three years; thus student militancy, unheard of in 1966, is now an accepted force in a dynamically changing political scene.

Apathy is a malaise induced by temporary political failure. It is the common expression of the sense of powerlessness felt by ordinary people, it is their resignation in the face of events. The reality of revolution depends on the mass of workers and students together refusing to accept their 'fate' and on their rejecting the *bourgeoisie*. Students and workers must unite in their common recognition of the efficacy of collective action on a mass scale to end, once and for all, the subordination of men to machines and the class which owns and manipulates them.

Soviets have never yet failed as a result of any supposed weakness in the idea; they have always been destroyed by the weight of counter-revolutionary capitalist or, as in the case of Hungary in 1956, Russian, armed might. The spectacle of real democracy in action has always been too much for the benefactors of the 'free' world to stomach. The real problem behind workers' control and self-government is not a technical one, for the specialists will still be there, they are after all workers, but the directors will go. The experts, the scientists, the specialists and all their equipment will be working alongside the shop-floor workers for a democratic enterprise in which those who work there will be able genuinely to declare : 'This is *our* factory, and this is *our* society.' For the democratic, revolutionary society will be shaped and moulded by the total participation of all those who live in it. It is simply the case that everything to do with efficiency and bureaucracy in society turns on the question of how that society is organized; on whether that society is organized for minority or majority participation in decision-making.

This is the 'crunch', this the political question underlying workers' power in modern industrial society. Behind the façade of technical sophistication, behind the complexity of modern industrial society, lies the basic conditioning factor of political command and economic power. Workers' control will inevitably remain merely a 'nice idea' until the workers themselves seize the power which is theirs to rid themselves of the technocratic assumptions embodied in the *status quo*. Such self-confidence can only be acquired through the act of revolution itself.

When that revolution comes, let us remember the ironical experience of the Bolsheviks and let us hope that we, unlike them, are able to keep pace with the political consciousness of the workers.

TARIQ ALI

The Extra-Parliamentary Opposition

The last few years have proved one fact quite conclusively, a fact which has been highlighted by the economic crises confronting the advanced capitalist countries of Western Europe. It is now abundantly clear that the problems which arise from the functioning of modern or neo-capitalism cannot be solved within the framework of the existing social structures. They can be dealt with in the short term by classic capitalist remedies (deflation, import controls, export subsidies, devaluation, etc.), but in the long run they will continue to plague capitalist societies. These societies will continue to be afflicted by the internal contradictions of the system; contradictions which will finally tear them apart.

The events of May 1968 in France, discussed elsewhere in this book, have proved beyond doubt the validity of the Marxist concept of alienation. The Renault workers are the highest paid in France : they were not on strike for higher wages, but for something much more far-reaching—control of the industries where they worked ! What France proved was that it is no longer necessary to have 1920-type slumps, that it is not essential to have twenty million unemployed before you have a crisis situation. A relatively small number of unemployed is sufficient to shatter confidence in the system. In France this confidence *was* shattered. French capitalism had to be saved by the French Communist Party, thus proving to all those who still needed proof that the PCF was in reality behaving in a

67

classic social-democratic fashion. Even Bernstein would have wept.

The trend in Western Europe today is a trend towards consensus government, towards a corporate state. The crisis in the international balance of payments has accelerated the process of political and economic authoritarianism. We have the Grand Coalition in Bonn; the tacit coalition in France; a consensus government in Britain. The political régimes in the advanced capitalist countries are beginning to grow more and more alike, more and more authoritarian, more and more repressive. The existing differences are quantitative rather than qualitative. The two important characteristics which bind these régimes together are (a) the complete interpenetration between economic and political power and (b) the institutionalization of the class struggle via the bureaucratic leaderships of the trade unions, which at worst act quite blatantly on behalf of the employers and at best contain the workers' struggle and attempt to channel it in limited, and mainly symbolic, forms.

Britain is no exception to this trend. It is not necessary to detail the iniquities of the Labour Government. By now most people should be aware of them. British social democracy is simply trying to fulfil its historic role—that of holding back the traditional organizations of the workers while cuts are made in workers' living standards in order to solve the economic problems facing British capitalism. Although the submission of the trade unions has been virtually accomplished, the economic problems have multiplied disastrously. Even the loyalist trade unions are beginning to show signs of strain because of the flagrant anti-trade-union policies of the Labour Government. The Labour Party, if anything, is crusading to save British capitalism; this crusade is one in which even the limited reformism envisaged in the Party's election manifestoes has been sacrificed on the altar of capitalist necessity. At home the Labour Government has adopted traditional Tory policies. It has pandered to racialist Tory demands and in some cases has gone even further to the right than the Tories themselves would ever have dared. In foreign affairs Labour has faithfully reflected the policies of the United States State Department. The first time Labour leaders dared to show their face in public was. at a public meeting in Hyde Park at the time of the Soviet invasion of Czechoslovakia—an invasion which was of course condemned. The *New Statesman*, a consistent apologist for the 'progressive' wing of the

Labour Cabinet, commented : 'It has always been an axiom of British foreign policy that *we* stand up for smaller nations.'[1] Forgotten was the betrayal of Jagan in Guiana; forgotten were the rights of the people of Vietnam, Greece, Portuguese Guinea, Zimbabwe (Rhodesia), South Africa, Portugal; forgotten was the butchery, which Britain helped the Federal Nigerian Government perpetrate, of the Biafrans.

It should be mentioned that in the face of these betrayals of the most elementary principles of reformist politics, the response of the reformist section of the parliamentary Labour Party was totally inadequate and half-hearted. How these well-meaning reformists were duped by Barbara Castle, Anthony Greenwood and Judith Hart under the direction of Harold Wilson is a story in itself that has been brilliantly recounted in great detail elsewhere.[2] Suffice it to say that the reformists were completely ineffectual. When finally they decided that some act of faith was necessary, they produced a document called the 'Socialist Charter'. Their weekly organ, *Tribune*, proudly described itself as the 'paper which supports the Socialist Charter'. It was left to a reporter of the revolutionary socialist bi-monthly, *The Black Dwarf*, to expose this fiction :

Just as the coffin is being lowered into the grave, alongside the hopes of those who have looked for a mass movement of Labour's Left against Wilson, there has come a faint knocking from the inside of the box. On reopening the coffin the corpse is seen to have a flicker of life still left. A weak smile hovers on its pallid face. Pinned to its chest is the undoubted document, written on parchment and entitled : THE SOCIALIST CHARTER. 'Sign here please !' mutters the corpse.[3]

And to prove that this was not mere rhetoric, the writer attacked the very corner-stone of the new Charter :

The Charter contains nothing new. Demanding 'Economic Independence' it plugs a utopian, reactionary, economic nationalism; it talks about planning, without asking WHO plans; demanding an extension of public ownership until the *public* sector dominates

[1] *New Statesman* editorial (September 6th, 1968).
[2] Paul Foot, *The Politics of Harold Wilson* (Penguin, 1968).
[3] *The Black Dwarf* (August 14th, 1968).

69

the private, it shows an extreme naïveté in imagining that the bourgeoisie will be expropriated *en masse* by their own state; it demands that profits, prices and dividends be 'controlled' : *this is impossible*. Either smash capitalism or a Labour Government (like Wilson's) will administer it according to its own laws.[4]

In these circumstances, therefore, it was inevitable that a mass-movement would begin to develop against labourism, against parliamentary hypocrisy and against the existing social structure. As in European countries, it was the youth who first came out on the streets. And in Britain as elsewhere the reason for the mass-mobilizations was the war in Vietnam.

VIETNAM VIETNAM VIETNAM

The struggle being waged by the Vietnamese people against United States imperialism has no precedent in history. It has shown the world that a superior form of political organization and political ideology can never succumb, not even to the power of the most advanced capitalist technology in the world. The resistance of the Vietnamese has exposed to the whole world (not least to the American soldiers involved in the fighting) the brutality and the viciousness which hides behind the myths of opulence and 'representative democracy'. It has exposed the acquisitive nature of neocapitalism and by its heroic resistance has reawakened a socialist consciousness in the West which had been virtually dormant since the beginning of the Cold War. And indeed the Vietnamese are aware of the historical importance of their struggle. They realize perfectly well that an American defeat in Vietnam would give a badly needed upsurge to the revolutionary movement in Asia and Latin America, and indeed the spectre of the Latin American revolution knocking on the doors of the United States itself is a heartening thought. In an interview with me in Hanoi in January 1967 the North Vietnamese Prime Minister stressed this fact time and time again : 'Tell the comrades in Western Europe that the Vietnamese people are fighting for them as well. . . . Internationalism is in our blood.'

[4] Ibid.

And there is little doubt that in times to come we will look back on this century as the years when the success of the Bolsheviks in 1917 inspired men to unheard-of feats of heroism and bravery. The Long March undertaken by Mao Tse-tung's peasant warriors will never be forgotten; Fidel's struggles in the Sierra Maestra and Che's selfless devotion to the cause of the Latin American Revolution will always be remembered; and the epic struggle of the Vietnamese will reverberate for centuries to come.

The Vietnam war has radicalized people throughout the world, and particularly so in the United States and Western Europe. In Britain the largest demonstrations since the Labour Government came to power have been on the issue of Vietnam. And the important fact to remember is that these demonstrations have not been pacifist in nature. The early demonstrations were organized by the Establishment Left—the reformists. These were the 'Left' Labour MPs, the British Communist Party and various other pacifist groupings. They believed in tokenism, in gestural politics, in petitioning the British Prime Minister, or in his absence sundry other members of the Government. They concentrated their action upon supporting U Thant's proposals and were attacked by the North Vietnamese for doing so. Their demonstrations were sparsely attended. It was in these circumstances that the Vietnam Solidarity Campaign was formed, largely on the initiative of the Bertrand Russell Peace Foundation and the International Marxist Group, which is affiliated to the Trotskyist 4th International.

The Vietnam Solidarity Campaign has stressed from its very inception its complete break with the politics of the reformist organizations. It has declared time and again its total solidarity with the National Liberation Front of South Vietnam. It has taken the movement off the reformist fence and committed it strongly to one side in the war—the Vietnamese people. And it was its espousal of a revolutionary political line in theory and its no-nonsense tactics on the streets which has won it the support of the new revolutionaries. Old-time socialists who had become cynical and disgusted with reformism found themselves getting interested in politics again. The result was the mass-demonstration of ten thousand people chanting 'Victory to the NLF!' on October 22nd, 1967. On reaching Grosvenor Square the demonstrators, not disconcerted by a thin blue line of policemen, charged through—some

71

of them actually reaching the steps of the citadel. That was the nearest they were ever to get to the United States Embassy. The charge, it should be recalled, was led by a group of militant workers from the Barbican site in the City, where there had been a long and partially successful strike that had ended a few days before the demonstration. The morning after the demonstration the national press became hysterical : 'THE GREAT PEACE PUNCH-UP', headlined the *Daily Express* on its front page, and its reporters described the demonstration in their typically 'objective' fashion : Mobs howling for peace in Vietnam warred with police up and down the West End last night. . . . The mob growing more furious, threw rocks at the police, at Embassy windows, at the press.'[5]

The 'impartiality' of the *Daily Express* was imitated in various degrees by the rest of the bourgeois press. The suggestion that we were 'peace-marchers' was still perpetrated as a means of discrediting us : it was asserted that there was a disparity between our 'aims', with which of course all right-thinking *Guardian* readers could sympathize, and our 'behaviour'—which was 'thuggish'. Completely ignored was the fact that we had specifically told the press and anyone else who was interested that we were not marching for peace but for a NLF victory. It was to take the mass-media quite some time to discover that politically we were 'hooligans' as well.

The first Vietnam Solidarity Campaign demonstration had come as a pleasant surprise to most revolutionary socialists. The movement was on the increase and in subsequent demonstrations the numbers doubled and trebled, as did the violence. The new revolutionaries were quite open about their aims : it was hypocritical to protest against violence at home while justifying it in Vietnam; we were not pacifists, and if a policeman hit us we would defend ourselves. Our violence was defensive—a response to the repressive violence of the State machine. Moreover, we were not going to be told how to demonstrate. We would occupy the streets, march with linked arms and not let our comrades be arrested. Solidarity with each other was as important as solidarity with the Vietnamese guerrillas. Tokenism was over.

Surprised and annoyed by the rapid growth of the new movement, Harold Wilson said in the House of Commons on March 12th, 1968 : 'Provided that those who demonstrate genuinely want peace

[5] *Daily Express* (October 23rd, 1967).

and not military victory for one side or the other, if it makes them feel good, I have no objection.' The *Morning Star* did not comment.

Meanwhile the demonstrations of the Vietnam Solidarity Campaign continued to be successful, despite the withdrawal of financial support by the Bertrand Russell Peace Foundation. Some sectarians described the VSC marches as 'adventures on the periphery of British politics' and themselves continued to work within the Labour Party. Finally the Young Communist League, under pressure from its militant rank-and-file, was forced to change its policy. It began to co-operate with the Campaign, albeit with caution.

The radicalization progressed rapidly. Those who had been radicalized by the war finally realized that they had absorbed even the most trivial detail about the war in Vietnam. They knew about the so-called Gulf of Tonkin incident. The Geneva Agreements were studied in detail, as were the various 'peace' moves by L.B.J. and his acolytes, among them Harold Wilson. The new revolutionaries used Vietnam to analyse the social structure of societies which were waging the war in Vietnam and this led many of them to extend their struggle against the capitalist system itself. The new revolutionaries were also becoming socialists.

The struggle against the Vietnam war has sparked off a whole anti-capitalist movement, one of whose facets is the revolt against the university structure, which, one hopes, will embrace the educational system as a whole. Because it is at school that the process of brainwashing begins; because the ideologies transmitted in schools are class ideologies; because the final goal of the school is to organize consent for society and the existing social relationships. In its place the university today is being called upon to discharge a function which is of cardinal importance to the smooth functioning of the capitalist system : the rapid production of technocrats and technicians who will form the core of the new bureaucracy and finally replace the 'fuddy-duddy dinosaurs' who constitute the Civil Service as it exists at present. The university revolt is analysed and discussed elsewhere in this book, but it would be wrong to place too much emphasis upon it in Britain. For in Britain, at any rate, the revolt against the bourgeois university involves only an active minority of the students. There are few examples where a majority of the students have been involved. And the second important point to remember is that this active minority consists largely of students studying social sciences rather than of technocrats—although doubtless the revolt will spread and embrace the university as a whole, particularly in view of the cut-backs in research grants.

The university revolt usually begins with demands for reform. These in turn gradually multiply until it is impossible for the university establishments to accede to them in the context of the existing social structure. It is at this stage that the reformers tend to become revolutionaries. The main enemy—capitalism—comes clearly into focus.

But this is not the place to discuss the student revolt in detail. It is done more than adequately elsewhere in this volume. Suffice it to say that the Revolutionary Socialist Student Federation is an important and vital sector of a movement which is gradually beginning to assume the responsibilities of an extra-parliamentary opposition.

BLACK POWER

Another crucial part of the opposition is the Black Power movement. It is far too easy to deride this new development; it is only too easy to adopt dogmatic Marxist stances and declare that the exponents of Black Power are black racists, or as some sections of the movement argue that 'they only galvanize the Right' : as if the Right in this country needed galvanizing!

It is important that socialists understand the nature of this movement. It is necessary that revolutionaries establish contact with the Black Power militants and engage in dialogue. Those who maintain that there is no race war, only a class war, are in the ultimate analysis perfectly correct; but the way they pose this question gives the impression that they are evading the problem of racism in Britain. It is well to remember that the first *political* strike organized by the British working class, or at any rate a militant segment of it, has been to demand a total ban on coloured immigration into Britain. There is no *colour* problem in this country. It is essentially a *white* problem, and denying its existence or denying black

74

militants the right to organize themselves to face this problem is overt racism. It is too facile an argument to suggest that there was discrimination against the Irish in the nineteenth century but that *they* were assimilated into British society. The Irish were whites. Assimilation was not difficult. Today's immigrants are black and this in itself is enough to prevent it, if indeed assimilation was a solution. In 1870 Marx could write :

Every industrial and commercial centre in England now possesses a working-class population divided into two *hostile* camps, English proletarians and Irish proletarians. The ordinary English worker hates the Irish worker as a competitor who lowers his standard of life. In relation to the Irish worker he feels himself a member of the ruling nation and so turns himself into the tool of the aristocrats and capitalists, thus strengthening their domination *over himself.* He cherishes religious, social, and national prejudices against the Irish worker. His attitude towards him is much the same as that of the 'poor whites' to the Negroes in the former slave states of the USA. This antagonism is artificially kept alive and intensified by the press, the pulpit, the comic papers, in short by all the means at the disposal of the ruling classes. *This antagonism* is the *secret of the impotence of the English working class,* despite its organization. It is the secret by which the capitalist class maintains its power. The latter is well aware of this.[6]

For Marx's Irishman substitute black, and the analysis holds good even today. By limiting coloured immigration alone, both Toryism and social democracy have pandered to racialism in Britain. Their objection to Enoch Powell's speeches is not that the *premise* of his 'argument' is wrong, but rather the 'immoderate' way in which he expresses himself. That is the only difference between him and the Labour and Tory front benches in the House of Commons. The British ruling class, let us not forget, is the oldest and most experienced ruling class in the world. It maintained its colonial empire in the old days by the classic policy of 'Divide and Rule'—India, Pakistan, Cyprus, Central Africa bear eloquent tes-

[6] Karl Marx, *Letters to Americans* (International Publishers, New York), p. 78.

timony to this fact. Is it unnatural then for the British ruling class to apply the same concept to preserve its long-guarded privileges at home? What newspaper in Britain has ever demanded an end to immigration control? Which politician has ever said, since the Wilson régime came to power, that immigration controls should be applied to everyone or no one? Do the politicians who agitate for Britain's entry into the European Common Market realize that one of the terms for entry is unlimited immigration in the member countries? And if they do, will they call for a complete ban on coloured immigrants on the grounds that the country is too full as it is? Those who attempt to raise these questions are either 'lunatic-fringe Trotskyite extremists' or black militants, and the Britain of Edward Heath, Harold Wilson and their respective followers looks with disfavour on both these groups. Why should anyone be surprised, then, if in these circumstances the Black Power militants organize the black community to protect itself? Black Power is not an end in itself; it is merely a transitional slogan coined by black people after years of humiliation, slavery and exploitation of the most brutal sort. And if the slogan 'Black Power' is effective in raising the political consciousness of the ordinary black people, either in Britain or in America or anywhere else, then it is a valid slogan and revolutionary socialists should give it support. Of course the situation in Britain is not the same as in the United States. Of course some of the Black Power 'leaders' in Britain are idle demagogues for whom brave words alone are enough, who are completely out of touch with the black communities and their needs. It took over a hundred years of slavery in the United States to produce a Malcolm X, a Stokely Carmichael or an Eldridge Cleaver. Leaders evolve through a process of struggle, and this must hold true for Britain. The ineffectiveness of certain Black Power spokesmen is no excuse to dismiss the movement as a whole; for as racialism increases, so also will the movement to combat racialism. Socialists will then have two options before them : either to participate in the struggle despite disagreements with those leading them; or stay aloof and from time to time offer analyses from the 'Marxist point of view'.

THE EXTRA-PARLIAMENTARY OPPOSITION

The time is coming when the different strands in the revolutionary movement in Britain will have to coalesce; isolated struggles invariably weaken the movement and many of the militants involved tend to veer towards an apathetic cynicism. What is needed in Britain at the moment is a united Revolutionary Socialist Party, but it could be argued that this need is not a new one. Indeed as far back as January 1957 a socialist militant could write :

No struggle 'within the constitution' will meet the needs of the working class in this new situation. The trade unions must be made to perform the functions for which they were brought into being. Instead of co-operating in the drive against foreign competition, they must mobilize the workers for struggle against the employers.

The unions belong to the workers, but they are, in the main, controlled by officials. The leaders are more concerned about helping the State than helping the workers. The struggle cannot be avoided. It will continue until it develops into a political struggle; a struggle for political power.

We hold the belief that to give guidance in this situation a new Revolutionary Socialist Party is needed. All sincere socialists should help to achieve this aim.[7]

The 'sincere socialist' who wrote this was none other, alas, than the present Labour Member of Parliament for Walton, Liverpool. The situation in 1968, however, is considerably different to what it was when Comrade Heffer wrote those words of wisdom. Today social democracy stands exposed and isolated, its credibility for the working class virtually destroyed. It is trying desperately to rationalize and humanize British capitalism but—needless to add—it will fail and this failure will continue to haunt those who support it, like a Greek tragedy. The British Communist Party, discredited over the years for its blind adherence to Soviet Stalinism, can continue to wait in the wings for ever. It reminds one more and more of an ageing ballerina who has never made the grade despite signs of

[7] Eric Heffer, editorial in *Socialist Revolt* (January-March 1957). This publication is now defunct.

early promise, and who refuses to admit it—not even to herself. Throughout the country there is a mood of cynicism and despair. Some are turning to Powellism and trying to avoid facing the real problems by blaming everything on the blacks. Others are simply fed up with the suffocating parliamentary cant. The definition of 'cant' I have in mind is Trotsky's : *'Cant* : A specific form of conventional lie, tacitly acknowledged by all through considerations of social hypocrisy. According to Carlyle, cant is the art "whereby a man speaks only what he does NOT mean". In Parliamentary-Protestant Britain this art has been carried to extraordinary heights —or depths.'[8]

The task of revolutionary socialists in Britain is crystal-clear : to work unceasingly for the formation of a Revolutionary Socialist Party; and although in essence this new party should be similar to Lenin's Bolshevik Party, we must remember also that Lenin wrote *What Is to Be Done* at the height of czarist oppression in Russia. Until such time as this party is formed, however, the different revolutionary tendencies and factions should group together to set up a formal Extra-Parliamentary Opposition and give some sense of socialist direction to the movement. Confrontations in the West End and elsewhere with London policemen, despite all the provocations, will simply not be sufficient to disguise the absence of a coherent policy and sustain a mass-movement. We must create an opposition whose demands at this particular juncture should essentially be transitional—STRUGGLE AGAINST IMPERIALISM ABROAD, STRUGGLE AGAINST CAPITALISM AT HOME. Let us sink our sectarian differences and move towards setting up the Extra-Parliamentary Opposition.

[8] Leon Trotsky, *Where Is Britain Going?* (Plough Press).

ELDRIDGE CLEAVER

Letter from Jail

I fell in love with the Black Panther Party for Self-Defense immediately upon my first encounter with it; it was literally love at first
sight. It happened one night at a meeting in a dingy little storefront
on Scott Street in the Fillmore district, the heart of San Francisco's
black ghetto. It was February 1967. The meeting was the latest in a
series of weekly meetings held by a loose coalition functioning under
the name of the Bay Area Grassroots Organizations Planning Committee. The purpose of the coalition was to co-ordinate three days
of activities with the worthy ambition of involving the total black
community in mass-action commemorating the fourth anniversary
of the assassination of Malcolm X. The highlight and culmination
of the memorial was to be the appearance of Sister Betty Shabazz,
Malcolm X's widow, who was to deliver the keynote speech at a
mass-meeting at the Bayview Community Center in Hunters Point.
    Among the topics on the agenda for this arranged meeting was
the question of providing security for Sister Betty during the
twenty-four hours she was to be our guest in the Bay Area. There
was a paranoia around—which I did not share—that assassins by
the dozens were lurking everywhere for the chance to shoot Sister
Betty down. This fear, real or imagined, was a fact and it kept
everybody up tight.
    I had arrived at the meeting late, changing at the last minute a
previous decision not to attend at all. I was pissed off at everyone in

79

the room. Taking a seat with my back to the door I sat there with, I'm sure, a scornful frown of disdain upon my face. Roy Ballard (if the normal brain had three cylinders, his would have one) sat opposite me, across the circle formed by the placement of the chairs. He, above all, understood the expression on my face, for he had done the most to put it there; this accounted, I thought, for the idiot grin on his own.

On Roy's left sat Ken Freeman, Chairman of the now defunct Black Panther Party of Northern California, who always looked to me like Dagwood, with his huge round bifocals and the bald spot in the front of his natural. On Roy's right sat a frightened-looking little mulatto who seemed to live by the adage, 'It's better to remain silent and be thought a fool than to open one's mouth and remove all doubt'. He probably adopted that rule from observing his big fat yellow wife, who was seated on his right and who had said when I walked in, just loud enough for me to hear, 'Shit! I thought we agreed after last week's meeting that *he* wouldn't be allowed to attend any more meetings!'

Next to her sat Jack Trueblood, a handsome, earnest youth in a black Russian cap who represented San Francisco State College's Black Students Union and who always accepted whatever tasks were piled upon him, ensuring that he would leave each weekly meeting with a heavy load. On his right sat a girl named Lucky. I could never tell why they called her that—not, I'm sure, because she happened to be Roy Ballard's old lady; maybe because she had such a beautiful smile.

Between Lucky and myself sat Marvin Jackmon who was known as a poet, because after Watts went up in flames he had composed a catchy ditty entitled 'Burn, Baby, Burn!' and a play entitled *Flowers for the Trashman*. (It is hard for me to write objectively about Marvin. My association with him, dating from the third week of December 1966, ended in mutual bitterness with the closing of the Black House. After getting out of prison that month, he was the first person I hooked up with. Along with Ed Bullins, a young playwright who now has a few things going for himself off-Broadway, and Willie Dale, who had been in San Quentin with me and was trying to make it as a singer, we had founded the Black House in January 1967. Within the next two months the Black

House, located in San Francisco, became the centre of non-Establishment black culture throughout the Bay Area.)

On my right sat Bill Sherman, an ex-member of the Communist Party and at that time a member of the Central Committee of the Black Panther Party of Northern California. Next to Bill was Victoria Durant, who dressed with what the black *bourgeoisie* would call 'style', or better yet, 'class'. She seemed so out of place at those meetings. We were supposed to be representing the common people —grassroots—and here was Victoria ready to write out a fifty-dollar cheque at the drop of a hat. She represented, as everyone knew, the local clique of black democrats who wanted inside info. on everything even hinting of 'organizing' in their stomping grounds —even if the price of such info. was a steady flow of fifty-dollar cheques.

Then there was Marianne Waddy, who kept everybody guessing because no one was ever sure of where or what she really was. One day she'd be dressed in flowing African gowns with her hair wrapped up in a pretty *skashok*, the perfect picture of the young Afro-American lady who has established a certain identity with and relationship to traditional African culture. The next day she would be dressed like a man and acting like a man who could cut the first throat that got in his way.

Next to Marianne sat a sneaky-looking fellow called Nasser Shabazz. Sitting between Nasser and Ken Freeman, completing the circle, was Vincent Lynch, as smooth and black as the ebony statues he had brought back from his trip to Nigeria and the only member of the Black Panther Party of Northern California I ever liked or thought was sincere. Somewhere in the room, too, was Ann Lynch, Vincent's wife, with their bright-eyed little son, Patrice Lumumba Lynch. Ann was the head of Black Care, the women's auxiliary to this Panther Party. These sisters spent all of their time talking about the impending violent stage of the black revolution, which was inevitable, and how they, the women, must be prepared to care for the men who would be wounded in battle.

I had come out of prison with plans to revive the Organization of Afro-American Unity, the vehicle finally settled upon by Malcolm X to spearhead the black revolution. The OAAU had never really gotten off the ground, for it was cut short by the assassins' bullets that felled Malcolm on the stage of the Audubon Ballroom in New York City. I was amazed that no one else had moved to continue Malcolm's work in the name of the organization he had chosen, which seemed perfect to me and also logically necessary in terms of historical continuity. The three-day memorial, which was but part of the overall plan to revive the OAAU, was to be used as a forum for launching the revival. In January, I had put the plan on paper and circulated it throughout the Bay Area, then issued a general call for a meeting to establish a temporary steering committee that would see after things until the start of the memorial. At this time we would have a convention, found the Bay Area branch of the Organization of Afro-American Unity and elect officers whom Sister Betty Shabazz would instal, giving the whole effort her blessings in a keynote address on the final day of the memorial.

By February the plan had been torn to shreds. If the plan was a pearl, then I had certainly cast it before swine, and the biggest swine of all, Roy Ballard, had hijacked the plan and turned it into a circus. It soon became clear that if the OAAU was to be reborn, it would not be with the help of this crew, because all they could see was the pageantry of the memorial. Beyond that, their eyes blotted out all vision. Far from wanting to see an organization develop that would put an end to the archipelago of one-man showcase groups that plagued the black community with division, they had each made it their sacred cause to ensure the survival of their own splinter group.

From the beginning, when the plan was first put before them, they took up each separate aspect and chewed it until they were sure it was either maimed for life or dead. Often after an idea had gone around the circle, if it still showed signs of life they would pounce upon it and rend it some more. When they finished, all that was left of the original plan was a pilgrimage to the site where a sixteen-year-old black youth, Matthew Johnson, had been murdered by a white cop, putting some pictures of Malcolm X on the walls of the Bayview Community Center, a hysterical speech by Ken Freeman and twenty-four hours of Sister Betty Shabazz's time.

In all fairness, however, I must confess that the whole plan was impossible to achieve, mostly because it did not take into account certain negative aspects of the black man's psychological heritage from four hundred years of oppression here in Babylon. Then, too, I was an outsider. Having gone to prison from Los Angeles, I had been paroled to San Francisco. I was an interloper unfolding a programme to organize *their* community. Fatal. It didn't matter to them that we were dealing with the concept of the Black Nation, of colonized Afro-America, and that all the boundaries separating our people were the stupid impositions of the white oppressors and had to be obliterated. Well, no matter; I had failed. Proof of my failure was Roy Ballard, sitting there before me like a gaunt buzzard, presiding over the carcass of a dream.

Suddenly the room fell silent. The crackling undercurrent, that for weeks had made it impossible to get one's point across when one had the floor, was gone; there was only the sound of the lock clicking as the front door opened, and then the soft shuffle of feet moving quietly toward the circle. Shadows danced on the walls. From the tension showing on the faces of the people before me, I thought the cops were invading the meeting, but there was a deep female gleam leaping out of one of the women's eyes that no cop who ever lived could elicit. I recognized that gleam out of the recesses of my soul, even though I had never seen it before in my life : the total admiration of a black woman for a black man. I spun around in my seat and saw the most beautiful sight I had ever seen : four black men wearing black berets, powder-blue shirts, black leather jackets, black trousers, shiny black shoes—and each with a gun ! In front was Huey P. Newton with a riot pump shotgun in his right hand, barrel pointed down to the floor. Beside him was Bobby Seale, the handle of a .45-calibre automatic showing from its holster on his right hip, just below the hem of his jacket. A few steps behind was Bobby Hutton, the barrel of his shotgun at his feet. Next to him was Sherwin Forte, an MI carbine with a banana clip cradled in his arms.

Roy Ballard jumped to his feet. Licking his lips, he said, 'For those of you who've never met the brothers, these are the Oakland Panthers.'

'You're wrong,' said Huey P. Newton. 'We're not the Oakland Panthers. We happen to live in Oakland. Our name is the Black Panther Party for Self-Defense.'

With that the Panthers seated themselves in chairs along the wall, outside the circle. Every eye in the room was riveted upon them. What amazed me was that Roy Ballard did not utter one word in contradiction, nor was there any yakkity-yak around the room. There was absolute silence. Even little Patrice Lumumba Lynch seemed to sit up and take notice.

Where was my mind at? Blown! Racing through time, racing through the fog of a perspective that had just been shattered into a thousand fragments. Who are these cats? I wondered at them, checking them out carefully. They were so cool and, it seemed to me, not unconscious of the electrifying effect they were having upon everybody in the room. Then I recalled a chance remark that Marvin Jackmon had once made. We were discussing the need for security at the Black House because the crowds were getting larger and larger and we had had to throw out bodily a cat who was high and acting like he owned the place. I said that Marvin, Ed, Dale and I had better each get himself a gun. As I elaborated on the necessity as I saw it, Marvin said, 'You need to forget about the Black House and go across the bay and get with Bobby Seale.' And he laughed.

' Who is Bobby Seale?' I asked him.

At first he gave no answer, he seemed to be carefully considering what to say. Finally he said, 'He's arming some brothers across the bay.' Though I pressed him, he refused to go into it any further, and at the time it didn't seem important to me, so I forgot about it. Now, sitting there looking at those Panthers, I recalled the incident with Marvin. I looked at him. He seemed to have retreated inside himself, sitting there looking like a skinny black Buddha with something distasteful and menacing on his mind.

'Do you brothers want to make a speech at the memorial?' Roy Ballard asked the Panthers.

'Yes,' Bobby Seale said.

'O.K.,' said Ballard. 'We have the programme broken down into subjects : Politics, Economics, Self-Defence and Black Culture. Now which section do you brothers want to speak under?' This was the sort of question which in my experience had always signalled the beginning of a two-hour debate with this group.

'It doesn't matter what section we speak under,' Huey said. 'Our message is one and the same. We're going to talk about black people arming themselves in a political fashion to exert organized force in the political arena, to see to it that their desires and needs are met. Otherwise there will be a political consequence. And the only culture worth talking about is a revolutionary culture. So it doesn't matter what heading you put on it, we're going to talk about political power growing out of the barrel of a gun.'

'O.K.,' Roy Ballard said. He paused, then added, 'Let's put it under Politics.' Then he went on to start the specific discussion of security for Sister Betty, who would pick her up at the airport, etc. Bobby Seale was jotting down notes in a little black book. The other Panthers sat quietly, watchfully.

Three days before the start of the memorial I received a phone call from Los Angeles. The man on the other end identified himself as Mr Hakim Jamal, Malcolm X's cousin by marriage. He would be arriving with Sister Betty, he said, and both of them wanted to talk with me. They had liked, it turned out, an article on Malcolm that I had written and that was published in *Ramparts*. We agreed that when they got in from the airport I would meet them at the *Ramparts* office in San Francisco.

On the day that Sister Betty and Hakim Jamal were to arrive in San Francisco, I was sitting in my office tinkering with some notes for an article. One of the secretaries burst through the door. Her face was white with fear and she was shouting, 'We're being invaded! We're being invaded!'

I couldn't tell just who her 'we' referred to. Were the Chinese coming? Had the CIA finally decided to do *Ramparts* in? Then she said, 'There are about twenty men outside with guns!'

I knew that Hakim Jamal and Sister Betty had arrived with their escort of armed Black Panthers.

'Don't worry,' I said, 'they're friends.'

'*Friends?*' she gasped. I left her there with her eyes bugging out of her head and rushed to the front of the building.

I waded through *Ramparts'* staff jammed into the narrow hallway, fending off frightened inquiries by repeating, 'It's all right, it's all right'. The lobby resembled certain photographs coming out of Cuba the day Castro took Havana. There were guns everywhere, pointed toward the ceiling like metallic blades of grass growing up out of the sea of black faces beneath the black berets of the Panthers. I found Hakim Jamal and Sister Betty surrounded by a knot of Panthers, who looked calm and self-possessed in sharp contrast to the chaotic reactions their appearance had set off. Out-

85

side, where Broadway ran in four lanes to feed the freeway on-ramp and to receive the heavy traffic from the off-ramp, a massive traffic-jam was developing and sirens could be heard screaming in the distance as cops sped our way.

I took Jamal and Sister Betty to an office down the hall. We talked for around fifteen minutes about Malcolm. Sister Betty, her eyes concealed behind dark glasses, said nothing after we were introduced. She looked cool enough on the surface, but it was clear that she felt hard-pressed. Huey P. Newton was standing at the window, shotgun in hand, looking down into the upturned faces of a horde of police. I left the room to get Sister Betty a glass of water, squeezing past Bobby Seale and what seemed like a battalion of Panthers in the hall guarding the door. Seale's face was a chiselled mask of determination.

A few yards down the hall, Warren Hinckle III, editor of *Ramparts,* was talking to a police lieutenant.

'What's the trouble?' the lieutenant asked, pointing at the Black Panthers with their guns.

'No trouble,' Hinckle said. 'Everything is under control.'

The policeman seemed infuriated by this answer. He stared at Bobby Seale for a moment and then stalked outside. While I was in the lobby a TV cameraman, camera on his shoulder, forced his way through the front door and started taking pictures. Two white boys who worked at *Ramparts* stopped the TV man and informed him he was trespassing on private property. When he refused to leave, they picked him up and threw him out the door, camera and all.

When it was agreed that it was time to leave, Huey Newton took control. Mincing no words, he sent five of his men out first to clear a path through the throng of spectators clustered outside the door, most of whom were cops. He dispatched a phalanx of ten Panthers fast on their heels, with Hakim Jamal and Sister Betty concealed in their midst. Newton himself, along with Bobby Seale and three other Panthers, brought up the rear.

I went outside and stood on the steps of *Ramparts* to observe the departure. When Huey left the building, the TV cameraman who had gotten tossed out was grinding away with his camera. Huey took an envelope from his pocket and held it up in front of the camera, blocking the lens.

'Get out of the way!' the TV man shouted. When Huey continued to hold the envelope in front of the lens, the TV man started cursing, and reached out and knocked Huey's hand away with his fist. Huey coolly turned to one of the score of cops watching and said : 'Officer, I want you to arrest this man for assault.'

An incredulous look came into the cop's face, then he blurted out, 'If I arrest anybody, it'll be you!'

Huey turned on the cameraman, again placing the envelope in front of the lens. Again the cameraman reached out and knocked Huey's hand away. Huey reached out, snatched the cameraman by the collar and slammed him up against the wall, sending him spinning and staggering down the sidewalk, trying to catch his breath and balance the camera on his shoulder at the same time.

Bobby Seale tugged at Huey's shirt-sleeve. 'C'mon, Huey, let's get out of here.'

Huey and Bobby started up the sidewalk toward their car. The cops stood there on the point, poised as though ready to start shooting at a given signal.

'Don't turn your back on these back-shooting dogs!' Huey called out to Bobby and the other three Panthers. By this time the other Panthers and Sister Betty and Jamal had gotten into cars and melted into the traffic-jam. Only these five were still at the scene.

At that moment a big beefy cop stepped forward. He undid the little strap holding his pistol in his holster and started shouting at Huey, 'Don't point that gun at me! Stop pointing that gun at me!' He kept making gestures as though he was going for his gun.

This was the most tense of moments. Huey stopped in his tracks and stared at the cop.

'Let's split, Huey! Let's split!' Bobby Seale was saying.

Ignoring him, Huey walked to within a few feet of the cop and said, 'What's the matter, you got an itchy finger?'

The cop made no reply.

'You want to draw your gun?' Huey asked him.

The other cops were calling out for this cop to cool it, to take it easy, but he didn't seem able to hear them. He was staring into Huey's eyes, measuring him.

'O.K.,' Huey said. 'You big fat racist pig, draw your gun!'

The cop made no move.

'Draw it, you cowardly dog!' Huey pumped a round into the

chamber of the shotgun. 'I'm waiting,' he said, and stood there waiting for the cop to draw.

All the other cops moved back out of the line of fire. I moved back, too, on to the top step of *Ramparts*. I was thinking, staring at Huey surrounded by all those cops and daring one of them to draw : Goddam, that nigger is c-r-a-z-y !

Then the cop facing Huey gave up. He heaved a heavy sigh and lowered his head. Huey literally laughed in his face and then went off up the street at a jaunty pace, disappearing in a blaze of dazzling sunlight.

'Work out soul-brother,' I was shouting to myself. 'You're the baddest mother-fucker I've ever seen !' I went back into *Ramparts* and we all stood around chattering excitedly, discussing what we had witnessed with disbelief.

'*Who was that?*' asked Vampira, Warren Hinckle's little sister.

'That was Huey P. Newton,' I said, 'Minister of Defense of the Black Panther Party for Self-Defense.'

'Boy, is he gutsy !' she said dreamily.

'Yeah,' I agreed. 'He's out of sight.'

The quality in Huey P. Newton's character which I had seen that morning in front of *Ramparts*, and which I was to see demonstrated over and over again after I joined the Black Panther Party for Self-Defense, was *courage*. I had called it 'crazy', as people often do to explain away things they do not understand. I don't mean the courage 'to stand up and be counted', or even the courage it takes to face certain death. I speak of that revolutionary courage it takes to pick up a gun with which to oppose the oppressor of one's people. That's a different kind of courage.

Oppressed people, Fanon points out, kill each other all the time. A glance through any black newspaper will prove that black people in America kill each other with regularity. This is the internalized violence of oppressed people. Angered by the misery of their lives but cowed by the overt superior might of the oppressor, the oppressed people shrink from striking out at the true objects of their hostility and strike instead at their more defenceless brothers and sisters near at hand. Somehow this seems safer, less fraught with dire consequences, as though one is less dead when shot down by one's brother than when shot down by the oppressor. It is merely criminal to take up arms against one's brother, but to step outside the vicious circle of the internalized violence of the oppressed and take up arms against the oppressor is to step outside of life itself, to step outside the structure of this world, to enter, almost alone, the no-man's-land of revolution.

Huey P. Newton took that step. For the motto of the Black Panther Party he chose a quotation from Mao Tse-tung's Little Red Book : 'We are advocates of the abolition of war; we do not want war; but war can only be abolished through war; and in order to get rid of the gun it is necessary to pick up the gun.'

When I decided to join the Black Panther Party the only hang-up I had was with its name. I was still clinging to my conviction that we owed it to Malcolm to pick up where he left off. To me, this meant building the organization that he had started. Picking up where Malcolm left off, however, had different meanings for different people. For cats like Marvin Jackmon, for instance, it meant returning to the ranks of Elijah Muhammad's Nation of Islam, denouncing Malcolm as a heretic and pledging loyalty to Elijah, all in Malcolm's name. For Huey, it meant implementing the programme that Malcolm advocated. When that became clear to me, I knew what Huey P. Newton was all about.

For the revolutionary black youth of today, time starts moving with the coming of Malcolm X. Before Malcolm, time stands still, going down in frozen steps into the depths of the stagnation of slavery. Malcolm talked shit, and talking shit is the iron in a young nigger's blood. Malcolm mastered language and used it as a sword to slash his way through the veil of lies that for four hundred years gave the white man the power of the word. Through the breach in the veil, Malcolm saw all the way to national liberation, and he showed us the rainbow and the golden pot at its end. Inside the golden pot, Malcolm told us, was the tool of liberation. Huey P. Newton, one of the millions of black people who listened to Malcolm, lifted the golden lid off the pot and blindly, trusting Malcolm, stuck his hand inside and grasped the tool. When he withdrew his hand and looked to see what he held, he saw the gun, cold in its metal and implacable in its message : Death-Life, Liberty or Death, mastered by a black hand at last ! Huey P. Newton is the ideological descendant, heir and successor of Malcolm X. Malcolm prophesied the coming of the gun to the black liberation struggle. Huey P. Newton picked up the gun and pulled the trigger, freeing the genie of black revolutionary violence in Babylon.

The genie of black revolutionary violence is here, and it says that the oppressor has no rights which the oppressed are bound to respect. The genie also has a question for white Americans : Which side do you choose? Do you side with the oppressor or with the oppressed? The time for decision is upon you. The cities of America have tested the first flames of revolution. But a hotter fire rages in the hearts of black people today : total liberty for black people or total destruction for America.

The prospects, I confess, do not look promising. Besides being a dumb nation, America is mad with white racism. Whom the gods would destroy, they first make mad. Perhaps America has been mad for too long to make any talk of sanity relevant now. But there is a choice and it will be made, by decision or indecision, by action or inaction, by commission or omission. Black people have made their choice. A revolutionary generation that has the temerity to say to America that Huey P. Newton must be set free, also invested with the courage to kill, pins its hopes on the revolutionary's faith and says, with Che : 'Wherever death may surprise us, it will be welcome, provided that this, our battle-cry, reach some receptive ear, that another hand reach out to take up our weapons, and that other fighting men come forward to intone our funeral dirge with the staccato of machine-guns and new cries of battle and victory.'

STOKELY CARMICHAEL

Black Power and the Third World*

'We greet you as comrades because it becomes increasingly clear to us each day that we share with you a common struggle. We have a common enemy. Our enemy is white Western imperialist society. (Note that we use the term white Western *society* as opposed to white Western *civilization*. The West has never been civilized. It has no right to speak of itself as a civilization.) Our struggle is to overthrow this system which feeds itself and expands itself through the economic and cultural exploitation of non-white, non-Western peoples—the THIRD WORLD.

'We share with you also a common vision of the establishment of humanistic societies in the place of those now existing. We seek with you to change the power base of the world, where mankind will share resources of their nations, instead of having to give them up to foreign plunderers, where civilizations can retain their cultural sovereignty instead of being forced to submit to foreign rulers who impose their own corrupt cultures on those civilizations they would dominate.

'Anglo society has been nearly successful in keeping all of us— the oppressed of the Third World—separated and fragmented. They do this for their survival, because if we felt our unity we would

---

* The following is the text of a speech made by Stokely Carmichael at the OLAS (Organization of Latin-American Solidarity) conference held in Havana in the period July 31st-August 10th, 1967.

know our strength. Especially here on this continent, where the Anglo is in the minority, he has for hundreds of years succeeded in keeping all of us who are oppressed from realizing our common plight. But the call of Che Guevara for a continental struggle against a common enemy would seem to ameliorate this fragmentation among those who would resist Western imperialism.

'We speak with you, comrades, because we wish to make clear that we understand that our destinies are intertwined. Our world can only be the Third World; our only struggle, for the Third World; our only vision, of the Third World.

'Until recently, most African-Americans thought that the best way to alleviate their oppression was through attempts at integration into the society. If we could enjoy public accommodations in the United States (motels, hotels, restaurants, etc.) our condition would be alleviated, many of us believed. This attitude was characteristic of the "Civil Rights movement" and clearly points up the bourgeois character of that "movement". Only the *bourgeoisie* are in a position to be concerned about public accommodations.

'The African-American masses, on the other hand, do not have any jobs, any housing worthy of the name "decent", nor the money to enjoy restaurants, hotels, motels, etc. The "Civil Rights movement" did not actively involve the masses, because it did not speak to the needs of the masses. Nonetheless, the "Civil Rights movement" was a beginning, and because its aims met resistance throughout the United States, depths of racism heretofore unrecognized were laid bare. It had been thought that the aims of the "Civil Rights movement" would be easily realizable, because the United States Constitution supported them. But thousands of African-Americans were jailed, intimidated, beaten, and some murdered, for agitating for those rights guaranteed by the Constitution, but only available to whites.

'Eventually, the United States Congress passed a Civil Rights Bill and a Voting Rights Bill, assuring us of those rights for which we had been agitating. By this time, however, more and more of us were realizing that our problems would not be solved by the enacting of these laws. In fact, these laws did not begin to speak to our problems. Our problems were an inherent part of the capitalist system and therefore could not be alleviated within that system.

'The African-American masses had been outside the "Civil Rights movement". For four years they watched to see if any significant changes would come from the non-violent demonstrations. It became clear to us that nothing would change and in the summer of 1964, only a couple of weeks after the Civil Rights Bill was passed, the first of what are now over one hundred rebellions occurred. The following year, the same year that the Voting Rights Bill was enacted, one of the largest rebellions occurred in Watts.

'These rebellions were violent uprisings in which African-Americans exchanged gunfire with policemen and army troops, burned down stores and took from the stores those commodities that are rightfully ours—food and clothing—and which we never had. These rebellions are increasing in intensity and frequency each year until now practically every major city has seen us rise to say, "We will seize the day or be killed in the attempt".

'The "Civil Rights movement" could never attempt and hold the young bloods who clearly understood the savagery of white United States and who are ready to meet this savagery with armed resistance. It is the young bloods who contain especially the hatred Che Guevara speaks of when he says, "Hatred is an element of the struggle . . . relentless hatred of the enemy that impels us over and beyond the natural limitations of man and transforms us into an effective, violent, selected and cold killing machine".

'The Black Power movement has been the catalyst for the bringing together of these young bloods : the real revolutionary proletariat, ready to fight by any means necessary for the liberation of our people. In exposing the extent of racism and exploitation which permeates all institutions in the United States, the Black Power movement has unique appeal to young black students on campuses across the country. These students have been deluded by the fiction that exists in white North America that if the black man would educate himself and behave himself he would be acceptable enough to leave the ranks of the oppressed and join white society.

'This year, when provoked by savage white policemen, students on many campuses fought back, whereas before they had accepted these incidents without rebellion. As students are a part of these rebellions they begin to acquire a resistance consciousness. They begin to realize that white North America might let a very few of them escape one by one into the mainstream of her society, but

93

as soon as blacks move in concert around their blackness, she will reply with a fury which reveals her true racist nature.

'We are moving to control our African-American communities as you are moving to wrest control of your countries—of the entire Latin continent—from the hands of foreign imperialist powers. Therefore there is only one course open to us.

'We must change North America so that the economy and politics of the country will be in the hands of the people. Our particular concern is our people—African-Americans. But it is clear that a community based on the community ownership of all resources could not exist within the present capitalist framework. For the total transformation to take place, whites must see the struggle that we're engaged in as being their own struggle. At the present time, they do not. Even though the white worker is exploited, he sees his own best interest lying with the power structure. Because of the racist nature of this country, we cannot work in white communities, but have asked those whites who work with us to go into their own communities to begin propagandizing and organizing. When the white workers realize their true condition, then there will exist the possibilities for alliances between ourselves and them. However, we cannot wait for this to happen, or despair if it does not happen.

'The struggle we are engaged in is international. We well know that what happens in Vietnam affects our struggle here and what we do affects the struggle of the Vietnamese people. This is even more apparent when we look at ourselves not as African-Americans of the United States, but as African-Americans of the Americas.

'At the present moment, the power structure has sown the seeds of hate and discord between African-Americans and Spanish-speaking people in the large cities where they live. In the State of California, Mexican-Americans and Spanish-speaking people comprise almost 50 per cent of the population, yet the two view each other with suspicion, and sometimes outright hostility. We recognize this as the old trick of "divide and conquer" and we are working to see that it does not succeed this time.

'Last week Puerto Ricans and blacks took to the streets together in New York City to fight against the police, which demonstrates success in this area. Our destiny cannot be separated from the destiny of the Spanish-speaking people in the United States and of

the Americas. Our victory will not be achieved unless they cele-
brate their liberation side by side with us. For it is not their struggle,
but our struggle.

'We have already pledged ourselves to do what we are asked to
aid the struggle for the independence of Puerto Rico, to free it
from domination by United States business and military interests.
And we look upon Cuba as a shining example of hope in our
hemisphere. We do not view our struggle as being contained within
the boundaries of the United States as they are defined by present-
day maps. Instead we look to the day when a true United States of
America will extend from Tierra del Fuego to Alaska, when those
formerly oppressed will stand together, a liberated people.

'Our people are a colony within the United States; you are
colonies outside the United States. It is more than a figure of speech
to say that the black communities in America are the victims of
white imperialism and colonial exploitation. This is in practical
economic and political terms true.

'There are over thirty million of us in the United States. For
the most part we live in sharply defined areas; in the rural black
belt areas and shanty-towns of the South, and more and more in
the slums of the northern and western industrial cities. It is estimated that in another five to ten years, two-thirds of our thirty
million will be in the ghettoes—in the heart of the cities. Joining
us are the hundreds of thousands of Puerto Ricans, Mexican-
American and American-Indian populations. The American city
is, in essence, populated by people of the Third World, while the
white middle class flee the cities to the suburbs.

'In these cities we do not control our resources. We do not control
the land, the houses or the stores. These are owned by whites who
live outside the community. These are very real colonies, as their
capital and cheap labour are exploited by those who live outside
the cities. White power makes the laws and enforces those laws
with guns and night-sticks in the hands of white racist policemen
and black mercenaries. The capitalist system gave birth to these
black enclaves and formally articulated the terms of their colonial
and dependent status, as was done, for example, by the *apartheid*
Government of Azania (South Africa), which the United States
keeps alive by its support.

'The struggle for Black Power in this country is the struggle to free these colonies from external domination. But we do not seek to create communities where, in place of white rulers, black rulers control the lives of black masses and where black money goes into a few black pockets : we want to see it go into the communal pocket. The society we seek to build among black people is not an oppressive capitalist society, for capitalism by its very nature cannot create structures free from exploitation. We are fighting for the redistribution of wealth and for the end of private property inside the United States.

'The question that may be asked is, how does the struggle to free these internal colonies relate to your struggle to destroy imperialism? We realistically survey our numbers and know that it is not possible for black people to take over the entire country militarily and hold large areas of land. In a highly industrialized nation the struggle is different. The heart of production and the heart of commercial trade is in the cities. We are in the cities. With our rebellions we have become a disruptive force in the flow of services, goods and capital.

'Since 1966, the cry of the rebellions has been "Black Power". In this cry, there was an ideology implied which the masses understood instinctively. It is because we are powerless that we are oppressed, and it is only with power that we can make the decisions governing our lives and our communities. Those who have power have everything; those who are without power have nothing. Without power we have to beg for what is rightfully ours. With power we will take our birthright, because it was with power that our birthright was taken from us.

'Black Power is more than a slogan; it is a way of looking at our problems and the beginning of a solution to them. It attacks racism and exploitation, the horns of the bull that seeks to gore us.

'The United States is a racist country. From its very beginning it has built itself upon the subjugation of coloured people. The Europeans who settled the United States systematically stole the land and destroyed the native population, the Indians, forcing them eventually on to reservations where they live today, a mere 0.3 per cent of the total population. And at the same time the United States was waging genocide against the Indians, it was raping the African Continent of its natives and bringing them to the Americas to work as slaves.

'To enslave another human being, one needs a justification; and the United States has always found this justification in proclaiming the superiority of whites and the inferiority of non-whites. We are called "niggers"; Spanish-speaking people are called "spics"; the Chinese "chinks"; the Vietnamese "gooks". By dehumanizing us and all others of colour, it therefore becomes just, in the mind of the white man, that we should be enslaved, exploited and oppressed. However, it becomes even easier to keep a man a slave when he himself can be convinced that he is inferior. How much easier it is to keep a man in chains by making him believe in his own inferiority! As long as he does, he will keep himself in chains. As long as a slave allows himself to be defined as a slave by the master, he will be a slave, even if the master dies.

'This technique has been successfully practised not only against us, but wherever people have been enslaved, oppressed and exploited. We can see it happening today in the schools of large United States cities, where Puerto Rican and Mexican children are not allowed to speak Spanish and are taught nothing of their country and their history. It is apparent in many African countries, where one is not considered educated unless one has studied in France and speaks French.

'Black Power attacks this brain-washing by saying, WE WILL DEFINE OURSELVES. We will no longer accept the white man's definition of ourselves as ugly, ignorant and uncultured. We will recognize our own beauty and our own culture and will no longer be ashamed of ourselves, for a people ashamed of themselves cannot be free. Because our colour has been used as a weapon to oppress us, we must use our colour as a weapon of liberation. This is the same as other people using their nationality as a weapon for their liberation.

'This coming together around our race was an inevitable part of our struggle. We recognize, however, that this is not the totality, only the necessary beginning. Black Power recognizes that while we are made to feel inferior, this is only so that we may be more easily exploited. Even if we destroy racism, we would not necessarily destroy exploitation. Thus, we must constantly launch a two-pronged attack; we must constantly keep our eyes on both of the bull's horns.

'Colour and culture were and are key in our oppression. Therefore our analysis of history and our economic analysis are rooted in these concepts. Our historical analysis, for example, views the United States as being conceived in racism. Although the first settlers themselves were escaping from oppression, and although their armed uprising against their mother country was around the aggravations of colonialism—"taxation without representation", etc. —the white European settlers could not extend their lofty theories of democracy to the Indian, whom they systematically exterminated as they expanded into the interior of the country. Indeed, in that same town where the settlers set up their model of government based on the theory of representative democracy—in that same town the first slaves were brought from Africa.

'In our economic analysis our interpretation of Marx comes not only from his writings, but from how we see capitalism's relationships to people of colour.

'The Labour movement of the United States, while in the beginning containing some great leaders in the struggle against the absolute control of the economy by the industrial lords, essentially fought only for more money. Those few who had the vision of extending the fight for workers' control of production, never succeeded in transmitting their entire vision to the rank and file. This Labour movement found itself asking the industrial lords not to give up their control but merely to pass out a few more of the fruits of this control. Unlike us, they do not raise questions of redistributing the wealth inside the United States.

'Thereby did the United States anticipate the prophecy of Marx and avoid the inevitable class struggle within the country by expanding into the Third World and exploiting the resources and slave labour of people of colour. United States capitalists never cut down on their domestic profits to share with the workers. Instead they expanded internationally and threw the bones of their profits to the American working class.

'The American working class enjoys the fruits of the labours of the Third World workers. The proletariat has become the Third World; the *bourgeoisie* is white Western society.

'The true potential revolutionaries in this country are the black youths of the ghettoes; those who have developed insurgence in the cities are African-American and Latin communities, where past rebellions have taught important lessons in dealing with the Government's armed reaction to our uprisings.

'These rebellions should not be taken lightly. In the past three years, there have been over one hundred uprisings in the internal colonies of the United States. These are no doubt reported to you as "minor disturbances initiated by a few malcontents". These are major rebellions with large numbers of participants who are developing a consciousness of resistance.

'It is with increasing concern that we see the United States will by any means necessary attempt to prevent the liberation struggles sweeping across the Third World. But in particular we know that the United States fears most the liberation struggle on this continent. In order to secure itself geographically, the United States must have Latin America—economically, politically and culturally. It will not do for the Anglos to be isolated on a continent of hostiles.

'Black Power' not only addresses itself to exploitation, but to the problem of cultural integrity.

'Wherever imperialism has gone, she has imposed her culture by force on other peoples, forcing them to adopt her language and way of life. When African slaves were brought to this country, the Anglo saw that if he took away the language of the African, he broke one of the bonds which kept them united and struggling. Africans were forbidden to speak to each other in their own language. If they were found doing so, they were savagely beaten into silence.

'Western society has always understood the importance of language to a people's cultural consciousness and integrity. When it moves into the Third World, it has moved to impose its own language. In Puerto Rico, where Yankee cultural imposition is at its height, English is taught in all high schools for three years, while Spanish is taught for two years.

'Anglo society learned other valuable lessons from the enslavement of Africans in this country. If you separate a man's family, as was done to the slaves, you again weaken his resistance. But carry the separation further. Take a few of the weaker slaves and treat them as house pets—the lighter skinned slave (the offspring of the master's rape of the African woman) was preferred. Give him the crumbs from the master's table and cast-off clothing and soon he

99

will fear to lose these small comforts. Then use his fears by getting him to report on the activities of the bad slaves, report the impending revolts and uprisings. Distrust and dissent is created among the Africans, and thus they will fight among themselves instead of uniting to fight their oppressors.

'Today's descendants of African slaves brought to America have been separated from their cultural and national roots. Black children are not taught of the glory of African civilization in the history of mankind; they are instead taught about Africa, the dark continent inhabited by man-eating savages. They are not taught of the thousands of black martyrs who died resisting the white slave masters. They are not taught of the numerous uprisings and revolts where hundreds of brave Africans refused to submit to slavery. Instead, their history books read of "happy slaves singing in their fields . . . content with their new lives". Those "few" slaves who did resist are called "troublemakers", "malcontents", "crazy".

'Black children in North America grow up aspiring only to enter white society—not only because white society eats better, is housed and clothed better and can make a better living, but also because they have been bombarded by the white-controlled communications media and educated by black teachers with white minds (our petty Yankees) that white IS better, white is beautiful. Anglo features, manner of speech and aspirations are to be acquired if one is to be successful, even *within* the black community.

'The white man hardly needs to police his colonies within this country, for he has plundered the cultures and enslaved the minds of the people of colour until their resistance is paralyzed by self-hate. An important fight in the Third World, therefore, is the fight for cultural integrity. Wherever Western society has gone, as Frantz Fanon tells us, she has imposed through force her culture. Through force and bribery (the giving of a few crumbs to a few petty Yankees) the people of a conquered country begin to believe the Western culture is better than their own. The young people begin to put aside the richness of their native culture to take on the tinsel of Western culture. They become ashamed of their roots and inevitably can only be trapped in a life of self-hate and private pursuit for self-gain.

'Thus does the West entrap whole peoples with little resistance.

'One of our major battles is to root out corrupt Western values, and our resistance cannot prevail unless our cultural integrity is restored and maintained. It is from our people's history, therefore, that we know our struggles and your struggles are the same. We have difficulty getting the information we need on what is happening in your countries. In so many ways we are illiterate of your heroes, your battles and your victories. We are working now to increase the consciousness of the African-American, so it will extend internationally. The United States fears this more than anything else, not only because such a consciousness would destroy within black communities the minority complex so carefully cultivated by the Anglos, but because it knows that if the black man realizes that the counter-insurgency efforts of this country are directed against his brother, he will not go, he cannot go. Then it will become crystal-clear to the world that the imperialist wars are racist wars.

'During the past year we have instituted a black resistance to the draft movement, not only because we are against black men fighting their brothers in Vietnam, but also because we are certain that the next Vietnam will be on this continent. Perhaps Bolivia, where there are now "special forces advisers"; perhaps Guatemala, Brazil, Peru or the Dominican Republic.

'The African-American has tried for the past four hundred years to exist peacefully inside the country. It has been to no avail. Our history demonstrates that the reward for trying to coexist peacefully has been the physical and psychological murder of our peoples. We have been lynched, our houses have been bombed and our churches burned. We are now being shot down in the streets like dogs by white racist policemen and we can no longer accept this oppression without retribution. We must join those who are for armed struggle around the world.

'We understand that as we expand our resistance and internationalize the consciousness of our people, as our martyred brother Malcolm X taught us, retaliation from the Government will come to us as it did to him. As the resistance struggle escalates, we are well aware of the reality of Che Guevara's words that the "struggle will not be a mere street fight . . . but will be long and harsh". In the end our common brotherhood sustains us all, as we struggle for our liberation by any means necessary.

'But Black Power means that we see ourselves as part of the

Third World; that we see our struggle as closely related to liberation struggles around the world. We must hook up with these
struggles. We must, for example, ask ourselves : when black people
in Africa begin to storm Johannesburg, when Latin Americans
revolt, what will be the role of the United States and that of
African-Americans?

'It seems inevitable that this nation will move to protect its
financial interests in South Africa and Latin America, which means
protecting white rule in these countries. Black people in the United
States, then, have the responsibility to oppose—at least, to neutralize
—that effort by the United States. This is but one example of many
such situations that have already arisen around the world—with
more to come.

'There is only one place for black Americans in these struggles,
and that is on the side of the Third World. Frantz Fanon, in *The
Wretched of the Earth*, puts forth clearly the reasons for this and
the relationship of the concept of a new force in the world :

' "Let us decide not to imitate Europe; let us try to create the
whole man, whom Europe has been incapable of bringing to
triumphant birth.

' "Two centuries ago, a former European colony decided to
catch up with Europe. It succeeded so well that the United States
of America became a monster, in which the taints, the sickness
and the inhumanity of Europe have grown to appalling
dimensions. . . .

' "The Third World today faces Europe like a colossal mass
whose aim should be to try to resolve the problems to which
Europe has not been able to find the answers. . . ."

'It is a question of the Third World starting a new history of
man, a history that will have regard to the sometimes prodigious
theses which Europe has put forward, but that will also not forget
Europe's crimes, of which the most horrible was committed in the
heart of man, and consisted of the pathological tearing apart of
his functions and the crumbling away of his unity.

'No, there is no question of a return to nature. It is simply a
very concrete question of not dragging men toward mutilation,
of not imposing upon the brain rhythms—which very quickly

obliterate it and wreck it. The pretext of catching up must not be used to push man around, to tear him away from himself or from his privacy, to break and kill him.

'No, we do not want to catch up with anyone. What we want to do is go forward all the time, night and day, in the company of man, in the company of all men.'

INTI PEREDO

We Will Return to the Mountains!
Victory or Death!

'And if we were all capable of uniting to make our blows more solid and more infallible, so that the effectiveness of every kind of support given to the struggling peoples were increased, how great and how near that future would be!'—Che Guevara

Guerrilla warfare in Bolivia is not dead!

It has just begun.

The Bolivian guerrillas are now fully on their way, and we will unflaggingly carry the struggle through to the brilliant victory of the revolutionary forces that will bring socialism to Latin America.

Our country has lived through—in principle—a revolutionary experience of undreamed-of continental proportions. The beginning of our struggle was accompanied by tragic adversity. The irreparable physical death of our friend and comrade Major Ernesto Che Guevara, as well as of many other fighters, has been a rude blow to us. They, who were the purest and noblest of our continent's generations, did not hesitate to offer up the only thing they could —their lives—on the altar of human redemption.

But these painful events, far from frightening us, strengthen our revolutionary awareness; increase our determination to fight for a just cause; make it stauncher; and forge, in the purifying and bloody crucible of war, new fighters and leaders, who will honour and pay homage to those who have already fallen.

We know what we are fighting for. We are not waging war for the sake of war. We are not wishful thinkers. We are not fighting for the sake of personal or party ambition. We have confidence in man as a human being. Our single and final goal is the liberation of Latin America, which is more than our continent; it is rather our homeland, temporarily torn into twenty republics. We are convinced that the dream of Bolivar and Che—that of uniting Latin America both politically and geographically—will be attained through armed struggle, which is the only dignified, honest, glorious and irreversible method that will motivate the people. No other form of struggle is purer. Guerrilla warfare is the most effective and correct method of armed struggle.

For this reason, as long as there is a single honest man in Latin America, guerrilla warfare will not die. Armed struggle will surge ahead vigorously until all of the people gain political awareness and rise up in arms against the common enemy, United States imperialism.

Guerrilla warfare in Bolivia is not dead; it has just begun.

Both enemies and friends of the revolution have analysed, more or less profoundly and from a great variety of viewpoints, the complex phenomenon of the guerrilla activity that went on in our country. Guided by petty reasons, they all reach the narrow and biased conclusion that guerrilla warfare is not the correct method for the seizing of power in Bolivia.

Dishonest documents have been put out; accounts have been given which are most biased and slanted; and thus world public opinion has been, to a certain extent, misled in connection with the events. But one thing has not been accomplished : the dulling of the faith and determination of our country's revolutionary forces. The clearest and most unconditional proof of this is the fact that our National Liberation Army (ELN) has remained and still remains staunchly faithful and firm in the struggle, despite the temporary setbacks we have experienced. Due to circumstances, the duty has fallen upon me to explain to the revolutionaries of this country and to those of the whole continent the reasons why we, even though we have recently lost a battle, insist upon our position in support of guerrilla warfare as the most effective and surest method for the seizing of power.

Any one of the comrades who have participated and fallen as heroes in this struggle would likewise have done his duty in this regard. I do so without in the least considering myself the immediate successor of Che Guevara. Being Che's successor would be an undeservedly high honour for me. I am, rather, acting in my capacity as an accidental heir to the last and most valuable teachings of the greatest revolutionary genius of Latin America. I harbour the hope that this document will be a contribution to the rich storehouse of revolutionary experiences of our peoples in their struggle for national liberation, and at no time do I seek to justify our mistakes.

Nor are these words the lamentations or complaints of an isolated survivor of the guerrilla struggle. On the contrary, they are the full expression of the forces making up the National Liberation Army representing our people and having at present the real, staunch and objective conviction that within the armed struggle guerrilla warfare is the specific method offering the best prospects for achieving our ideals of liberty and social justice.

Specious arguments are being put forth in an effort to prove that the opposite is true. It is adduced that 'the guerrilla forces were crushed' in a relatively short time. For us, guerrilla warfare is a form of struggle utilized by the people to seize power, it being understood that one essential characteristic of this form of struggle is its more or less protracted nature.

The first phase of any guerrilla struggle consists in the guerrillas being able to survive until they have established deep roots among the people, mainly among the peasants. The guerrilla nucleus will thus be in a position to renew its forces indefinitely until a stage of development is reached that will render it invincible. From that moment on the guerrilla forces deal the regular army repeated blows, causing it to become demoralized and progressively weaker until it is finally overcome and destroyed completely, along with the régime it supports.

In our own case, the newly established guerrillas were not able to surmount the first phase; but other guerrilla groups will appear and will attain full development and eventually crush the enemy.

Based on this circumstance, our critics have come to the conclusion that our method is the wrong one. They fail to mention and avoid analysing the causes of our partial and temporary defeat. The reason they do not do so is that, in so doing, they would have to judge themselves. They observe our struggle from afar. What is more, isolated they refused to co-operate and carried on anti-guerrilla propaganda against our struggle within the ranks of their own organizations. Later, in order to keep up their 'anti-imperialist' posture, each one of their organizations issued a declaration of 'solidarity' with the guerrilla struggle. But, in fact, that 'solidarity' was mere lip-service in the guise of moral support which they could not avoid giving to a small group of 'romantic dreamers'.

Dreamers! Yes. But those dreamers constituted and still constitute the only force in Bolivia that has set itself the task of seizing power by and for the people. The CPB leadership speaks of the Party's preparations for seizing power by 'all methods'. All of the people should and must take part in the seizing of power. For this reason, the people should be prepared to do so, and it is wrong to talk to the people about 'all' methods at a time when preparations for using one of the methods are being made. When a party or a group sets itself the task of seizing power, that party or group must choose a specific method; not to do so is tantamount to not thinking seriously of seizing power.

In an amusing manner, they want the guerrilla method to be scrapped after the first attempt results in failure, and they insist on the feasibility of the 'democratic' or 'reformist' approach in spite of the permanent failure of the latter method. Let us rule out elections! No serious revolutionary can consider this the road for the taking of power in Bolivia or in any other Latin American country.

How many peaceful demonstrations have been held, in which thousands upon thousands of workers and ordinary people have been violently suppressed—with casualties running into the hundreds—by the Government's repressive apparatus? Still fresh in our minds are the events of May and September 1965, during which factory workers and miners were brutally murdered, almost without offering any resistance. We can never forget the bloody 24th June 1967, when humble and defenceless miners were slaughtered in cold blood even as our guerrilla force, made up of scarcely

107

forty men, dealt the murderous army hard blows, inflicting considerable casualties and demoralizing it internally. We are not against the people's struggles for the sake of obtaining economic and social gains. But we feel sure these struggles will be much more fruitful and effective when they are waged against a government frightened and weakened by the actions of a guerrilla *foco*.

It is this guerrilla *foco* that will prove to the people—with facts —that it is possible to face the power of imperialism and its puppets, and that it is not only possible to face that power, but also that it is possible to win victory over it. The people—and especially the peasants—will not support something they do not consider as being real. To expect the peasants' support for armed struggle when this struggle has not yet come into being is to play at insurrection in the same way some 'theorists' of armed struggle do when they demand the prior widespread support of the peasantry. The peasants will only give concrete support to a guerrilla *foco* when the latter can show that it is strong. That is why, in the first phase, the aim is for the guerrilla force to grow in strength, to survive on the field of operations. During this phase it is essential for the guerrilla force to be given aid from the cities. Our guerrilla *foco* was denied this aid by political forces that knew of the existence of our movement.

The political parties that seek to play the vanguard role in our people's anti-imperialist struggle are duty-bound to be honest and to account to the people for their actions. These parties are also duty-bound to admit their mistakes when they feel they have erred and to explain their actions, if they believe these actions to be correct.

How can these parties pay homage to fallen guerrillas when they attacked them as the guerrillas were preparing to fight? How can the fact be explained that Monje sounded the warning among the ranks of his party against a 'factionist group' deviating from the Party 'line' and that Zamora had Comrade Moises Guevara—who led a group of followers to join the guerrillas—expelled, for the same reason, from the pro-Chinese CPB?

The people demand and are awaiting an explanation for this double-dealing.

We do not intend to blame the CP for our temporary failure. We do not blame anybody for the outcome of this first phase. Our object is to establish the historic responsibility of the parties which in our country claim to be anti-imperialist fighters.

Some people think that we are a force in the process of dispersal. They are wrong. We are at the point of reorganizing our armed command cadres; and we will again take up the struggle in the mountains, because we firmly believe that this is the only road that will lead us to the liberation of our people and of Latin America from the clutches of Yankee imperialism.

We are not seeking the formation of a political party. We shall succeed in the structuring of an armed force capable of facing and defeating the army, the main prop of the present régime in our country. But we are not going to be the 'fighting arm' of any political party.

We are fully convinced that the guerrilla force is not an auxiliary instrument of some other 'higher form of struggle'. On the contrary, we believe—and international experience so proves it—that this form of struggle will lead to the liberation of our peoples.

In the heat of the struggle the different forces that have set themselves the goal of liberating their country will unite, and our National Liberation Army will be joined by militants from the various parties. Then the true alliance of anti-imperialist forces will be a reality.

The forces of the Left will progressively support and join the guerrilla *foco*. Our short experience has already proved this fact.

The leaderships of the various political parties representing the people, whose militancy demands a clear-cut anti-imperialist policy, had to support the guerrilla movement. We know that this support was simply formal, but once the guerrilla force passes beyond its first stage the masses will force the leaders to convert this formal support to *de facto* support, lest they be completely isolated from the masses, without anyone to lead. Only then will the political instrument that the people need for the functioning of their future government emerge.

The liberation of our people can never be the work of one single group or one single political party. In that we agree with the parties of the Left. We need a broad, anti-imperialist front. The question is how to achieve this.

Our short experience has shown us that much more was accomplished in a few months of armed struggle than in many years of sitting around tables. Actually, all the parties that expressed their sympathy were uniting around the guerrilla *foco*, whether or not they want to admit it. We have to ask ourselves how these parties would have acted had the guerrilla struggle continued and become stronger. Positions would have been clearly defined, since in an atmosphere of armed struggle, which demands a clear-cut attitude, there isn't much room for demagogy and deceit.

The title vanguard of the people, or of the working class, is not self-bestowed. It is won by leading the people or the class which should become the vanguard in the struggle towards their objective —in this particular case, towards national liberation—by joining the anti-imperialist struggle everywhere.

The issuing of mere expressions of solidarity with a given form of anti-imperialist struggle—anti-imperialist in essence and in deed —can only place us in a rearguard position as regards the leadership of any revolutionary movement. That is why it is not enough to sympathize with the guerrilla force. One must participate in it and attain its leadership by proving that one is the truest exponent of this form of struggle.

To have pretentions of leading the movement before starting it, or to make one's participation in an anti-imperialist movement conditional on who is leading it, is demonstration of sectarianism, which conflicts with the call to 'anti-imperialist unity'.

It will be the people, and only the people, who will bestow the title of vanguard upon those who lead them to their liberation.

The sectarianism of the so-called vanguard is also made evident in its demands for subordinating the guerrilla leadership to the political leadership. This would lead to the question : to whose political leadership?

Is it, perhaps, a case of dividing the struggle into armed struggle and peaceful struggle, by subordinating armed struggle to peaceful struggle? Or would this be an attempt to use armed struggle as a mere instrument of pressure for the 'political struggle' in the cities?

Why not think, instead, of a sole politico-military leadership, considering that, in a state of war—and guerrilla warfare creates a state of war—the most skilled and able revolutionary cadres are to take care of the war?

The struggle waged in the cities must constitute a support for guerrilla action; therefore, the cities cannot lead the guerrillas. It is the guerrillas, as the armed vanguard of the liberation movement, who should lead the movement. This comes naturally. To try to do the opposite would be tantamount to rendering the guerrillas inoperative, bogging them down. In short, it would lead them to defeat.

The struggle itself will bring forth its leaders. The true leaders of the people will be forged in the struggle, and no one who considers himself a true revolutionary should insist upon leading or fear that his position will be taken from him.

The prolonged nature of the struggle is conducive to a clear awareness of one's goal. The opposing forces become defined, and the principal enemy, Yankee imperialism, shows its true nature. The people are able to see clearly how the imperialists demand that their puppets toe the line more assiduously and that they make clear their intentions. The imperialists are not about to abandon their markets, to surrender their colonies. That is why the people must prepare themselves for a long, hard struggle. To think that we are going to seize power without making sacrifices is to daydream and to create conformism among the people. The struggle will be a cruel and bloody one, and it will be waged throughout the country—even in the most humble huts and isolated regions.

In the face of the constant violence of the Yankee imperialists, we—and the people with us—have chosen the way of revolutionary violence, a violence that punishes the oppressors and that, once it has crushed them, gives way to socialist humanism. In short, we do not preach violence for its own sake, but rather advocate the people's organized retaliation against organized oppression, in order to achieve full freedom. Therefore, it will be the entire people, each and every one of the inhabitants of this country, who will contribute by direct action in the cities and in the countryside towards bringing about the insecurity, fear, panic and final defeat of our enemies.

The national liberation movements all over the world are dealing hard blows at the common enemy, imperialism. The criminal war in Vietnam, despite the fact that it balances the United States economy by converting it into a war economy and thus staving off a crisis, is creating serious problems for the imperialists. All the military power of the Yankees has already been proved ineffective in holding back that glorious people-in-arms. The struggle of our Vietnamese brothers is the struggle of all the revolutionaries of the world. They are fighting for us, and we must fight for them. Their war is our war.

The Yankee imperialists cannot withstand another Vietnam. And it is up to us and our peoples to create this second Vietnam, faithful to the legacy left to us by our heroic Major Ernesto Che Guevara. The idea of creating several Vietnams is no mere whim or the figment of a warmonger mentality, as our enemies and the pseudo-revolutionaries would have others believe; it is an idea in keeping with reality. The Yankee imperialists will not surrender their positions willingly, and on our continent—through their Ministry of Colonies, the OAS—they will order their lackeys in the various countries to join forces to crush any people that may rise up in arms.

The time for a continental revolution has come. We must respond to the united front of the continent's military against the revolution with the unity of all the national liberation movements of the continent. The frantic squealing of the reactionaries and some pseudo-revolutionaries who oppose the participation of patriots from other countries in our people's liberation struggle is nothing but a reflection of their vain attempts to isolate our movement and collaborate with the enemy by creating feelings of chauvinism among the people.

Our guerrillas were attacked by soldiers of the Bolivian Army advised by Yankee 'instructors' (veterans of the war in Vietnam) and equipped with weapons and rations supplied by the armies of Argentina and Brazil. We are sure that, once the guerrillas become a force to be reckoned with in our country and the regular army feels powerless to destroy them, it will receive immediate aid from the armies of several neighbouring countries, in the form not only of war material but also of soldiers. But then the revolutionary war will extend to those countries, bringing about the same state of insecurity and powerlessness among their respective armies. At this point the Pentagon will be forced to change its policy of 'advising' to one of 'direct', ever-growing participation by its troops, as is happening in Vietnam.

Some pseudo-revolutionaries tremble at such a prospect. They wish to spare the people this 'tragedy'. They do not realize that, by acting as they do, they are not avoiding anything. On the contrary, their attitude only serves to keep the people under the scourge of poverty, hunger and death, sacrificing them on the sacrosanct altar of conformism. This is no 'tragedy', weighed against what the people would have to suffer if they were kept under their present yoke for ever, their only prospect being that it would weigh heavier and heavier upon them. This is no 'tragedy', weighed against the miserable lives that our people are forced to lead.

Mining towns are nothing but concentration camps, where the inhabitants don't have any rights—not even the right to amuse themselves, and even less, of course, the right to protest. The massacres that have been systematically perpetrated are tyranny's answer to the just demands of those who bear upon their shoulders the weight of the economy of the country and the luxury of the military castes. No movement of protest or people's demand is tolerated by the military tyranny, the pillar of the present 'democratic' régime. Such movements are violently repressed, to set an example and maintain the 'principle of authority'. Anyone who rebels against such principles will be made to feel the full weight and brutality of the military régime.

Faced with this brutal reality, should we be held back by the prospect of the sacrifices involved in a just war? Our struggle will not demand any more sacrifices than those made by our people under this tyranny. That is why the creation of a new Vietnam does not constitute a 'tragedy'. It is an honour and a duty we will never refuse.

We have lost a battle, a battle in which the foremost leader of the oppressed people, Major Ernesto Che Guevara, gave his life. But our war continues, and we will never stop, because we who fought at Che's side do not recognize the word 'surrender'. His blood and that of other fighters, spilled on the soil of Bolivia, will give life to the seed of liberation and will turn our continent into a volcano spewing forth fire and destruction on imperialism. We will be the triumphant Vietnam that Che, the romantic and heroic visionary, dreamed of and loved.

We are determined to win or die for these ideals.

Cuban comrades died for these ideals.

Peruvian comrades died for these ideals.

Argentinian comrades died for these ideals.

Bolivian comrades died for these ideals.

Honour and glory for Tania, Joaquin, Juan Pablo Chang, Moises Guevara, Jorge Vazquez, Aniceto Reynaga, Antonio Jimenez and Coco Peredo. Honour and glory for each and every one of those who died with weapons in their hands, because they understood that, as Che said : 'Wherever death may surprise us, it will be welcome, provided that this, our battle-cry, reach some receptive ear, that another hand reach out to take up our weapons, and that other fighting men come forward to intone our funeral dirge with the staccato of machine-guns and new cries of battle and victory.'

Our banners bear crêpe, but will never be lowered.

The ELN considers itself the heir to the teachings and example of Che, the new Bolivar of Latin America. Those who cravenly murdered him will never kill his thought and his example.

Let the imperialists and their lackeys withhold their songs of victory, because the war has not ended; it has just begun.

Bolivia will again resound to our cry, VICTORY OR DEATH !

BILL LUCKIN

Students and the Chinese Cultural Revolution

Students in twentieth-century China have many times been militantly involved in political struggle. It was a students' parade in the streets of Peking in 1919, protesting against territorial concessions in favour of Japan in the Versailles Treaty, that first made the West aware of nascent Chinese nationalism, antagonistic to foreign imperialism and impatient of a corrupt republic at home. Students later suffered terribly at the hands of Chiang Kai-shek in the urban purges of the 1920s, especially in Shanghai. Some —Chou En-lai among others—left and were partly educated in Europe. Others, like Mao himself, who was also a part-time, self-educated student, first worked underground to push the industrial working class towards direct action; then, the 'Russian' period of the Party over, turned his attention to the peasant movement. Nevertheless, many young intellectuals, liberal and Marxist, students and young teachers, stayed in the cities and worked as propagandists in the 'thirties, while an increasingly Maoist rural army, evading Chiang's 'round-up' and 'encirclement' campaigns, later embarked on the Long March. Progressive students in the cities were periodically terrorized and executed. Some—including the partly self-educated Liu Shao-chi—survived to take their place in the new régime in 1949.

After the Sino-Japanese war, it was younger and more politically conscious students who staged demonstrations against, and helped to demolish, the last feeble columns of the Nationalist régime in the great urban offensive of 1946-49. These were the mainly bourgeois students who were to become teachers, administrators and cadres in the new China. Mao Tse-tung, who spoke in 1949 of the need for a united front among all the organizations and parties which had fought against Chiang—urban and rural, liberal and Marxist/Maoist—in the new republic, appreciated the value of the student and intellectual effort. The generation of students of the 'thirties and 'forties was unrepresented in the hierarchy of the *politbureau*. But in the early days of the republic they became the new élite of economists, teachers and technologists.

Not all of China's intelligentsia were Marxist or Maoist and, in the early 1950s, the Party scrutinized ever more carefully the class origins of both teachers and students. If China was to become a socialist state it must necessarily have a socialist system of education. Yet virtually all the existing corps of teachers had been educated in the Western style—mainly in missionary schools—hence the re-education drives of 1950 and 1953 and the intermittent rectification campaigns which were often directed nearly as intensively at bourgeois students and the young intelligentsia as at former *rentiers* and businessmen. The Party now demanded 'redness' as well as expertise. Some bourgeois teachers lost their jobs, only to be reinstated later; others were quietly pensioned off in the same way as the urban capitalists, who continued—particularly in the east coast cities where Chinese *compradores* had been most heavily concentrated—to lead a quiet and, in Chinese terms, affluent life, supported by interest paid by the Government for the plant that it had confiscated.

The attempt in the 1950s to 'sinicize' education was not successful. Partly, it was a matter of resources—there were simply not enough teachers to support nominally universal primary education as well as an extensive university system. The other reasons were ideological. Many teachers could not adapt to either politicization or the practical—i.e. manual—sections of the new curricula. The young were amenable to the new ideology and there were institutions—the Young Pioneers, the Young Communist League—ready to confirm their enthusiasm. Most of the teachers, on the other hand, had not experienced the revolution that had steeled the Party leadership and which was already a legend revered by the young. Chinese schools, despite the strivings of multifarious ministries, remained at worst obstinately European in teaching method and at best a weak duplicate of the Russian technocratic model. The typical Chinese classroom was a dull place. Children sat bolt upright at their desks, their hands behind their backs, and only spoke to the teachers when they were spoken to. Rote learning and the drudgery of calligraphy, the traditional banes of Chinese education, had not been eradicated. This was as true of the early 'sixties as of the 'fifties. China was producing more and better graduates, especially in fields such as medicine and geology, and contrary to most Western opinion, the new graduates were successfully modernizing industry and, more importantly, agriculture. But, lower down, for the mass of the people at primary and secondary level, reforms were needed. Mao stressed the importance of linking practice to theory, and students and schoolchildren went to communes during vacations; but young people became increasingly dubious of curricula that tied them for so long to the classroom, while cadres outside went about the more heroic and more advertised job of continuing and consolidating the revolution. A Western fallacy about Chinese education before the cultural revolution was that Chinese students spent all their time producing blast furnaces and building dams, and little on 'formal' education. In fact, they worked a classroom day probably longer than any in the world (there was a lot of pre-revolutionary ground to be made up) and did a certain amount of practical work in their spare time.

Not all students in the early years were ideologically committed to the new régime. This became especially clear during the Hundred Flowers episode in 1957. A minority of students, and rather more than a minority of teachers, revealed themselves quietly or openly anti-Maoist and anti-socialist. Bourgeois students were resentful of manual labour; peasant students who had been lucky enough to get into university claimed that they were discriminated against and that their courses were anachronistic and irrelevant. On the one hand, the *bourgeoisie* saw an opportunity for *revanchism*; on the other, the underprivileged said that the Government had not dealt harshly enough with a materially and culturally affluent *bourgeoisie*. From one side, Mao was called a totalitarian dictator; from the other, he was adjured for Rightism. Mao went into retreat, pondered on the distinction between antagonistic and non-antagonistic contradictions among the people, and in late 1957 decided on communalization and the Great Leap Forward.

It was at this stage—in the late 'fifties—that policy differences first seriously divided the *politbureau*. The rifts were not public : to the outside world the Chinese élite seemed the most stable in all the socialist states. Nor was there any proven attempt to dethrone Mao himself or discard the charisma of Maoism. But a group of the *politbureau*—probably Liu Shao-chi, Teng Hsiao-ping and the rising Peng Chen—disagreed with their leader over several central issues : the relationship with the Soviet Union; the pace of collectivization; and the question—never properly settled—of material incentives. It is probably true to say that the opposition was more 'moderate' than Mao. It wanted consolidation, especially during the disastrous 'hard years' of the early 'sixties, when three successive harvests failed; a 'professional' rather than a guerrilla army, in case of a possible war with the United States; and a more conciliatory attitude towards the Soviet Union.

These early rifts are important because they contained the seeds of the cultural revolution and help partly to explain the students' role in it. On the one hand Mao advocated 'self-reliance' and a continuation of his own version of the 'perpetual revolution' : the cult of the personality burgeoned and young people were adjured more than ever before to emulate 'the heroes of the revolution' for whom, in the 1930s, nothing had proved impossible. On the other hand, the opposition—and especially Teng Hsiao-ping as General Secretary of the Party and Liu Shao-chi as President of State— were supporting their own men in the provinces and the armed forces—cadres quietly or, as in the case of Wang En-mao in distant Sinkiang, very nearly openly anti-Maoist. Beneath the facile unity of the cult of the personality, China was threatened with political schizophrenia. Mao himself was out of contact with the Party. He was isolated in the *politbureau*. (He was later quoted as saying of Liu and his supporters : 'They talked of me as though I was already in the grave.') The inner tensions were bound to erupt into open conflict, involving every section of society. The clash was not so much about who should succeed Mao (the facile interpretation of most Western sinologists), but about the choice of national policies.

During the next period—1960-62—students especially were

vulnerably and ambiguously placed. Food was desperately short. (I was told by one graduate of the Shanghai Foreign Languages Institute that she ate meat only once during 1960.) A Government directive laid down calory quotas for manual and non-manual labourers. At some universities classes ceased and the students were advised to spend as much time as possible in bed to conserve their energy. Other universities disbanded altogether and went labouring on the communes. They took their ideology with them. Some of them got on well with the peasants; others did not. The peasants would not make allowances for urban customs, resented giving food to cadres and students who were physically unable to do a full peasant's day's work and were jealous of industrial workers who had higher fixed wages—although food prices for urban workers were generally higher.

At the same time there was more effort to make a nominally comprehensive educational system comprehensive in reality. This implied an artificial weighting of places in favour of the peasants. But it was soon found that peasants came to secondary and further education much less well prepared than the sons and daughters of cadres, workers and bureaucrats. The Maoist concept was that selection should be based increasingly on class background, and that examinations in specialized subjects should contain a sizeable political element. Thus a peasant's son who did badly in his English exams at a special foreign languages institute was marked up simply because he was the son of a peasant. The procedure was politically defensible but led inevitably to dissension and disagreement both among the pupils themselves and between peasant pupils and teachers, many of whom, at specialist institutes, tended to be more 'expert' than 'red'. 'Cultivated' Shanghai students, sons of workers and Party members, were notoriously 'quick' at picking up knowledge : peasants, owing to the poor quality of primary education in rural areas, were slower. Some of the privileged town-dwellers were contemptuous of their rural classmates' way of life and dress. Furthermore, in a city like Shanghai, it was well known that graduates with influential Party connections could avoid being posted to jobs in far-flung areas like Changsha, when they might want to get married at home. All that was required was a doctor's certificate saying that their health would not stand up to the climate. (The Chinese tend to be obsessively pernickety about frail health, a legacy perhaps from an age when so many children died in infancy from malnutrition or disease.)

When the cultural revolution proper began in 1966 these social and class grievances came into the open. Peasant and poor worker pupils accused their bourgeois teachers of discrimination. Because they had been selected primarily on 'political' criteria, they complained that the courses were not political enough. 'Khrushchevite' Party careerists, 'taking the capitalist road', had denied them the opportunity of gaining the best jobs on graduation. The Party and the Young Communist League had become a closed shop, easily open to those whose parents were Party members, but often closed to those with a peasant background.

In the early days of the cultural revolution, in June 1966, some of these criticisms were formally drafted by the fourth class of the senior grade of No. 1 Girls' Middle School of Peking in a letter addressed to the Party Central Committee and Chairman Mao. The letter complained that entrance to higher education was in the control of 'reactionary elements' and that all middle-school graduates should spend a certain time working and studying with the army workers and peasants. Such work ought to qualify the pupil for a new variety of 'ideological diploma'. Furthermore, admission to higher education ought to be based on the recommendation of workers, peasants and soldiers. The Maoist response was rapid enough to make it seem likely that the 'petition' had in fact been drafted by Chen Po-ta, Mao's amanuensis, rather than by Peking's dissatisfied middle-school girls.

Within a week the State Council and the Central Committee had issued a directive announcing the abolition of the old entry requirements for further education : no new students would be enrolled for a period of six months. Those who were to have gone to university or college were to be encouraged to work on the communes and in the factories. The political upheaval gave the 'underprivileged' among China's students the opportunity to pay off old scores. Embezzlement, lechery, playing an unproletarian piano, buying Western-style perfume for wives—of all these crimes could teachers, professors and principals be accused, and on the very best authority—Mao Tse-tung's. Some of the accusations were true; some were not. The Red Guards were encouraged to 'rebel' and re-educate bourgeois teachers and given a set of rules—the sixteen-point directive of June 1966—upon which to base their rebellion. At the high point of the student phase of the cultural revolution, the summer and autumn of 1966, these rules were largely ignored and, even discounting deliberate misinformation from Washington and Moscow, very serious excesses took place. Later, the Government said it deplored the excesses and warned the Red Guards that there would be punishments for those using violence against class enemies. At the time, however, there was very little the Government—or even Mao himself—could do : many of his rebels had run in the wrong direction and attacked the wrong people. At the height of the violence Lin Piao said, 'Don't hit any-one'. As it was, the hitting had already occurred and only now, as the triple alliances are being drawn painfully together, are some of China's more valuable teachers returning to the lecture-room, back from lavatory-cleaning and coal-carrying.

The cultural revolution, then, provided the opportunity both for settling accounts and for securing reforms which may bring a genuine 'sinification' to all sectors. When finally the whole educational system is again functioning, there will almost certainly be a greater equality between the teacher and pupil : a finer balance between the theoretical and the practical (half a day in the school, half a day in the workshop or on the commune); and a higher political (Maoist) content in all lessons and courses. This is what many of the rebels demanded, and it seems that most of the demands will be met. This is a very remarkable example of success-fully applied student power.

But it would be wrong and naïve to see the Red Guard's role in the cultural revolution in purely educational terms, for to the Chinese—and to Mao himself—the issues are much more broadly political. Certainly specific educational injustices did lead to rebellion, and rebellion to change : equally, much of the student activity was genuinely spontaneous, and not controlled by the Government. Yet it is also true that the Maoists made as much political use of student power as did the students of their freedom to suggest reforms.

To understand why Mao should need to harness student power to bolster up his own—and his *politbureau* supporters'—authority, it is necessary to recapitulate the events which led to the first phase of the cultural revolution in the late spring of 1966. These events have been underpublicized in the West, but are well documented in a series of pamphlets published by the Chinese under the title, *The Great Socialist Cultural Revolution in China*.

Number 2 in the series is particularly intriguing for its revelations of criticisms of Mao by politicians and literati in Peking. The most cutting rebukes came as early as 1961 from Teng To, secretary of the Peking Municipal Committee and a journalist. The attacks in the journal *Frontline* are sometimes oblique and sometimes expressed in allegory:

. . . Recourse to even the finest words and phrases is futile, or rather, the more such clichés are uttered the worse the situation will become. [A reference to Mao's *Thoughts*.]

. . . When a man plans everything himself, flatterers will seize the chance to say things to please him. [A reference to the cult of personality.]

Later, using an obscure historical analogy about a man who suffered from amnesia during the Ming dynasty, Teng To wrote of the amnesiac's 'cure': '. . . he must promptly take a complete rest and say nothing and do nothing, and if he insists on speaking and acting, he will come to grief'.

As early as 1962, then, Mao was being advised to retire: he was also politically threatened. We can only speculate on what occurred in the *politbureau* between 1962 and 1966, but the opposition—and especially Peng Chen with his stronghold in the powerful Peking municipality—clearly gained ground. Whether, early in 1966, there was an attempt to force Mao to step down from the *politbureau* in favour of Liu Shao-chi or Peng Chen, or a coalition, or whether Mao himself finally decided to move against the dissidents, is not of central importance. Whatever the motivation, Mao decided that he had to act. Without the open approval of Liu or Teng, the Peking Party was purged. Peng Chen and his hierarchy were dismissed. The dismissals were not easily accepted either by Party members in Peking or by workers, among some of whom Peng was particularly popular. By early summer Teng and Liu, who may previously have been involved with Peng in an attempted *coup*, found themselves no longer able to support openly what was developing into the cultural revolution.

To whom, then, could Mao turn for ideological and political backing? He was unsure of the loyalty of many of the Party provincial leaders and he had been threatened in Peking. He must therefore find a new power base for consolidating his position and a new organization to harangue and convince dissident cadres of their errors. The power base was near to hand—the PLA (Peoples' Liberation Army) : hence the reappearance of Lin Piao, after years of absence from the political scene through illness. The new organization was the Red Guard movement, which would replace the Young Pioneers and Young Communist League, in Mao's eyes tainted with incipient careerism and revisionism.

To a certain exent Mao's critique of the existing youth organizations can be substantiated. Entry to the Young Pioneers was almost automatic for all but the most bourgeois or unruly of children. (At the school at which I taught, children who misbehaved might be told : 'If you go on like this you won't get into the Young Pioneers.' There is a parallel with gaining 'badges' in the Boy Scouts in Great Britain.) The Young Communist League had also tended, especially in the cities, to be too exclusively open to those who could mouth the right Maoist slogans at the right time. There was little knowledge of Marxism among applicants (there is now little knowledge of Marxism anywhere in China), and certainly no League members had been 'steeled' by any of the required 'revolutionary experience'. In this sense, Mao's invitation to rebel, form communes and reorganize schools and universities under joint teacher/student revolutionary committees both shook up a section of the Party apparatus that had become torpid, and provided doorstep revolutionary experience.

But Mao and his supporters—the committee that included the propagandist Chen Po-ta, Lin Piao and, a little later, the somewhat sinister Chiang Ching (Mrs Mao)—had other tasks for the young revolutionaries. First, they were to break down the power of the 'revisionists' in Peking and Shanghai; then they were to move to other regions, purifying recalcitrant Party cadres, factory managers, workers and peasants. In the first of their tasks they succeeded. At a series of mass-rallies in Peking, Peng Chen, Teng Hsiao-ping and other leaders were harangued and denounced. There was no semblance of 'socialist justice' in these so-called trials. Mao's former long-standing colleagues were prejudged and destroyed. Teng

Hsiao-ping attempted suicide : Peng Chen is now probably dead. Only Liu Shao-chi, because of his popularity and influence among provincial Party leaders, could not be similarly humiliated. Liu was not even publicly named in the Chinese press, and was consistently and euphemistically referred to as 'the most prominent Party person following the capitalist road'. Red Guards called for his head, but throughout the summer Liu remained in his home, surrounded by loudspeakers. He made a self-criticism, then allegedly withdrew it. So far as we know, he is still at home and still nominally President of State.

The Red Guards' other business, outside Peking, proved more testing, and there were many reasons for their partial failure. First, many of them were too young. The Young Communist League had recruited its members principally from university students, those who had already passed through further education and from among young workers. The ethos of the Red Guards—'rebel, destroy the old and bring in the new throughout the country'—appealed more to the senior grades of secondary schools than to the eighteen- to twenty-five-year-olds. These latter groups certainly took part in the 'conversion' campaigns throughout the country, but many preferred to stay behind and reform their own institutions—universities, technical institutes and factories. They chose neither to travel on free passes around the country, dossing down wherever they were tolerated, nor to undertake mini-Long Marches.

Because of the youth and the occasional hysteria of the Red Guards it was always possible for an anti-Maoist official in the provinces to organize his resistance well in advance. Wang En-mao in Singkiang had his own 'Red Guards' waiting at the station when the battalions arrived from Peking. The Maoists were stopped at the ticket-barrier and put on the first train back to the capital. In the factories, also, the Red Guards met resistance from workers whose loyalty lay with long-serving Party cadres and managers. In Peking a group of factory workers put up a *da tse bao* (poster) which read : 'These students are gangsters. Do not let them into the factory. Shoot to kill.' There were many armed clashes. In September Mao, almost as if to incite violence, was alleged to have told the Red Guards that they were 'an *armed* [my italics] revolutionary youth organization'. Near Canton, peasants with hoes chased a group of Red Guards armed with wooden clubs off a commune. Railway workers struck in protest against Red Guard vandalism. Genuine 'opposition' groups, under a hundred different names always with the word 'red' somewhere in their title (mainly based upon legendary military groups of the Civil War period), fought for local officials and bureaucrats. They were condemned by the Maoists as a 'small minority of active counter-revolutionaries'. To confuse matters further, the opposition groups also called themselves Maoists. The 'genuine' Maoists denounced this as 'waving the red flag to hide the red flag'.

The total confusion of the ideological and physical battles that took place throughout the summer and autumn of 1966 and the spring of 1967 has been well described by a dispassionate observer, Andrew Watson, a teacher of English in Sian, the capital of Shensi province in north-west China. After a long and gruelling battle, the Maoist Red Guards finally managed to overthrow the North-West Bureau of the Central Committee of the Party in January 1967. Yet this caused a deepening rather than a healing of social rifts in the region. Some leaders of the student group wanted rapid unification with the workers, but others pointed out that, during the struggle for control in Sian, it had been the workers who had put up the most stubborn and reactionary resistance. For their part, the workers accused the students of 'left-wing' opportunism and misinterpretations of Mao's thought. The crisis reached boiling point when each group in turn tried to gain control of the city's street broadcasting system. Scuffles broke out and the relay system changed hands a number of times. The workers in Mr Watson's hotel were divided among themselves, although all claimed to be Maoists. Both sides took prisoners and wrote posters —'royalist workers surround and beat three hundred students'— which bore no relation to what had actually occurred. In this instance the duel had been mainly verbal, each side yelling Maoist edicts at the other, rather than physical. Significantly, the PLA, a number of whom were present during the conflict, were undecided about which side to support—hardly surprising, since both sides professed themselves to be Maoist so vociferously. Mr Watson's summary of the event is trenchant and illuminating :

No one was the true victor in February . . . in Sian. The only lasting product was increased tension and animosity between the workers, former conservatives, and the students, extreme rebels. This situation appears in many respects to be typical of the situation throughout China now. The social discord and apparent anarchy which is preventing the Chinese people uniting behind Mao seems to be more the product of newly formed social enmities than any anti-Maoist front. However, such a situation is fertile ground should any real anti-Maoists wish to take advantage of it.[1]

That the prevailing 'freedom to criticize' could not be allowed to continue at such a vociferous pitch had been accepted much earlier by the hierarchy—including Mao—in the autumn of 1966. Red Guard control commissions, often liaising with the PLA, were set up to deal with 'hooliganism'. The commissars, who wore grey as distinct from red arm-bands, nominally counted Mao and Lin Piao among their numbers. 'Extremist anarchism' was denounced, as were texts such as Lenin's *Left-Wing Communism—An Infantile Disorder*, which had been listed as required reading by the earlier enthusiasts for the 'Paris communes'. Left-wing opportunism, officially denounced, included trying to change the name of Peking to Red Capital, substituting another colour for 'red' as the stop sign at traffic-lights, renaming streets, French Revolution style, and attacking such stalwarts of early revolutionary days as Soong Ching-ling, the widow of Sun Yat-sen. The students were told not to interfere with production and to go out into the countryside to help the peasants bring in the autumn harvest. Some obeyed Mao's and Lin's directives : others stayed on the rampage. It was intended to reopen some of the schools and universities early in 1967, but in many cases this proved impossible—the pupils had travelled elsewhere and the teachers were too terrified to return to their posts. Many schools were torn apart by the upheaval and it is safe to say that large numbers of teachers were forced to flee.

By mid-1967, the heyday of the students and schoolchildren had

[1] 'An Experience of the Red Guards in Action', *The Times* (August 18th, 1967).

been officially curtailed. This is not to imply that the cultural revolution itself had moved anywhere nearer to a meaningful climax, but merely that the theatre and forces of combat had changed. By that time the outcome had come to depend much more on the loyalties (and divisions) among the PLA—the ultimate upholders of law and order—than on skirmishes between Red Guards and Party officials and bureaucrats. The turning point may well have been the now famous 'Wuhan incident' of July 1967, when two of Mao's close collaborators—Vice-Premier Hsieh Fu-chi, the Minister of Public Security, and Wang Li, Director of Propaganda in the cultural revolution group—were held captive by Chen Tsai-tao, commander of the Wuhan district. Chen was accused of massacring hundreds of Maoist supporters (the figures were probably grossly exaggerated on posters in Peking), but from this time onwards the hierarchy, intermittently at war within itself, had foreseen the dangers of a possible national war, and advocated moderation and the formation of 'triple alliances' between the army, emergent Maoist rebels and those of the Party and bureaucracy who had proved themselves Maoist. The order is significant. The army came first, the Red Guards second, and the formerly downgraded but now less denounced Party, third. Many Party members who had been ousted by Red Guards were admitted to have been over-criticized, and students were quietly but firmly told—usually by Chou En-lai, the perpetual middleman—that veterans of the revolution such as Chen Yi, the Foreign Minister, were 'good elements' and should no longer be castigated.

At the time of writing it is not altogether clear who is 'winning' the cultural revolution, but about half of China's provinces are now officially claimed to be operating under effective triple alliances. The revolution is, at least provisionally, following the traditional Chinese pattern of unity-criticism-unity, although the criticism, especially from the young, has exceeded in ferocity that of all previous campaigns in China's 'perpetual revolution' since 1949. But the ferocity is now channelled and institutionalized in a way that it was not in the high, rebellious summer of 1966. The formalization of the Red Guard movement, the confession of absolute devotion to pure Maoism, came in a declaration of the 1st Congress of the Red Guards, which was held in Peking in February 1967. Ten thousand young militants from three 'headquarters' heard a great deal of rhetoric about the creation of communes and new institutions, but much more about dedication to democratic central-ism, Maoism and their abhorrence of Liu Shao-chi. Part of the declaration read :

The Marxist principle of smashing the old State machinery must be carried out in those organizations which have become rotten because a handful of persons in the Party who are in authority and taking the capitalist road entrenched themselves there for a long time.

Elsewhere the declaration confessed rather lamely : 'We must strengthen . . . our sense of organization and discipline.'

In the space of eight months the young rebels had become potentially orthodox Maoist cadres—Maoist in the sense that they had pledged to use their power exclusively to overthrow Mao's enemies. Meanwhile, in the universities, rival factions—anarchist, leftist and moderates—began to form coalitions for a resumption of academic life.[2]

The late Isaac Deutscher said of the cultural revolution in 1966 :

Young people are called upon to rebel against established authority. The Red Guards have been urged to elect their leaders according to the rules established by the Paris Commune, so that every leader could be revoked or deposed by the electors at any time. These evocations of a Marxist-Leninist tradition would be convincing if at the same time you could hear any genuine debate going on in the country, any genuine discussion, any genuine exchange of opinion. Then this movement could be regarded as a manifestation of a new democracy from below. In fact, all that one has been allowed to hear are Mao's and Lin Piao's denunciation of their 'revisionist' opponents, right or left; you don't hear any dissenting voice; you are not allowed to find out for yourself what Mao's critics have been saying, or on what grounds they have been opposing him. . . . I'm sorry to have to say this; I would have preferred to applaud these Red Guards.

[2] See John Collier, 'Cultural Revolution in Canton', *New Left Review* (March/April 1968).

But they have really acted—unfortunately I can find no other, more adequate expression—in a hooligan-like manner, stopping any debate and muzzling any criticism of the Maoist line.[3]

Part—a great part—of Mr Deutscher's thesis is indisputable. The 'opposition', which is strong and obstinate, has not been granted any access to the media. Only by a very careful sifting of the evidence from official media is it possible to deduce the opposition's strength or policies. Red Guard groups have been allowed to publish their own newspapers : their opponents have not. The Central Committee has continued to be muzzled, presumably because the cultural revolution committee is uncertain of its loyalties. Indeed, had there been general loyalty to the Maoist line in the first place, the cultural revolution and the Red Guards might never have come into being. As with the Hundred Flowers campaign, 'minority' views will probably only be heard *post hoc*, although this time the 'minority' will be vastly bigger, even if it does not ultimately reveal itself to be the 'majority'. This last hypothesis implies a long-drawn-out struggle (the revolution has already lasted for over two and a half years), with the eventual winners, the 'anti-Maoists', no doubt governing China for a period with the cult of Mao as their public ideology, but gradually modifying Maoist policies.

Yet, as I have tried to point out in an earlier section of this article, it would be wrong to see the Red Guard movement—or the criticism movement among the workers—as entirely negative activities. Chinese schools and universities can never again be as academically stultifying as they have been in the past; and if it is argued that the singing of 'Mao Is Our Great Helmsman' for half an hour a day is not good education, it can equally well be argued that it is more exciting than the repetition of traditional Chinese calligraphy and memorized recitation. Furthermore, whatever the 'excesses' of the Red Guards, the activists have at least gained valuable experience in political struggle.

This is the central issue. For too long internal contradictions in Chinese society have remained hidden beneath a (perhaps) politically necessary cult of the personality. Now this cult has been threatened by senior Party members who, after a long period of

[3] Isaac Deutscher, *The Chinese Cultural Revolution* (Bertrand Russell Peace Foundation pamphlet).

passivity, have decided that they can no longer support some of the more crucial Maoist policies. The schisms have now been publicized. It is too easy to conclude that the schisms have been solely created and exploited by Mao. The reality is quite different. Mao and Maoism are the products, not the moulders or destroyers of, contemporary Chinese society. After Mao the internal contradictions will continue for as long as the 'permanent revolution' continues. And the most significant factor in the years to come, as the Chinese people move towards genuine unity and nationhood, will be the policies of the United States. The phenomenon of the Red Guards is as much a creation of American aggression in South-East Asia as of the propaganda department of the cultural revolution committee in Peking.

Since the above was written, the most significant developments have been : first, Liu Shao-chi's official dismissal; and second, a further consolidation of the triple alliances and the revamped Maoist Party. However, this crucial question remains : by whom, and how democratically, will China be governed after Mao's death?

JACEK KURON and KAREL MODZELEWSKI

Poland

THE GENERAL SOCIAL CRISIS OF THE SYSTEM

No social system has collapsed solely because it exploited and oppressed the masses. On the other hand, no class can maintain its rule for any length of time if it is based only upon coercion, victimizing the rest of society.

To achieve some minimal viability, a ruling class must provide other classes and strata, within the framework of its system, with improved material and spiritual conditions of life, the basis of which is economic development. If it cannot do that, even bayonets will not help. Thus, as long as the conditions of production underlying class rule of the central political bureaucracy favoured rapid economic development (the period of forced industrialization), mass social advancement improved the lot of millions of people and raised the cultural level of society as a whole, enabling the bureaucracy to establish its hegemony. And during the post-October (1957) period of stabilization, although social mobility was limited, the working class and almost all social strata, nevertheless, saw a positive increase in their individual incomes. But what can the bureaucracy give them today, when the system is in economic crisis?

In the nature of things, the working class is the chief opponent of the bureaucracy. The worker stands on the lowest level of the social ladder, with everyone from the foreman to the prime minister above him and no one below him. Because the exploitation of the worker constitutes the material basis maintaining the system, the

131

entire apparatus of power and coercion is directed primarily against the working class. This is the way it was in the past and the way it is now. But during the periods 1949-55 and 1956-59 the workers' lot improved, although for different reasons in each of these two periods. However, according to official statistical data, in the 1960-63 period the average real income per capita among families of industrial workers only rose by 2.6 per cent (0.6 per cent yearly on the average). Taking into account the hidden increase in living costs due to changes in lines of goods and, in recent years, the price rise of articles of prime necessity, the standard of living of the working class has actually declined during the last four years. This state of affairs was particularly painful for the majority of families : none of them benefited and the number of wage-earners did not increase.

The Plan for the 1967-70 period provides for the creation of 1.5 million new jobs, at the enormous cost of 830-40 million *zloty* (57 *zloty*=£1) set aside for investment. Yet, according to the calculations of the demographers (Holzer's article in *Trybuna Ludu* published before the 15th Plenum of the CC of the PUWP), the increase in the working age population during that period will amount to two million. This means that if the Plan is fulfilled, there will be no jobs for about 500,000 people. At the 4th Party Congress, no increases in real wages were promised; from published data (28 per cent increase in individual consumption alongside an 18 per cent increase in unemployment), one may conclude that, if the Plan is executed ideally, the average real wage will increase by about 10 per cent—about 2 per cent yearly—during the Five-Year Plan period. However, Professor Kalecki has shown that necessary raises alone consume nearly 2 per cent of the wage fund every year.

Apart from this, there is a growing differential between the earning levels of workers, on the one hand, and managers, engineers and technicians, on the other. According to official data, in the 1960-63 period, the average real income per capita in families of white-collar workers employed in industry rose by 11.6 per cent, while the increase for workers' families was only 2.6 per cent. In the CC's report to the 4th Party Congress, it was mentioned that the investment fund has been so calculated as to make possible 'at least a stabilization of real wages'—that is, at the edge of the inflationary barrier. This means that workers' real wages in the coming five years must be lowered somewhat if the Plan is to be realized. But in all the twenty years of the Polish Peoples' Republic, investments have always cost more than planned and have never achieved fruition within the allotted time. Nothing indicates that the coming Five-Year Plan period will be an exception. The sum of 840 billion *zloty* will probably prove to be insufficient for carrying out a businesslike programme of investment, and the collapse of this programme will mean a drastic rise in unemployment. It will be necessary to find additional means for the realization of the investment programme. Since these means can only be found by drawing from the consumption fund, the assumption that real wages can be stabilized will prove false. A substantial fall in real wages will result and the inflationary barrier will be broken.

The possibilities of supplementing the investment fund by lowering real wages are limited, however, for economic and political reasons. Therefore, it is likely that the investment programme for the 1966-70 period will not be fulfilled after all and no way will be found of creating the 1.5 million new jobs. The number of people for whom there will be no jobs will, then, exceed half a million.

The mass proportions of unemployment will probably compel the economic bosses to employ some of these people despite the shortage of jobs. In that case, the nominal wage fund will rise, while production will not increase. This will cause a disruption in the balance of the market. Prices will soar and real wages will fall further, while hundreds of thousands of people of working age will still find no work.

As can be seen, in a growing crisis the system not only deprives the working class of the prospect of an improved material situation; it is not even able to assure the maintenance of earnings at the present level or the retention of jobs.

By treating social consumption as a necessary evil, the bureaucracy tries to keep the earnings of numerous categories of hired workers at subsistence levels. These include not only industrial, construction and transport workers, but also the large majority of white-collar employees in telecommunications, the communal economy, trade, the health services, education and the lower echelons of the civil service. This mass of low-paid white-collar employees differ in no way from the working class in terms of their material situation and future prospects. Everything we have said about the workers' material conditions of existence when the system is in economic crisis applies to the large majority of all employees outside agriculture.

Industrialization has brought a substantial improvement to the social and cultural conditions of the working class. Education has become universal and the young have been given an opportunity to advance since university education has become accessible to all. Many of these achievements—State housing at low rents, free medical care, social benefits, etc.—constitute an indispensable part of the historically determined subsistence level, given the low level of the working wage. In crisis conditions, the bureaucracy first limits all expenditures which might be called 'investments in the human being', and this hits the poorest categories of the population hardest : the working class, the low-paid white-collar employees and the poorer peasantry.

Despite the very bad housing situation, Poland is one of the last on the European list in meeting the demand for housing construction. It has adopted a co-operative system which is supposed to supply 60 per cent of the apartments in the next Five-Year Plan. That is why the costs of building apartment houses were transferred from the State budget to individual incomes, which means that apartments will not be obtained by those who need them most, but by those who can pay for them. For a worker, whose wages are hardly sufficient to survive, it is practically impossible to get an apartment.

Cuts in cultural expenses together with higher prices in this area cause a decline in cultural activities. Theatre audiences are smaller and the quantity of periodicals and books, including textbooks, drastically decreased. This particularly hurts workers' families, who exist on a minimum subsistence level and for whom the higher prices of books, theatre and movie tickets, etc., amount to giving up many elementary cultural goods.

Cuts in expenses for higher education, in particular for scholarships, student cafeterias and dormitories, make it difficult for youngsters from workers', peasant and lower-middle-class families to attend universities. Their percentage in higher education decreases : a money standard limits their rights to education and social advancement.

In a growing crisis, working conditions inevitably deteriorate.

The growing danger of unemployment makes managers and supervisors more refractory and greatly facilitates official pressure on the workers. Formerly, exploitation was covered up by compulsory, sloganized and sometimes authentic enthusiasm. The powers-that-be liked to put on overalls and prided themselves on their working-class origins. They decorated shock workers and found it unfitting to pay the manager ten times as much as the worker. Today, the authorities wear elegant suits and the manager who knows best how to squeeze the surplus product out of the workers is a positive hero of socialist construction, while his villa and car are visible symbols of his social prestige and civic virtue. Today, exploitation is evident and visible to all, and its tool is not propaganda or forced enthusiasm but the whip of economic penalty, of administrative coercion and—in cases of organized attempts at resistance—of police violence. Today, the trade unions, jointly with the Government and together with the managements, execute resolutions and decisions on firing workers (Operation 'R').

Thus the crisis worsens the material, cultural and social situation of the working class, intensifies the degree of its captivity in its place of work and completely deprives if of prospects for the realization of its minimal interest within the framework of prevailing production and social relations. *It forces the working class to come out against the system in defence of the present level of its material and spiritual existence.*

The bureaucracy will not willingly give up to the working class even one *zloty* and, in conditions of economic crisis and lack of reserves, it has nothing to give up under pressure. In this situation, any large-scale strike action cannot but transform itself into a political conflict with the bureaucracy. For the working class, it is the only way to change its situation. *Today, at a time when the system is going through a general crisis, the interest of the working class lies in revolution* : the overthrow of the bureaucracy and the present relations of production; gaining control over one's own labour and its product; control over the production goals—the introduction of an economic, social and political system based on workers' democracy. The interests of the vast majority of white-collar employees coincide with those of the working class.

For the countryside, the crisis means mass-reductions in the number of worker-peasants, the resurgence of rural overpopulation and the loss of sources of income outside agriculture that support poor peasants and a large number of small farms. For the majority of peasants, it means not only a lack of prospects for improvement, but an absolute worsening of their material situation and a danger of their farms' failing. Only the small minority of rich peasants can benefit from this through an increased supply of cheap labour and cheap land which will open possibilities for capitalization. But even this richest group feels the fiscal pressure of the State as a limitation on its possibilities of accumulation and capitalist development. Therefore, despite the fact that the present agricultural policy is relatively the most suitable from its point of view, its attitude towards the system is hostile and it will not lend active support to the ruling bureaucracy.

If society in general is deprived of perspectives, it is the *youth* who experience this most painfully. Unemployment is a disaster for the working class as a whole, but young people just reaching working age are the first to be jobless. Transition to co-operative building deprives the majority of city dwellers of the chance to improve their housing situation; while young people about to marry and start a family find it most difficult to find a place of their own. The danger of rural overpopulation threatens the well-being of the majority of peasants, but most of all the members of the younger generation who, if it became a reality, would not find jobs in industry, while at the fathers' or elder brothers' farms they would, at best, have the status of agricultural labourers. Inadequate investments for higher education retard the development of the whole of society, but inflict the greatest damage on the children of workers, peasants and small town dwellers.

Since the youth are finding it particularly difficult to secure a place in the life of the community and are among the most seriously hurt by the economic, social, ideological and moral crisis, they constitute a potentially revolutionary element in every stratum.

It would appear that today the *technocracy* is the chief pillar of bureaucratic power in society, since it is bound to the ruling class by its privileges and special role in the productive process. Reality would undoubtedly conform with appearance if this technocracy could achieve its natural aspirations within the framework of the existing system. Before 1956, it was a stratum of badly paid supervisors whose salaries were much smaller than those of the small prewar groups of administrators at the service of capital. But along with the postwar impetus to industry, a managerial cadre emerged and the directors' chairs were filled by people who owed their advancement, and everything else, to the system.

Today, the technocracy has become a stable stratum conscious of its own interests. It enjoys the privileges of high consumption and is in conflict with the working class in its daily supervisory function and in its hankering for a form of 'managerial socialism'. On the other hand, we have seen that the class goal of production under the present system is alien to the interests of the technocracy, which acts against the goals set up by the bureaucracy whenever it has an opportunity to exercise any initiative. That is why the managerial stratum is deprived, not only of all influence on general economic decision-making, but also of the right to decide on matters of fundamental significance for its own plants and its own work. In the existing system, the technocrats can be nothing more than executors and supervisors who cannot realize their own aspirations. They yearn for decentralization of management based on the Yugoslav model, thereby seeking a change in the production relations. The slogan 'power to the experts', popular with this group, expresses both the managers' opinion of what the social range of democracy should be in their kind of socialism as well as their hostility towards the existing system and the central political bureaucracy at its head.

The interests of the technocracy, exceeding the limitations of the existing system, drive it into opposition to the ruling bureaucracy.

We have seen also that the entire working class, the majority of low-paid salaried employees, almost the entire peasantry (with the exception of the richest group), the youth—in other words, the overwhelming majority of the population—have no prospect of improving their lot within the framework of the existing system. On the contrary, the growing crisis worsens their material, social and cultural living conditions. In these circumstances, the bureaucracy is deprived of social support and must rely on blatant economic, administrative and political coercion, which clearly reveals the class nature of its dictatorship. The control of the political police over society is tightened, not because it is again to become a Moloch that will devour the Party itself but because, in all strata, hostility to the ruling bureaucracy is sharpening and any autonomous organization of social forces in this situation signifies mortal danger for the system. The legislation of total Stalinist dictatorship—the so-called 'Small Criminal Code'—has been dusted off.

By its very nature, the bureaucracy destroys initiative, since its rule is based on a monopoly of social organization and the atomization of independent social forces. This tendency is reinforced during times of crisis, when any authentic social initiative becomes a more dangerous threat to the bureaucracy. Initiatives connected with the development of social thinking and with the enrichment of cultural and ideological life—discussion clubs, cultural societies, etc.—are subjected to strict control and treated by the authorities as a potential danger. The same applies to all signs of independent ideological/ political activity and to discussions in the livelier youth and Party organizations, something that the members of the Party and SYU at the university know from their own experience.

Since it no longer has the possibility of imposing its hegemony on the rest of society, the bureaucracy has no ideology of its own; nothing has replaced the official Stalinist doctrine which was shattered in 1956-57. The bureaucracy justifies its political and economic moves in the name of the 'national interest'. The national interest, if it is not the interest of the various classes and strata in society, can only be the interest of the class in whose hands State power resides. No matter how hard the bureaucracy tries to obscure its class interest by presenting it as the general national interest, nationalism preached from a position of power in a period of social crisis has little chance of gaining social support.

Having no official, coherent ideological system, while at the same time controlling the sum total of collective life and all forms of ideological life in the country by means of organizational, administrative and police methods, the bureaucracy seeks to eliminate all signs of ideological independence in a time of general crisis. For ideology is the consciousness of people acting socially in conditions of crisis. When the interests of the overwhelming majority of society can no longer be satisfied within the framework of the system, and they are turned against it, then authentic ideology and social activity reflecting the interests of given strata must, ultimately, turn against the bureaucracy.

This situation has especially sharp repercussions on the creative intelligentsia, for its social function is the scientific formulation of social thought and the artistic expression of ideas. The ideological crisis in society signifies a crisis in creativity for this stratum and all attempts to overcome it and achieve ideological independence for its creative members are administratively repressed. Engaged scholars, writers and artists are discriminated against by publishing houses and cultural policy-makers. They are denied access to mass-media—that is, the chance to practise their profession; socio-literary periodicals that exhibit even a minimum degree of independence are replaced by publications which are then boycotted by the most eminent creative people; the intensification of censorship narows down still further the already small margin of professional freedom among the creative intelligentsia. In this way, the ideological crisis becomes the source of a crisis in cultural creativity.

The ideological crisis also brings in its wake a crisis of moral values and norms, especially for youth in the process of forming their views and ideals. What results is cynicism, crude careerism, hooliganism; mass-thefts, too, are not just an economic phenomenon.

As the economic crisis cannot be overcome within the framework of present production relations, so, too, the general social crisis cannot be overcome within the limits imposed by prevailing social relations. A solution is possible only through the overthrow of prevailing production and social relations. *Revolution is a necessity for development.*

No social class sides with the bureaucracy in crisis. At best, the rich peasants and *petite bourgeoisie* might remain neutral. But only the working class, because of its conditions of life and work, *is compelled* to overthrow the bureaucracy. The essential origins of the economic and social crisis lie, as we have seen, in the production relations that prevail in the sector of heavy industry; that is, in the relationships into which the working class and the central political bureaucracy enter mutually in the productive process. Revolution is thus, first of all, the conflict between these two fundamental classes in an industrialized society. That is why the working class must be the chief and leading force of revolution. The revolution that will overthrow the bureaucratic system will be a proletarian revolution.

It is often said that a tremendous power apparatus, having at its disposal modern means of material coercion, is sufficient for the ruling class to perpetuate its power even without any social backing. Despite appearances of modernity in the argument, this is an error as old as class society and the State itself. In October 1956, we saw that a powerful coercive machine in Hungary proved helpless and collapsed within a few days. The working class produces and transports weapons, serves in the armed forces, produces the entire material potential of the State. The walls of prisons, barracks and arsenals are durable, not because they have been built of solid materials, but because they are guarded by the authority of the powers-that-be, by fear and accommodation to the prevailing social order. These psychological walls allow the ruling powers to secure their position atop the walls of brick. But a deepening social crisis undermines the psychological walls that are the real defence of the ruling powers and, as a revolutionary situation matures, the walls of brick, too, will crumble. In view of the impossibility of overcoming the crisis within the framework of the bureaucratic system, *revolution is inevitable.*

THE INTERNATIONAL PROBLEMS OF THE REVOLUTION

We are told : 'We live in the centre of European conflicts. The world is divided into camps, and both sides have atomic weapons. All revolutionary movements in this situation are crimes against the nation and against humanity. The Polish *raison d'Etat*, following from the international situation and our geographical situation, demands our silence and obedience. Otherwise, we are menaced with atomic annihilation or, at best, with intervention by the tanks of a friendly power, as happened in Hungary. Under such conditions, to analyse social structures, to discuss surplus value, to work out political programmes—these are occupations which are either irrational or simply harmful. In order to build socialism one must first of all *exist.*'

Since this is a political argument, it is not a matter of indifference who says it and why. It is said first of all by the very representatives of the ruling State power, although they do not always dot all the 'i's'. It is also said by people who reluctantly admit to connections with the Government, but willingly suggest that, at the bottom of their souls, they are opposition-minded. They, nevertheless, proclaim obedience to the ruling State power, since they defend it. As propagandists of the system they speak; as alleged members of the opposition they are silent; their resistance does not go beyond the intimate area of their spiritual experience. In point of fact, therefore, they belong in the camp of the ruling State power and they plead the cause of the ruling bureaucracy.

This argumentation is, to put it delicately, somewhat equivocal : the leaders and propagandists of a system which has at its disposal all means of coercion and destruction, call on the masses for obedience in the name of maintaining peace. As a typical argument 'from a position of strength,' this blackmail can be rational and convincing. Let us therefore calmly consider this reasoning without deluding ourselves that it is a form of gentle persuasion.

(1) This thinking is based on the assumption that revolution is the result of a criminal conspiracy against internal or world peace. It is the traditional argument of all anti-revolutionary ideologies and well known in the history of the workers' movement. It is typical police thinking. In reality, revolutions are the result of economic and social crises.

From the social point of view, revolution is always an act of force which pits the strength of a social movement against that of the ruling power. But revolution is the act of an enormous majority of society directed against the rule of a minority that is in political crisis and whose apparatus of coercion has been weakened. That is why revolution does not necessarily have to be carried out by force of arms. The possibility of avoiding civil war depends on such factors as the level of consciousness and organization of the revolutionary movement which limit the degrees of chaos and the possibilities of armed counteraction. The real crime against the internal peace of the country is committed by the ruling bureaucracy, which first tries to disorganize the masses, deprive them of political consciousness, and then uses armed force to try to break their revolutionary movement. We remember Poznan and Budapest.

(2) The argument of Soviet tanks. It is said that an eventual revolution in Poland would inevitably lead to Soviet armed intervention, the result of which, from the military point of view, is not

open to doubt. Those who advance this view assume that everything takes place in 'one country in isolation' which, by way of exception, is torn by class struggles, while in neighbouring countries there are no classes but only regular armies with a given number of planes and tanks. For them, the revolution neither crosses national boundaries nor has an effect beyond them.

This typical 'political realism' completely contradicts historical experience. Revolutionary crises have always been of an international nature : 1956 was no exception, but the bureaucracy then had at its disposal economic and social reserves which enabled it to handle the crisis by a reform manoeuvre. This made it possible to put a brake on the development of the revolution in Poland, to prevent a revolutionary situation from arising in Czechoslovakia, the GDR and the USSR and, thereby, permitted the Hungarian Revolution to be isolated and crushed. The present phase of the crisis is marked by a lack of the necessary reserves for such a manoeuvre. This is true not only of Poland but also of Czechoslovakia, the GDR and Hungary, and even of the USSR itself. It is difficult to foresee in which of these countries the revolution will begin; it is certain, however, that it will not end where it begins. The crisis in these countries cannot be mitigated, even temporarily, by reforms and concessions, because there is nothing more to concede or to reform within the framework of the system. Under these conditions, the revolutionary movement must spread to the whole camp, while the possibilities of armed intervention on the part of the Soviet bureaucracy (if it is still in power) will not be measured by the number of its tanks and planes but by the degree of tension of class conflicts within the USSR.

The anti-bureaucratic revolution undoubtedly undermines the political stabilization of neo-capitalism, although it obviously more directly menaces the central political bureaucracy. In any case, it is improbable that Western imperialism, which would gladly take the place of the overthrown bureaucracy, would resort to intervention for that purpose. The working class in the developed Western countries has won a relatively wide margin of democratic freedoms for itself and for society. Therefore, war requires proper preparation of public opinion. Understanding this, an armed crusade against the countries of the anti-bureaucratic revolution is most implausible, since it would run counter to public opinion, lead to mass-resistance and an active anti-war struggle by the working class which, over there, is a well-organized and powerful political force. Moreover, neo-capitalism is threatened by the colonial revolution. A final deterrent to imperialist intervention against an anti-bureaucratic revolution is that it would threaten to escalate into a suicidal, world-wide conflict.

(3) The atom bomb is a modern addition to the traditional arsenal of anti-revolutionary arguments. Today, when the stocks of nuclear weapons are more than enough to destroy the world, the governing élites of the two great blocs which share power in the world decry revolution as a crime against internal peace and humanity. Those who possess the arsenals filled with the means of nuclear annihilation, the leading circles of imperialism and the international (central political) bureaucracy, demand obedience from the masses in the name of avoiding a world-wide nuclear war.

A world nuclear conflict would be absurd from the point of view of the goals of both great blocs; it would lead to the destruction, if not of the whole of mankind, at least of the major powers and of the parts of the world that are most thickly populated and economically and culturally advanced. It would be suicide. The two great blocs do not want mutual destruction in any case, but are engaged in an economic, political and diplomatic competition based upon a division into spheres of influence. In their struggle against revolutionary movement, atomic weapons are a means of blackmail. It is a well-known fact, however, that since the end of the Second World War, revolutionary wars have been waged continually in various parts of the world, while at the same time, and *independent of them*, the two great blocs, having atomic weapons at their disposal, carry on their politics of tension and *rapprochement*. This was pointed out recently by the leaders of the Chinese bureaucracy when their conflict with the Soviet bureaucracy and attempt to strengthen their independence and international position drove them to an alliance with the forces of the colonial revolution.

The bureaucracy speaks a great deal about the need to maintain peace on the basis of the *status quo*. But every time its rule has been threatened, it has not hesitated to use armed might. It used tanks against the demonstrating Berlin workers in June 1953; it did the same against the Poznan workers in 1956 and against the workers of Novocherkassk in 1962; it launched a regular war against the working class in Hungary.

The leaders of the imperialist countries compete with the bureaucracy in peace phraseology. But the history of the last twenty years is rife with armed interventions and wars against the colonial revolution : from the crushing of the liberation struggle of the Greek partisans, through Korea, Vietnam, Algeria, Cuba and right up to the Congo and aggression against the Democratic Republic of Vietnam.

(4) It is understandable that the ideological spokesmen of the ruling classes do not like to reflect upon the social causes of the war danger, while they hold as undesirable 'surplus value considerations'. In reality, this matter has never been as urgent as it is today, when the alienation of labour assumes material forms that threaten the existence of mankind, when the surplus product created by the workers of the West, by the nations exploited by imperialism, and by the workers of the USSR is turned against them in the classical form of police, prisons, marines and tanks, to which may be added the means of atomic annihilation.

The sources of the war danger are the growing social conflicts that give birth to and deepen the crisis in the world rule of the system of anti-popular dictatorship. This is true in the first place of imperialism which, being unable to maintain its rule over the backward countries, wages wars of intervention and continually embarks on new political adventures of 'brinkmanship'. But this is also true of the international bureaucracy : we remember the Berlin crisis of 1961, the provocative installation of Soviet rocket-launching sites in Cuba and the threat to the Cuban Revolution and world peace which followed; we remember the operations undertaken by Soviet tanks in Berlin and the war of intervention launched against the Hungarian Revolution.

Every assault on revolutionary movements strengthens anti-popular dictatorships and increases the risk of war. The danger of war can be done away with finally only by eliminating its social sources—imperialism and bureaucratic dictatorship. The possibilities for limiting this danger today and of its complete elimination in the future are afforded mankind by an organized international revolutionary movement conscious of its goals.

(5) Bureaucracy and the revolutionary movement in the world :

The young Soviet Republic was able to defend itself successfully against the intervention of the imperialist countries, thanks to the struggle of the working class in the West and the wave of revolutionary movements that shook the world towards the end of the First World War and after the triumph of the Russian Revolution. The maintenance and general development of Soviet Russia as a *workers' state* depended on the results of the revolutionary struggles in other countries, especially in the industrialized countries of the West. Lenin, Trotsky and the other Bolshevik leaders realized that only another revolutionary power could be a genuine ally of the proletarian dictatorship. That is why the ideology and foreign policy of Soviet Russia in that early period had an internationalist character. As the Soviet state became bureaucratized and the ruling élite was transformed into a ruling class, an international revolutionary movement could not serve as a natural ally of the Soviet bureaucratic class. The movement had to be—and was—subordinated to the directives of the Soviet bureaucracy, to provide a convenient bargaining counter and tool for the realization of the State interests of the USSR's ruling bureaucracy. We know the results.

On the other hand, every independent and victorious revolution is a menace to the bureaucracy. For revolution is a sovereign act by the masses, whose example and contagious ideas strike at the ideological hegemony of the bureaucracy over its own subjects. Moreover, victorious revolutions do not subordinate themselves to the dictates of the Soviet bureaucracy; hence they threaten the rule of the international monolith, which is also dangerous for the internal monolith. The first country where an independent, victorious revolution took place after the Second World War was Yugoslavia, the second China. We know the results.

That is why the Soviet bureaucracy follows this principle : 'socialism' will reach as far as its army. In the name of this principle, it first tried to subordinate to its own police and its own bureaucrats the Spanish Revolution, which it then betrayed; it forbade the French and Italian communists to carry on a struggle for power in the 1945-46 revolutionary situation; it betrayed the Greek Revolution; it tried to pressure the Chinese communists to abandon the struggle against Chiang Kai-shek's army.

Snatching countries from capitalist domination has always been a factor that favours the revolutionary struggle against imperialism.

But the bureaucratization of those countries is a factor that puts a brake on the development of the colonial revolution and on the struggle of the working class of the highly developed capitalist countries. Through its foreign policy based on the sharing of spheres of influence with imperialism and on maintaining the *status quo*, through its ideology which sanctions this policy, and finally through its influence on the official communist parties, the international bureaucracy opposes the anti-capitalist revolution. The colonial revolution, however, escapes its control; it is successfully organized and directed by groups which stand outside the official communist parties. Witness Cuba, witness Algeria.

The control exerted by the international bureaucracy over the world communist movement is going through a crisis that has been deepended profoundly by the first anti-bureaucratic revolutions in Poland and Hungary. A victorious anti-bureaucratic revolution will put an end to the dictatorship's control and prove to be the natural ally of the world revolutionary movement.

PROGRAMME

Thus far we have considered the revolution as the gravedigger for the old order. It also creates a new society. Is the working class, which must be the main and leading force of the revolution, capable of developing a real, viable programme?

The class interest of the workers demands the abolition of the bureaucratic ownership of the means of production and of exploitation. This does not mean that the worker is to receive, in the form of a working wage, the full equivalent of the product of his labour. The level of development of the productive forces in a modern society necessitates a division of labour in which there are unproductive sectors, supported by the material product created by the worker. Therefore, under conditions of a workers' democracy, it will also be necessary to set aside from the total product a part earmarked for accumulation, for the maintenance and development of health services, education, science, culture, social benefits and those expenditures for administration and for the apparatus of political power which the working class will recognize as indispensable. The essence of exploitation is not that the working wage represents only a part of the value of the newly created product, but that the surplus product is taken away from the worker by force and that the process of capital accumulation is alien to his interests, while the unproductive sectors serve to maintain and strengthen the rule of a bureaucracy (or *bourgeoisie*) over production and over society, and thus in the first place, over the labour and social life of the working class.

To abolish exploitation means, therefore, to create a system in which the organized working class will be master of its own labour and the resulting product; in which it will set the goals of social production, decide on the sharing and use of the national income, hence define the size and purpose of investments, the size and disbursement of expenditures for social benefits, health services, education, science and culture, the amount for the power apparatus and its current tasks. In brief, a system in which the working class will exercise economic, social and political power in the State.

How should the working class and its state be organized in order to rule over its own labour and its product?

(1) If there is no workers' democracy in the factory, there can be none in the State on any long-term basis. For it is only in the factory that the worker is a worker, that he fulfils his fundamental social function. If he were to remain a slave in his place of work, then any freedom outside the place of work would soon become 'Sunday freedom', fictitious freedom.

The working class cannot rule over its own labour and its product without controlling the conditions and goals of its toil in the factory. To that end, it must organize itself in the plants into workers' councils, in order to run the factories. The manager must be made into a functionary subordinate to the council, controlled, hired or dismissed by the council.

However, these days, all key decisions relating to the management of an enterprise are made centrally. Under these conditions, the workers' council would, in practice, be deprived of power. The manager is closely bound up with the offices which make the decisions—the central apparatus of economic management. In this situation, the workers' council would inevitably be reduced to an adjunct of the management, as is the case with the present-day Conferences of Workers' Self-Government.

To manage enterprises through its workers' councils, the working class must make the enterprise independent, creating the preliminary conditions for workers' democracy and, at the same time, adapting management relationships to the new class goal of production. (As we have already shown, the system of centralized management is an organizational tool of production for the sake of production, whereas production for the sake of consumption requires a decentralized system.) Thus, while taking the first step towards realizing its programme, the working class achieves that which is most far-reaching and progressive in the programme of technocracy : the independence of enterprises. However, the working class and the technocracy imbue this concept with fundamentally different social contents. To the technocracy, independence of an enterprise means that management has full powers in the factory. For the working class, it means self-government for the working force. That is why the working class must go beyond plant management via the councils. Workers' self-rule, limited to the level of the enterprise, would inevitably become fictitious and a cover for the power of management in the factory and for the rule of a new technocratic bureaucracy; exploitation would be maintained and the former state of chaos would return in a new form.

Basic decisions relating to the sharing and use of the national income naturally have a general social character; that is, they are made on an economy-wide scale and, therefore, they can only be made centrally. If these central decisions were to remain outside the influence of the working class, it would not rule over the product that it has created and over its own labour.

(2) That is why, in addition to factory councils, the working class will have to organize itself into a nationwide system of councils of workers' delegates, headed by a central council of delegates. Through the system of councils, the working class will determine the national economic plant and maintain permanent control over its execution. As a result, the councils at all levels will become organs of economic, political, legislative and executive power. They will be truly elective offices, since the electors, organized according to the natural principle of production, will be able at any time to recall their representatives and appoint new ones in their place. In this way, the representatives of working forces in the factories will become the backbone of proletarian State power.

(3) If, however, the workers' representatives in the central

council of delegates were to have only one draft plan for the division of the national income laid before them by the Government or by the leadership of the sole political party, their role would be limited to a mechanical act of voting. As we noted earlier, a monopolistic ruling party cannot be a workers' party; it inevitably becomes the party of the dictatorship over the working class, an organization of a bureaucracy designed to keep the workers and the whole of society disorganized and in line.

For the council system to become the expression of the organized will, organized opinion and organized activity of the masses, *the working class must organize itself along multiparty lines.* In practice, a workers' multiparty system means the right of every political group that has its base in the working class to publish its own paper, to propagate its own programme through mass-media, to organize cadres of activists and agitators—that is, to form a party. A workers' multiparty system requires freedom of speech, press and association, *the abolition of preventive censorship,* full freedom of scholarly research, of literary and artistic creativity. Without the freedom to elaborate, publish, express various ideological trends, without full freedom for the creative intelligentsia, there is no workers' democracy.

In the workers' multiparty system, various parties will propose plans for the division of the national income to the central council of delegates, creating conditions for discerning alternatives and for freedom of choice for the central representatives of the working class and for factory workers electing and recalling their delegates.

We speak of a workers' multiparty system, although it would serve no purpose or even be possible to limit membership in the parties to workers only. The working-class character of the multiparty system would follow from the nature of the State power, organized as a system of councils. This means that parties seeking to influence the centre of political power would be obliged to win influence among the workers.

By the same token, we are against the parliamentary system. The experience of both twenty-year periods shows that it carried no guarantee against dictatorship and, even in its most perfect form, it is not a form of people's power. In the parliamentary system, parties compete for votes. Once the votes have been cast, election programmes can be tossed into the waste-basket. The deputies in parliament feel close only to the leadership of the party which nominated them. The electorate, artificially arranged in purely formal districts, is atomized and the right to recall a deputy is fictitious. The citizen's participation in political life is reduced to his reading statements by political leaders, listening to them on radio or watching them on television, while once every four or five years he goes to the ballot-box to decide which party's representatives are to rule him. Everything happens with his mandate, but without his participation. In addition, parliament is a purely legislative body, which permits executive power to emerge as the only real authority. Thus, in the parliamentary system, the working class and the whole of society, on the strength of their own vote, are deprived of influence on the centre of power.

As against this formal, periodic voting, we propose the regular participation of the working class, through its councils, parties and trade unions, in economic and political decision-making at all levels. In capitalist society, above parliament, stands the *bourgeoisie*, disposing of the surplus product; in the bureaucratic system, above the fiction of parliament, the central political bureaucracy rules invisibly. In a system of workers' democracy, if it takes a parliamentary form, the working class will stand above it, organized into councils and having at its disposal the material basis of society's existence—the product of its labour.

(4) The working class cannot decide directly, but only through its political representation at the central level, how to divide the product it has created. But as its interests are not entirely uniform, contradictions between the decisions of workers' representatives and the aspirations of particular sections of the working class are unavoidable. The very fact of separating the function of management from the function of production carries with it the possibility of alienation of the elected power, at the level of both the enterprise and the State. If the workers were deprived of the possibility of self-defence in the face of the decisions of the representative system, apart from their right to vote (i.e. apart from that very system), then the system would turn against those whom it is supposed to represent. If the working class was deprived of the possibilities of self-defence in its own state, workers' democracy would be fraudulent. This defence should be assured by *trade unions completely independent of the State and with the right to organize economic*

and political strikes. The various parties, competing for influence in the trade unions, would struggle for the preservation of their working-class character.

(5) To prevent the institution of workers' democracy from being reduced to a façade, behind which the old disorder would make a comeback, its democratic forms must be the living expression of the activity of the working masses. Administrators, experts and politicians have the necessary time and knowledge to bother with public affairs, while the worker is obliged to stand next to his machine. To take an active part in public life the worker, too, must be provided with the necessary time and knowledge. This requires a certain number of hours to be set aside weekly from the required paid working time to ensure *the universal education of the workers.* During those hours, workers grouped into production complexes will discuss draft economic plans submitted by different parties for the country, factory or region which are too difficult for popular presentation only if an attempt is made to conceal their class content. The representatives of political parties participating in these hours of workers' education will bring both their programmes and the working class closer to each other.

(6) In a workers' democracy it will be impossible to preserve the political police or the regular army in any form. The anti-democratic character of the political police is obvious to everyone; on the other hand, the ruling classes have had more success in spreading myths about the regular army.

The regular army tears hundreds of thousands of young people away from their environment. They are isolated in barracks, brainwashed of independent thinking by brutal methods, and taught, instead, to carry out mechanically every order issued by their professional commanders, who are locked in a rigid hierarchy. This organization of armed force is separated from society in order that it may, more easily, be directed against society. The regular army, like the political police, is by its very nature a tool of anti-democratic dictatorship. As long as it is maintained, a clique of generals may always prove stronger than all the parties and councils.

It is said that the regular army is necessary to defend the State. This is true in the case of an anti-democratic dictatorship, where, other than by terror, it is impossible to force the large mass of people to defend a state that does not belong to them. On the other hand, if the masses were allowed to carry arms outside the military organization, they would constitute a dangerous threat to the system. Consequently, for such a system, a regular army is the only possible form of defence force.

We have already seen, during the revolutionary wars in Vietnam, Algeria and Cuba, that the armed workers and peasants—if they know what they are fighting for and if they identify their interests with those of the revolution—are not worse soldiers than those of the regular army. This is especially true of small countries threatened by the counter-revolutionary intervention of a foreign power. It has no chance with a regular army; it can defend itself successfully by a people's war. Regular armies are necessary to aggressors who undertake colonial wars and wars of intervention; they are necessary to the anti-democratic dictatorships, in order to keep the masses obedient. This is evident especially in Latin American countries where the army has exclusively the internal function of the police. It can also be observed elsewhere—in Poland, too, as we saw during the events in Poznan. Whether or not the army and the workers actually clash, the regular army always remains an instrument of tyranny over the working class and society, just as a club always remains a means of beating, whether or not its owner actually puts it to that use. In a system of workers' democracy, the regular army does not ensure defence against the counter-revolution; on the contrary, it may become the source and the tool of the counter-revolutionary camp. It must therefore be abolished.

To make democracy indestructible, the working class should be armed. This applies, first of all, to the workers in larger industries who should be organized into a workers' militia under the aegis of the workers' councils. The military experts who will train the workers' militia will be employed by the workers' councils and remain subordinated to them. In this, the basic military repressive force in the State will be directly tied to the working class, which will always be ready to defend its own state and its own revolution.

For technical reasons, it is unavoidable to maintain permanent military units within specialized divisions such as the navy, air force, rocketry, etc. The soldiers for those divisions should be recruited among the workers of heavy industry, and during their military service they should remain in touch with their factory teams and retain all their workers' rights.

(7) Agricultural production plays an essential part in the economy, and the peasantry has too important a role in society for the workers' programme to by-pass the affairs of the countryside. The future of agriculture lies, without doubt, in large, specialized, industrialized and nationalized enterprises. The technical base for such an organization of agricultural production can only be created by the industrialization of agriculture. This requires enormous investments, whose realization is a problem for the distant future. Under present technical-economic conditions, all attempts at collectivization mean depriving the peasant of the land he owns, which can be achieved only against his will through the methods of police dictatorship. The result means a fall in production and a police dictatorship victimizing the working class itself. Such collectivization can be reconciled only with a bureaucratic system; it spells death for workers' democracy.

The free, unlimited interplay of market forces, under conditions of individual ownership of land, and given the present structure of agriculture, leads to capitalist-type farming. It deprives owners of small and scattered holdings of the possibility of concentrating their means of investment, necessary for their development, and consequently shifts the major part of the means of investment in the countryside to the richest farms. It means the rationalization of the rural economy by way of a severe crisis, bankrupting the poorest holdings; and it means unemployment and high prices for necessities for the industrial working class. This is acceptable to the technocracy, which is naturally sympathetic to capitalist farming, but unacceptable to a workers' democracy.

For the working class, the goal of production is the development of the consumption of the broad mass of people who today live at subsistence level. As we have already seen, the bureaucracy pushes the consumption of the majority of villages even below that level, deprives the peasant economy of its surpluses and agriculture of any prospects of development, because it seeks to minimize the real expenditure on labour and regards social consumption as a necessary evil.

The interests of the working class lie in overthrowing these relationships between the peasant economy and the State; it demands a rapid development of agricultural production—the basis for increased consumption—through the development of the mass of small and medium individual holdings. This makes the working class the spokesman for the majority of peasants and creates the basis for a real alliance between them. To realize their common interests it is necessary, first of all, to overcome the 'price scissors' that deprive small and medium peasant holdings of the material base for development, and to tax progressively the richest farms. Second, that part of the product of the peasant's labour intercepted by the State in the form of taxes or in any other way must be, after subtracting sums corresponding to the peasants' contribution to administrative expenditures, returned to the countryside in the form of social and cultural investments and as State economic and technical aid to assist small and dwarf holdings.

To achieve this, the peasantry needs to organize itself on an economic basis and elect its own political representatives. It must set up its own production organizations and find new perspectives for the almost 60 per cent of the peasantry which vegetates on small holdings and has labour surpluses; it is inadmissible to allow investments in industry to be blown up out of all proportion. This requires the proper use of labour surpluses in intensive additional production, such as livestock breeding, vegetable and fruit cultivation and such industries as meat-packing and fruit-canning. This is very difficult, and in the case of processing plants, impossible to achieve with the scattered forces of small holdings. The precondition for success is the creation of associations of small and medium holdings, having at their disposal a labour surplus. These associations, based on the land they possess, on co-operation and on State aid in the form of low-interest credits, participation in small investments, transport guarantees, etc., will then set up small processing plants and, also in common, organize their supplies and marketing. This is the cheapest way to increase the production of deficit-bearing agricultural produce and to invigorate the underdeveloped food industry. It is also the only way of intensifying the work of dwarf and small holdings and simultaneously employing, on the spot, the existing labour surplus.

Peasant holdings must be provided with conditions favouring the specialization of production, without which there can be no rational husbandry. At the same time, in their contacts with State purchasing enterprises, peasant producers must be organized to defend themselves against artificial lowering of prices. For the isolated peasant producer who enters into a 'voluntary' accord with the State is helpless when faced with the State's monopoly of the market. Accordingly, apart from creating production organizations, the rural population must form its own universal *supply and marketing organization* for the peasant holdings. The richest farms, which are relatively few in number but play an important role given their size and economic strength, will then have no chance to transform themselves into capitalist enterprises; they will be short of cheap labour and cheap land that would otherwise be provided by the failure of weak holdings. The richest farms, however, will have the chance to increase their production on the basis of their own means of investment, provided they are able to solve the manual-labour shortage by utilizing machines.

Inasmuch as industry plays the decisive role in the economy, the direction of industrial production will determine the general direction of the national economy. And the working class, which will have control of its own product, will thereby create a general framework for the functions of the other sectors, including agriculture. But within these most general limits, determined by the level, structure and development of industrial production, the peasants must also control the product of their labour. The plans for development, for investments, for economic aid, should not be imposed by the State on the peasant population. Otherwise, a specific apparatus of control would come into being and would, finally, also obtain control over the working class. *That is why political self-government by the peasants* is a must for the good of workers' democracy. It is made possible because the interests of the workers and peasants converge.

Economic organizations of peasant producers are not enough to give peasants control over that part of their product taken over by the State and which is to be restored to the countryside in the form of direct State investments and State aid to peasant holdings. This can be assured only by the *political representation of peasant producers on a national scale*, elected on the basis of economic organizations and peasant political parties.

(8) We do not consider the anti-bureaucratic revolution to be a purely Polish affair. The economic and social contradictions we have analysed appear in mature form in all the industrialized bureaucratic countries : in Czechoslovakia, the GDR, Hungary and the USSR. Nor do we view the revolution as the exclusive affair of

the working class in bureaucratic dictatorships. The bureaucratic system, passed off as socialism by official propaganda in both East and West, compromises socialism in the eyes of the masses of developed capitalist countries. The international bureaucracy and its leading force—the Soviet bureaucracy—fear all authentic revolutionary movements in any part of the world. Seeking internal and international stabilization of its own system, based on the division of the world into spheres of influence with capitalism, the bureaucracy suppresses revolutionary movements at home and uses its influence over foreign official communist parties to impede the development of revolutionary movements in Latin America, Asia and Africa. The anti-bureaucratic revolution is, therefore, the concern of the international workers' movement and of the movement for colonial revolution.

Like every revolution, the anti-bureaucratic revolution threatens the established world order and, in turn, is threatened by the forces guarding that order. The international bureaucracy will try to crush the first country or countries of the victorious revolution in proportion to the internal forces it will still have at the moment of crisis. Western imperialism will try to take advantage of our revolution to supplant the dictatorship of the bureaucracy with the dictatorship of the capitalist monopolies, which is in no way better.

Our ally against the intervention of Soviet tanks is the Russian, Ukrainian, Hungarian and Czech working class. Our ally against the pressures and threats of imperialism is the working class of the industrialized West and the developing colonial revolution in the backward countries. Against an eventual accord between the international bureaucracy and the international imperialist *bourgeoisie*, which maintain systems of anti-popular dictatorship in their spheres of influence, we utter the traditional working-class slogan : 'Proletarians of all countries, unite !'

The working class must carry out all these changes in the area of political, social and economic relations in order to realize its own class interest, which is the command over its own labour and its product. Is this programme realistic?

Following the initial step towards its realization—making the enterprise independent—the working class would create the conditions for adapting production to needs, eliminating all waste of the economic surplus and ensuring proper use of the intensive factors of economic growth. The same would be carried out by the technocracy, the difference being that the production goal of the working class is consumption by many, not the luxury consumption of privileged strata. That is why workers' control of production would assure the most radical resolution of the contradiction between an expanded productive potential and the low level of social consumption which impedes economic growth today.

The workers' separate class interest coincides with the economic interests of the mass of low-paid white-collar employees and of the small and medium holders in the countryside. Their numbers combined, they comprise the overwhelming majority of the rural and urban population. Since the slavery of the working class is the essential source of the slavery of other classes and strata, by emancipating itself, the working class also liberates the whole of society.

To liberate itself, it must abolish the political police; by doing so, it will free the whole of society from fear and dictatorship. It must abolish the regular army and liberate the soldier in the barracks from nightmarish oppression. It must introduce a multiparty system, providing political freedom to the whole of society. It must abolish preventive censorship, introduce full freedom of the press, of scholarly and cultural creativity, allow social thinking to progress unimpeded. It will thereby liberate the writer, artist, scholar and journalist; it will create, on the widest possible scale, conditions for the free fulfilment by the intelligentsia of its proper social function.

It must subject the administrative apparatus to the permanent control and supervision of democratic organizations, changing existing relationships within that apparatus. Today's common civil servant will become a man free of humiliating dependence on a bureaucratic hierarchy. It must assure the peasant control over his product, as well as economic, social and political self-government. It will thereby change the peasant from the eternal, helpless object of all power into an active citizen sharing in making decisions which shape his life and work.

Because the worker occupies the lowest position in the productive process, the working class, more than any other social group, needs democracy; every incursion on democracy is first a blow against the worker. That is why workers' democracy will have the widest social base and will create the fullest conditions for the free development of the whole of society.

Because the workers' class interest most closely corresponds to the requirements for economic development and to the interests of society, the working-class programme is a realistic one. Will that programme be realized? That depends upon the degree of ideological and organizational preparation of the working class in a revolutionary crisis, and therefore also depends upon the present activities of those who identify with workers' democracy.

PIERRE FRANK

Czechoslovakia: First Assessment, First Lessons

Czechoslovakia, which was economically the most developed of the people's democracies, was also the one least affected by 'de-Stalinization'. Rigid bureaucracy had resulted in stagnation in the economic sphere, and the technological gap between Czechoslovakia and the industrialist capitalist countries was widening. For the masses, the standard of living had been declining for some years. All social activity was at a standstill. The Communist Party had become more and more isolated from the vital forces of the nation, and especially from the young people whose independent creative initiative was being completely stifled by the strictness of the régime.

An element in the economic sector of the State, and also in the Party executive, realized that certain changes must be made, and began to contest Novotny's leadership. For several months there was a certain interaction between, on the one hand, the struggle within the Party executive, and on the other, demonstrations and demands by students and intellectuals.

Finally, Novotny was relieved of his duties, first as secretary of the Party, and then as State leader, his leadership of the Party being taken over by Dubcek who won a small majority in the Central Committee. The Soviet executive, whose help Novotny called for, was at first willing to accept this change, since at the time Dubcek's policies seemed harmless enough. He had no intention of abandoning the Warsaw Pact, for instance, to make any other alliances; who could possibly imagine a Czechoslovak government even considering an alliance with West Germany under the existing political conditions? Nor did the Soviet Government have any objection to Czechoslovakia's strengthening its economic ties with the West, to its applying economic reforms of a technocratic nature in order to stimulate its economy. The fact that at this period the Kremlin accepted Dubcek's policies is evidence enough, if evidence were needed, that some of the criticisms levelled at him by the Kremlin today are motivated by propaganda, and do not constitute the chief reason for the invasion of Czechoslovakia.

WAS THERE ANY DANGER OF A RESTORATION OF CAPITALISM?

The economic and social consequences of the 'economic reforms' introduced in several of the people's democracies had for some time provoked fears in the international workers' revolutionary movement of capitalism being re-established in those countries. The international relations of some of them, both with other people's democracies and with the capitalist countries, supported those fears. The case of Yugoslavia appeared a typical one; and the sympathy of the new Czechoslovak leaders for Yugoslav policies gave further cause for alarm.

This right-wing tendency in home and foreign policy (which was largely a reaction against the policies of the Kremlin leaders and their use of force against the smaller people's democracies) was certainly to be deplored; but it could hardly be described as a restoration of capitalism. That in effect would suggest that a people's democracy could gradually change into a bourgeois one, a non-capitalist economy into a capitalist one; in other words, into a kind of reverse reformism. There is capitalism only where the middle class is in power; that is, where the means of production and surplus profits are in the hands of individuals. The restoration of capitalism would only be possible if a new middle class were to take over the major means of production and overthrow the people's democracy, replacing it with a new state geared for its own ends. Nothing of the sort has happened in Yugoslavia, nor was it likely to happen in Czechoslovakia. In Yugoslavia the strikes in 1966 and

1967, and the student demonstrations in June 1968, were an indication that if the right-wing policy of the country's leaders had created serious contradictions in the economy and in society, those who were the closest adherents to socialism were capable of resisting any policies designed to favour the *petits bourgeois* classes.

In Czechoslovakia there was no evidence that any pro-capitalist class could so organize itself as to attempt to re-establish private ownership of the means of production and appropriate any profits. On the contrary, in this state, where the peasants were only a tiny minority of the population, and the proletariat the vast majority, with a long tradition of class-consciousness, there was a rapid orientation towards socialist democracy, and it was the proletariat who soon came to set the pace in the march of events.

THE STIRRING OF THE MASSES

Initially, the Czechoslovak workers seemed hesitant and even suspicious of the changes put forward, for they feared, not unreasonably, that economic reforms might lead to a rise in prices, a lowering of their standard of living and to unemployment. Among the policies of the new government there was no call to any real control by, or greater equality for, the workers. Far from it, for the 'liberal' wing of the bureaucracy actually demanded more privileges. But the struggle between the two wings of the bureaucracy, and the resistance of Novotny, led to discussions all over the country and to the revival of political life as a whole, a revival that affected the working class and penetrated every kind of organization—Party groups, union groups, youth groups, and so on. This led to an effort to rehabilitate those who had fallen victim to the Stalinist purges, the creation of political clubs, the fight for real freedom of the socialist press and the abolition of censorship, the dismantling of the secret police and their repressive machinery. Clearly workers had reached new heights of understanding and activity. Various Party committees were reshuffled from top to bottom. The delegates to the 14th Party Congress were elected either by rank-and-file members of the movement, or by popular acclaim. The plan for new Party statutes was evidence of pressure from people who wanted to restore Leninist standards of democracy within the life of the Party. This, together with the fight for the abolition of press, radio and television censorship, formed the pivot of the political battle going on all over the country.

The Soviet leaders began to be anxious when, independent of Dubcek's authority, and in spite of it, there gradually developed a mass-movement which was not content with the snail-like pace of de-Stalinization, nor with a 'liberalization' dependent upon the whims of the leaders of the country and of the Party, but demanded instead the establishment of a genuine social-democratic régime. Worse still, it was quite clear that Dubcek and his colleagues were aware of this growing pressure from the masses and that it was becoming increasingly harder to resist.

The situation considerably alarmed the Kremlin leaders and their satellites for reasons that extended far beyond the frontiers of Czechoslovakia. All the indications were that the 'Czechoslovak spring' was being followed with great interest and sympathy throughout Eastern Europe, and especially in the Soviet Union where, for two years, the régime had been becoming more and more authoritarian, withdrawing, among other things, the 'freedoms' that the intelligentsia had enjoyed a few years before. The Kremlin leaders knew better than anyone the situation in their own country, and the repercussions that a restoration of a workers' democracy could have there. In all the states of the 'socialist camp', aspirations towards socialist democracy were growing stronger; and voices were managing to penetrate the bureaucratic censorship to re-emphasize the basic truth that a socialist society ought to be freer and more human than even the most democratic of bourgeois societies. And now here were the workers, the students and the intellectuals of Czechoslovakia beginning to prove by their action the real possibility of such socialist democracy in an economically developed country. Considering also that the 'Czechoslovak spring' was attracting great interest among the working class in the economically advanced capitalist countries, showing them, for the first time since the October Revolution, socialism associated with a régime of political democracy, this example seemed all the more likely to arouse hopes, and if it proved successful, movements and risings among the workers in the Soviet Union and other people's democracies at present ruled by the iron hand of bureaucracy. The rule of bureaucratic power was thus directly and dangerously threatened.

The first attempts of the Kremlin and its associated bureaucracies to put a halt to what was going on in Czechoslovakia, and especially the Warsaw letter sent by the Five, had the opposite result to what was intended. The masses no longer hesitated, but united more firmly round the leadership of Dubcek, who seemed not only aware of their aspirations but also resistant to Kremlin pressure. It was not against a non-existent 'danger of a return of capitalism', but against this situation, in which the Kremlin could clearly see the arrival of an anti-bureaucratic political revolution, that, in a burst of anger and panic, it decided to send its armoured divisions into the Socialist Republic of Czechoslovakia.

The invasion, less than three weeks after the Czerna and Bratislava conferences, though totally unheralded, did not produce the instant intimidation and fear which the Soviet leaders and their allies undoubtedly expected. On the contrary, the movement of the people continued with unparalleled force and quite incredible political ingenuity. Workers, students, intellectuals, all refused to assist the occupiers in any way; clandestine papers and radio stations continued to inspire the people to stand firm; a clandestine Party congress took place in one of the big factories in Prague, with the workers standing guard. Unannounced strikes and various forms of sabotage (such as removing street signs) paralysed the occupiers physically, while the people talked to the soldiers, telling them quite plainly of the lies they had been fed, so that they could come to grips with the true situation in the country and realize what had motivated the 'counter-revolutionary' mission they were being forced to carry out.

There occurred the unprecedented phenomenon of a communist party forced into hiding, and receiving mass-suport such as it had never had before, because the party militants were in the forefront of the battle.

Though militarily successful, the occupation was a political fiasco. None of the known Kremlin supporters in the Czechoslovak Party dared declare themselves in favour of this intervention, or put themselves forward as a possible puppet government for the occupiers. Thus the whole operation presented grave dangers to the Kremlin. The Soviet and allied troops were confused and powerless. In addition, they could see for themselves an example of the beginnings of a workers' state, free of the dead hand of bureaucracy, functioning democratically through popular action in the very teeth of the Soviet tanks.

The Kremlin, in this totally unforeseen and extremely dangerous situation, changed its tone : contact with Dubcek and his colleagues was resumed, and those who had just been castigated as the 'leaders of a minority clique' and arrested, the very same leaders the Kremlin had tried to remove, were now asked to sign an agreement. According to the *Tass* communiqué, that agreement was supposed to be based upon 'principles of mutual respect for equality, territorial integrity, socialist solidarity and independence', but it was in fact simply a *diktat*. This same 'agreement' declared that 'the troops of the allied nations which have temporarily entered Czechoslovak territory will not interfere in the affairs of the Socialist Republic of Czechoslovakia', and would leave the country 'as soon as the situation there is normalized'. But what made the situation abnormal was the presence of foreign troops in the country, as well as that of Soviet functionaries (particularly those in the secret services) in the Czechoslovak ministries, above all in the Ministry of the Interior.

Despite their indignation and anger, and the strength they had shown, the Czechoslovaks are now politically immobilized. They have to submit, for an indefinite period, to an occupation which they resisted for a week in an absolutely extraordinary way. For the moment 'order' seems to reign in Prague.

These events which have affected Czechoslovakia so painfully have a world-wide significance. They prompt many fundamental questions. Why and how could they happen? What do they mean? Why did the movement stop so suddenly? What are the implications for the Soviet régime, the Czechoslovak Communist Party, the Vietnam war, international relations, the international workers' movement? What are the prospects?

The action of the Soviet Government has dealt a heavy blow to the cause of socialism and communism. The essential problems it raises must be examined in depth and faced unflinchingly, so that militants and the Labour movement may find means to remedy the situation it has created, and prevent its recurrence; they must be able once and for all to rid the world-wide cause of socialism of the gangster tactics which have characterized the rule of Stalin and his successors.

NO REFORM OF BUREAUCRATIC RULE

The first conclusion this use of force brings to mind inevitably concerns the Soviet bureaucracy itself, and the 'de-Stalinization' that it achieved after Stalin's death. As the 4th International persisted in saying from the start, 'de-Stalinization' was a means of self-defence, rather than self-liquidation, for the bureaucracy. The bureaucracy shook off certain particularly unattractive aspects of the Stalin régime, not so much because it found them repugnant as because keeping them would have been dangerous. Eliminating them was the price it was prepared to pay in order to preserve its essential privileges and keep its power over Soviet society. This latter point was of particular importance. The Party machine has shown peculiar determination in defending its hegemony over society, for it is in fact increasingly under attack from the intelligentsia, technologists, all kinds of scientists, who can compare the tremendous advances the Soviet Union has made in their particular areas with the effect this same machine exerts upon the rest of society, which it encloses in a cocoon without freedom of thought, expression or political activity, imposing upon it the most grotesque intellectual and artistic constraints.

The 'de-Stalinization' begun about fifteen years ago had raised the hopes of many groups in Soviet society. For several years the limitations of that 'de-Stalinization' had been obvious, and there were stirrings within Soviet society directed towards knocking down those barriers. Faced with what seemed a serious threat to its political power, the bureaucracy of the Kremlin reacted against the Czechoslovaks with the utmost brutality, abandoning all established rules as regards their own people who received from a controlled press nothing but a succession of lies about the whole event, lies which as time passed became more scurrilous and shameless. It also showed complete disregard for the people of those countries of Eastern Europe whose governments were involved, because of the Warsaw Pact against NATO, in the military invasion of a 'sister country' and were interfering with the leadership of its communist party. Finally, it showed its contempt for communist parties all over the world, for the proletarian and colonized masses everywhere.

After what has happened, no one can continue to think that this bureaucratic class is open to any kind of reform, or will ever voluntarily abandon its political privileges to yield to a régime of socialist democracy. The arrival of the tanks in Czechoslovakia was a warning to the masses in the Soviet Union, to its youth and its intellectuals, that they must give up all hope of socialist democracy or be forcibly repressed.

There is no way of establishing a democratic socialist régime in the Soviet Union and other people's democracies other than by getting rid of these hateful bureaucrats through revolution—that political revolution of which Trotsky was the first exponent, and whose potential strength and benefits were first demonstrated by the 'Czechoslovak spring'.

NO 'NATIONAL PATHS' TO SOCIALISM

What the Kremlin has done in Czechoslovakia—which, alas, presents many features in common with what the Americans are doing in Vietnam—also throws light on the question of 'national paths' to socialism, which for the post-Stalinists means simply adapting to a new situation the concept of the 'one-country socialism' defended by Stalin. There is no doubt that since every country has its own social structure and its own history, the socialist revolution will have certain specifically national characteristics in every case. But that does not call for any special theory, for it does not by any means indicate that there is a 'national path' for each country whereby it will be able to construct a socialism suited to its own territory, and independent of what takes place outside it. It is clear that the socialist revolution in Vietnam is an international problem, since the need there is not so much for defeating the forces of the native *bourgeoisie* as those of American imperialism. Soviet bureaucracy has shown that the struggle for socialist democracy in Czechoslovakia is also an international problem; victory could only be won by defeating the bureaucracy that governs in the Kremlin, and that has, in the past, used its power to put pressure on Yugoslavia, China, etc. As long as that bureaucracy has control over the resources of the Soviet State, as long as the Soviet masses fail to re-establish socialist democracy in their homeland, no people's democracy will be safe from pressure or even ultimately from military intervention by the Kremlin.

After Vietnam, Czechoslovakia shows more powerfully than ever the international nature of the struggle for socialism. The victories of the Vietnamese revolution over American imperialism are victories of socialism and of the masses all over the world. The action of the bureaucracy against the cause of socialism in Czechoslovakia is a crime, a blow against socialism and the masses all over the world. The democratic right to independence and national self-determination for all nations, especially small and weak nations, is a revendication basic to the Labour movement, but that right can only be secured by international action on the part of the working class.

WHY HAS THE MASS-MOVEMENT NOT BEEN SUCCESSFUL?

The strength of the mass-movement in Czechoslovakia, displayed in its remarkable tenacity in the face of the armoured divisions of the Warsaw Pact 'allies', is evidence of how the will of a people can hold in check an army whose military power is nowhere in doubt. We must therefore ask : how has it happened that that movement which was so powerful, so utterly extraordinary, should have suddenly, and one presumes temporarily, collapsed?

The failure of the movement was certainly not due to any weakness among the people themselves. The numerous militants (Party cadres, rank-and-file members, journalists, intellectuals, workers) who outstripped each other in the ingenuity of their resistance to the troops, to such an extent that the latter were in many cases quite worried about the task they had been assigned, were not crushed, nor even put to the test. The cause of the weakening must be laid squarely at the door of the Dubcek leadership. We certainly do not deny the appalling treatment to which the members were subjected—not only arrest, but physical brutality and moral constraint being used. Nor do we deny the courageous defence they put up in the weeks preceding the invasion, during the invasion itself, and in the interviews they had in Moscow with their Brezhnev-style jailers —during which, unlike the Czerna and Bratislava conferences, they were isolated from their country and people. Even now, they make no attempt to gloss over the 'agreements' they signed in Moscow, and in their statements on their return home they did not try to deceive the Czechoslovak people as to the fate the occupiers had decreed for them. There is no doubt of their courage or personal honesty. The problem is a political one, which Smrkovsky, one of their number, partially expresses thus :

> We could have refused all compromise, and let things go as far as the setting up of an occupation régime, with all the consequences for the sovereignty of the State, political rights, the economy, and even eventual loss of life, that such a development would undoubtedly have involved. . . . Thus we decided to choose the second alternative, that of a compromise allowing of the hope that it might be possible to continue along the way marked out by the January plenum. This was accepted by the other party as the basis for a possible solution.
>
> We were aware that our decision might be considered by the Czechoslovak people and by history either as a wise solution, or as treason.

The Dubcek leadership was not made up of intransigent Bolsheviks whose political rigidity was immovable, but of men whose training had been basically bureaucratic, and who had been raised in the system that had turned against them. They had come to oppose the rigidity of Novotny's policies, but did not understand the real essence of the Soviet bureaucracy. As liberals, they had often enough been on the receiving-end of the brutal interventions of the Moscow bureaucracy, but what they had not grasped was that that bureaucracy was essentially preoccupied with its narrow national interests, and quite ready to sacrifice everything else to them. Finally, and above all, because of their bureaucratic training, they did not fundamentally have confidence in the people; they might if need be, in some circumstances, make use of them, as they had done at one point in order to break down Novotny's final resistance, but certainly they would not have dreamt of pushing too far the idea of mobilizing the masses. They made no move to do so at the time of the first Soviet pressures; it was only from the rank and file that the inspiration came which stimulated every mass-action. They were partly aware of this movement among the masses, but at no time were they at its head, at no time did they lead this process of nascent political revolution in Czechoslovakia. That is why, finding themselves finally in conditions which forced them to see the evil of the Kremlin leadership, they did not rely upon the people but resolved the dilemma described by Smrkovsky so disastrously. As prisoners, they stood in relation to the Soviet leadership in such a position that their only power lay in the failure of their adversaries to find quislings to govern Czechoslovakia. By beginning to 'negotiate' an 'agreement', they surrendered their only trump card. Bolshevik leaders would have demanded to go back home unconditionally, and without any pseudo-negotiations. Such an attitude would have intensified the resistance of the Czechoslovak people. Accepting the 'negotiations' put the Dubcek team on a downward slope from which it would have been difficult, if not impossible, for them to escape. The people found themselves confused, then immobilized, with a weakened fighting spirit from which the occupiers were not slow to profit.

We do not know about most of the concessions that Dubcek and his colleagues agreed to in Moscow, but what they signed was not enough for the Soviet leaders : the latter took advantage of their superior strength to make up to some extent the ground they had lost during the first days. The sole reason they engaged in discussions with the Dubcek group was to force them into a position in which they had to make more and more concessions, and thus lose the authority and prestige they had won by their resistance earlier on. The Soviet leaders will continue to play this game until they think they can safely get rid of them and replace them with new leaders whom they can trust. This scheming on the part of the Soviet leaders, like that which led them to invade Czechoslovakia in the first place, rests upon false premises. But their assessment of the Dubcek leadership was correct : it can only collapse. The movement of the Czechoslovak people will start up again and go forward, but not under that particular leadership.

THE PROSPECTS

The consequences of the invasion are in a general way, for the moment at least, favourable to all that is reactionary, whether in the capitalist camp or the Labour movement. These consequences, however, are only temporary. We are no longer in the world situation that prevailed in Stalin's day, nor is there the same 'Cold War'. For some years, thanks chiefly to the magnificent and triumphant resistance of the Vietnamese people against the counter-revolutionary intervention of American imperialism, we have had a hopeful period, a time of revolutionary upsurge which extended in a quite remarkable way during the year 1968.

The victorious Têt offensive created a crisis in United States politics which may well fail to be resolved during the new presidential term. Then, in France, following the action of the students, there was a real revolutionary crisis—a general strike involving ten million workers that came near to overthrowing the autocratic régime of de Gaulle. In addition it brought to an end the period of stagnation and apathy which had prevailed for the last twenty years in Western Europe. In August came the unleashing of the potential forces for political revolution in Czechoslovakia which, as we have said, provided an object-lesson for the workers in the Soviet Union and the other people's democracies of Eastern Europe. Furthermore, we are now witnessing in Latin America (where for some years the various revolutionary movements have centred upon the peasant masses) more and more forceful mass-demonstrations in the large cities, from Mexico to Argentina.

These are not isolated episodes leading nowhere. In the years after the Second World War the revolutionary movements in Europe were quite soon liquidated, particularly because of the policy of collaboration between the social-democratic and the Stalinist régimes : economic prosperity did the rest, for a generation. After Stalin's death, a series of 'de-Stalinizing' measures led to the beginnings of a reformist spirit in the Soviet Union and the people's democracies of Eastern Europe, and in 1956 the bureaucracy put a stop to movements in Poland and Hungary—the latter with a bloody repression. In the last twenty years only the colonial revolution has developed as an effective wing of the world revolution. It has been extraordinarily vigorous and, despite reverses, even the most cruel repressions have not succeeded in crushing it. In 1968 the reawakening of the workers' movement in Europe, which began in May in France, and the rise of political revolution as witnessed in Czechoslovakia, indicate that we are entering a period when world revolution will advance on three fronts : that of proletarian revolution in the economically advanced capitalist countries; that of colonial revolution in the economically underdeveloped countries, whether formally independent or not; and that of political revolution against the omnipotent bureaucracy oppressing all the people's democracies.

The mass-movements of 1968 certainly did not achieve all the objectives they might have, but they were neither extinguished nor totally halted. If there is one fact that the year 1968 has revealed to us it is that, in the extremely tumultuous world situation we have at the moment, any struggle, even if in its first phase it is unsuccessful, will succeed in stimulating others in other countries, and will itself recur. We are at a stage not of bankruptcy, but of the maturing and developing of a revolutionary movement unlike anything the world has ever known.

The mirages of the 'consumer society', of neo-colonialism, of 'peaceful coexistence', of 'peaceful and constitutional advance', are tending more and more to disappear, especially in the eyes of the younger generation, nor are they likely to be restored. The young are rediscovering revolutionary programmes and forms of struggle which the old reformist mass-leaderships—whether social-democrat, or post-Stalinist—had managed to suppress for forty years. The movements that came to the fore in 1968 have shown that there exists a vast revolutionary potential which can be unleashed in perhaps unexpected forms. But they have also shown that, however powerful or popular a movement might be, it cannot achieve victory by spontaneity alone; that for its success there must be a revolutionary leadership armed with a definite programme and an international vision of the battle, organized into a politically coherent party, in touch with ordinary people and ready to act boldly.

The call put out by the 4th International—if only by its existence and work during the years of reaction—for the creation of new popular revolutionary Marxist parties, and for a popular revolutionary International, has under present circumstances become urgent and indeed imperative. Among the tasks facing revolutionary militants as part of the major struggles which have begun, this particular one of creating new Marxist parties is of paramount importance if we are to prevent the whole revolutionary potential from being frittered away in a succession of movements, each in turn resulting in failure. The sooner new revolutionary leaderships can be formed, the sooner the socialist revolution will advance and triumph all over the world.

THE TASKS

What are the immediate tasks resulting from the Soviet intervention in Czechoslovakia and the situation it has created? Every militant, every worker devoted to the case of socialism must consider the *diktat* of Moscow null and void. The workers in Czechoslovakia must be helped to reject it. The honour and the whole future of socialism are at stake. The international organization must be strengthened so that it can assist the Czech and Slovak revolutionaries whose work has been rendered illegal by the military occupation.

The mass-movement for socialist democracy in Czechoslovakia has been disoriented, weakened for the moment, but not defeated or eliminated. The Dubcek leadership has not had the strength to resist, and as history has shown more than once in such circumstances, to imagine it can recover would be to give credence to miracles. On the other hand, the movement for political revolution will start up again. From among those thousands and tens of thousands of militants who took action in the week of August 21st-27th there will arise new groups and a new revolutionary leadership. A new vanguard will learn the lessons of the 'Czechoslovak spring'. It will readopt everything that was put forward then as part of a programme of authentic socialist democracy, a workers' power stemming from democratically elected workers' committees, supporting freedom to organize parties which respect the socialist relationships in production, and the right to express differences, and against the attempts of any sector of the bureaucracy to seize possession of or wield power over any social sphere. It will be reformed in a spirit of proletarian internationalism, standing in the front line of the struggle for world revolution on all fronts. It will organize a clandestine resistance which, under various forms, from the most powerful to the most flexible, will in the end annul the *diktat* of Moscow, and complete the political revolution begun in 1968.

All over the world, workers' demonstrations of a quite unambiguous kind will proliferate, demanding the immediate and unconditional evacuation of Czechoslovakia. There will be demonstrations to demand that the Soviet police do not arrest the so-called 'forty thousand hooligans'—in actuality the communist militants, journalists, students, intellectuals, cadres of factories—who were the moving spirit behind the resistance in the first week of the occupation. But action for Czechoslovakia cannot stop with these immediate objectives. This is only the most recent crime in a series of crimes against socialism by the Kremlin bureaucrats who, for the past forty years, have wrongfully claimed the October banner as their own. Stalinism and its progeny still prevail in the Soviet Union, in the people's democracies and in the international Labour movement. They must be extirpated.

The invasion of Czechoslovakia demonstrated on the one hand a military force of the first rank, and on the other, a difficult political situation producing a panic reaction from the Soviet leaders.

We salute the courageous men and women who, having in previous months publicly defended the writers unjustly condemned by a judicial system that is a disgrace to the Soviet Union, were brave enough to demonstrate in Red Square their opposition to the invasion of Czechoslovakia. They too must be rescued from the jails. The campaign for their liberation, like the campaign to get the foreign troops out of Czechoslovakia, will act as a stimulus to the Soviet masses.

The workers, the young people, the intellectuals of the Soviet Union, must realize that there is no longer anyone in the Labour movement who is deceived by the lies of the Kremlin leaders and their lackeys, and that any action on their part to remove them from power would have enthusiastic support from workers all over the world.

In the other countries which sent troops for the invasion there have also been brave men to stand up against that crime. In Poland, since March, various people have been imprisoned, including the leaders of the communist revival, Modzelewski and Kuron, who had already had several years' detention for being the first to formulate a programme of anti-bureaucratic revolution in the days of the Left opposition. Opposition—sometimes on quite a large scale, in factories among other places—has been shown to be the crime of the bureaucracy. International workers' action for solidarity with the Czech people must be extended to include all those who are pioneering the anti-bureaucratic battle in those other countries as well.

Tito in Yugoslavia and Ceaucescu in Rumania both protested against the invasion of Czechoslovakia, but their opposition was essentially that of heads of state. Tito did not want the mass-demonstrations that took place in his country—in June 1968 he had his hands full with a student revolt against the governing bureaucracy in Yugoslavia. Ceaucescu began by organizing armed workers' militias, but soon diminished the force of his protests, and in any case still maintains a rigid political and bureaucratic régime in his own country.

Throughout this part of the 'socialist camp' the desperate action of the Kremlin leaders and their satellites should be the signal for a determined struggle for socialist democracy. The official communist movement is now in a desperate state of ideological collapse and organizational weakness. The kind of balancing-act performed by the leadership of the French party, for instance, to keep their links with the Kremlin without losing their links with the left wing of the middle class and the French social democrats, will end by saving nothing. A great number of militants were completely destroyed by Stalin and the post-Stalinists, who sought refuge in a more marked social-democratization of the communist parties, or in political inactivity. But to those who have not lost confidence in communism, and who have found new hope in the events of the past few months, we would say : stop the ostrich-like approach to the crisis that is shaking your movement; approach the essential questions courageously, and don't be afraid to develop that crisis into a convulsion. The trouble that has for so long been dogging the Communist Party can only be got rid of by forceful remedies, probably even by surgery. Be prepared to co-operate in the formation of new revolutionary Marxist leaderships with the militants who have for so long been waging this battle under the banner of Trotskyism, and with the new young revolutionaries who have come forward in recent years.

The crime recently committed by the Kremlin, far from being fatal for socialism, by pointing to the depths of ignominy and infamy to which the bureaucracy has fallen, may well be the beginning of a forceful renewal of the communist movement. The highly revolutionary conditions of the world at present are favourable to it. Military force—as has been proved beyond doubt—cannot defeat a powerful, popular movement that enjoys firm and bold leadership. What happened in Prague does not mark this as a time for despair and retreat, but for attack.

Down with the armed counter-revolutionary intervention of the Kremlin bureaucracy in the Socialist Republic of Czechoslovakia!

We want the immediate and unconditional evacuation of all foreign troops from Czechoslovak soil! Hands off the Czechoslovaks who resisted the invasion of their country!

Solidarity with the heroic Vietnamese people! Send the Soviet tanks out of Czechoslovakia and give them to the fighters in Vietnam!

Long live the socialist world revolution!

PIERRE FRANK

**From a Student Upheaval
towards a Proletarian Socialist Revolution**

PARIS

May 1968 has gone into French socialist history as the month of
the Latin Quarter 'riot'. This 'riot' led to the general strike of
May 13th, ten years to the day since the *coup* of the generals and
'pieds noirs' (French colonialists) in Algiers that precipitated de
Gaulle's rise to power. The 'riot' constituted the opening of the
period that will liquidate the Gaullist régime. How did it occur
and what happened?

Day by Day

We must go back to the Algerian war to find the roots of the intense
politicization in the student and university world. The Algerian
war, the influence of Cuba, the martyrdom of Che Guevara, and
also, to a certain extent, the 'cultural revolution' in China, height-
ened this political development and turned it more sharply away
from the policy of 'peaceful coexistence', from the 'peaceful and
parliamentary road' to socialism.

It was in this context that the specifically university problems,
resulting from the outmoded character of the educational system
and methods, were posed. The latest events began on March 22nd
at the University of Nanterre. This new university, recently founded
in the Paris suburbs, was to be the Government's most modern edu-

cational institution, equipped with every imaginable improvement. But the Government located it where it became exposed to a number of social contradictions. It was built next to a shanty-town. The municipality is under the thumb of the Communist Party; and the local CP looked with disfavour on the agitation, political discussion and factional ferment that groups largely led by militants expelled at different times from the UEC (Union des Etudiants Communistes) introduced into this suburban town. And a large proportion of the students came from the 16th *arrondissement* and other west Paris neighbourhoods, the most bourgeois in the city. The Nanterre students, unlike those at the Sorbonne, had no congenial off-campus community; they were forced to discuss university and social problems among themselves. And they connected up these two sets of problems.

What the established authorities thought about this may be gathered from the remarks of the Minister of National Education in Parliament after the street-clashes had gone on for several days : 'What sort of machinations did these Nanterre "madmen" carry on daily? . . . Under the label "critical university", the most absurd lucubrations were voiced in auditoriums renamed, to serve the cause, Fidel Castro, Che Guevara, Mao Tse-tung, Leon Trotsky.'[1]

The university officials decided to take reprisals against a group of students, including Daniel Cohn-Bendit. The latter had already had a run-in with a minister who came to the university to dedicate a swimming-pool. The Sorbonne students decided to extend solidarity to the students at Nanterre, who were threatened with expulsion, and to hold a meeting in support of them on Friday, May 3rd, in the Sorbonne courtyard. At the same time, a fascist group, Occident (the West)—the group is insignificant numerically but its connections permit it to carry out attacks with virtual impunity— declared that it was going to 'clean out' the Latin Quarter.

During the afternoon of May 3rd, the leaders and most of the militant elements of the university movements met in the Sorbonne courtyard. The marshals of these groups were also there to block any fascist movement. But at the end of this meeting, which had proceeded without incident, the police invaded the Sorbonne and arrested several hundred of those present. The police had come on to the university grounds in accordance with a written request from

[1] *Journal Officiel*, No. 26 A.N. (May 9th, 1968), p. 1606.

the rector, Roche. But, although this does not lessen his responsibility for the action taken, there is no doubt that the police operation was part of a plan conceived higher up.

The Government thought that the unrest among the students was the work of small groups with no real following. It was convinced that all that was needed to end it was a show of determination on its part; all the more so, since exams were in the offing. Furthermore, this same day, the organizational secretary of the French Communist Party, Marchais, had scathingly denounced these 'grouplets' in *l'Humanité*, speaking of 'the German, Cohn-Bendit'. The Government must have thought that repression of the students would not provoke the workers' organizations to express solidarity with them.

The arrest of the student cadres, which were hauled away in police vans before the eyes of everybody on the boulevard St Michel, touched off an immediate reaction. Students attacked the police cars and clashes of a violence not seen in years broke out spontaneously. Politically unaffiliated students played leading roles.

The next day, the UNEF (Union Nationale des Etudiants de France) and the SNES (Syndicat National de l'Enseignement Supérieur) called an unlimited strike for Monday, May 6th. After a hastily convoked court had served several demonstrators with stiff prison sentences, the strike began that day with three demands as prior conditions for all negotiations : release and amnesty for the sentenced students; withdrawal of the police from the Sorbonne; reopening of the university with full political and trade-unions rights for the students.

From early in the morning, May 6th threatened to be a stormy day. In the afternoon, still more violent fighting than in the preceding week began. In the evening, in St Germain des Prés, clashes lasted for several hours, producing casualties on both sides. Outraged by the brutality of the police, the people of the district displayed their sympathy with the demonstrators.

On the morning of the following day, the bourgeois press did not support the police. The UNEF and SNES leaders called a meeting for 6.30 p.m. at the place Denfert-Rochereau. The strikers occupied this square at the appointed hour and held their meeting. The police let it be known via the press that the meeting had not been authorized (no one had asked for any authorization) but had been 'tolerated'! After the meeting, a procession formed and with red banners flying marched about twelve miles through the streets of Paris, going up the Champs Elysées to the place de l'Etoile.

The bourgeois press and *l'Humanité* left one feature of this demonstration unmentioned. But in Parliament the next day a UNR (Union pour la Nouvelle République) deputy could not contain his indignation : '. . . The *Internationale* was sung there [at the tomb of the unknown warrior at the Arc de Triomphe] and red flags were made by tearing up red-white-and-blue ones [the French tricolour].'[2]

That day, as most often in the course of the battle, the demonstrators improvised, but what improvision! On the night of May 7th-8th there were violent encounters in the area between St Germain des Prés and Montparnasse.

On May 8th, the Government, in the person of the Minister of National Education, made equivocal statements before the National Assembly. False promises without definite commitments were made, conditional upon the restoration of order in the Latin Quarter. Confronted with an eminently difficult situation the UNEF and SNES leaders hesitated, and the day ended with a demonstration which dissipated itself for lack of an objective.

On Friday, May 9th, the students again gathered on the boulevard St Michel, not to demonstrate but to discuss what was to be done. By the afternoon, it was evident that the movement had not succumbed to the Government's manoeuvre and that it was spreading to the provinces.

The organizations in the lead called another meeting for Friday, again at the place Denfert-Rochereau at 6.30 p.m., and reaffirmed that there would be no negotiations until the three preliminary demands had been met. The new upswing in the movement continued into evening of May 9th. A month before, the JCR (Jeunesse Communiste Révolutionnaire) had planned a meeting for that day on the theme 'From Revolt to Revolution' in the Salle de la Mutualité. They wanted to explain the causes and objectives of the student movement developing in several countries. The events gave an acute timelessness to this meeting.

[2] Ibid., p. 1620. Tearing up the tricolour to make red flags was a sacrilege that no daily newspaper dared reveal.

During the day, the JCR announced that after the slated speakers had spoken, the meeting would be turned over to the students to continue their debate. An audience of four to five thousand persons gave the meeting the air of a revolutionary assembly by their enthusiasm and militancy. Italian, Dutch, Belgian, German and Spanish students affirmed their solidarity with the French students. The speakers forcefully stated that this struggle was not a reformist one, that it challenged capitalist society, that it would not end until the working class went into action in a revolutionary struggle for socialism.

The second part of the meeting given over to discussion was no less important. For nearly two hours speakers with differing political points of view aired their positions, their suggestions and their perspectives. Although it was not an assembly of elected representatives, it suggested a student soviet (council). Above and beyond the specific problems of the struggle, two concepts dominated the discussion : (1) The student struggle could be no more than a part of the struggle for socialism; and the fundamental social force in this struggle was the working class. No remarks of a Marcusian or similar type were listened to. There was abundant discussion of means for linking up the student struggle to that of the workers. (2) Democracy was vital to the movement's development. Differences were normal and the existence of political groups a matter of course. But these groupings must not try to impose their leadership upon the movement or disrupt it by raising extraneous questions.

When they broke up at about 1 a.m., several thousand fighters found themselves politically united for the big day of May 10th, which was to prove decisive.

May 10th

This day consisted of three successive phases, each with unforgettable characteristics. The morning began first of all with the spread of the movement to the medical students and, most important, with the high-school strike which had been announced at the May 9th meeting in the Mutualité. Where did this high-school movement come from? The Vietnam war sensitized very young students. They joined the Comité National Vietnam. When they tried to take this question into their schools they ran head-on into an administration —and too often a lack of understanding from many teachers, even those of the left wing—that regarded the high schools as nothing but barracks for teenagers, who must not concern themselves with politics.

Incidents occurred in the high schools. The expulsion of a student from the Lycée Condorcet led to a demonstration by students from several hundred high schools in front of this school and, above all, to the formation of the CAL (Comités Action Lycéens) in November 1967. This organization's activity developed over a period of several months. The organization of high-school students was helped along by the fact that they live together all day long in their schools like workers in a plant. A pamphlet should be written just on this movement—on the seriousness and perseverance of these very young militants from fourteen to sixteen years old.

Their strike began a little like that of the workers. A few schools 'broke the ground.' At 9 a.m. the students of these schools marched out into the streets of Paris and went from one school to another to call the students out on strike, holding meetings of between one to two thousand high-school students in the squares and quadrangles of Paris. Their basic demand was for the right to discuss politics and social questions in general in the high schools. They decided to meet at 6 p.m. at the place des Gobelins, to march on the place Denfert-Rochereau in order to take part in the university student action. 'Your problems will be our problems tomorrow,' they explained to the older students. In the afternoon, about eight thousand high-school students massed in a procession which reached the place Denfert-Rochereau at 6 p.m.

The second part of the day began. After a meeting at this spot, which was, rather, an assembly to discuss the movement and the course to be followed, a procession set out on the boulevard Arago and passed in front of the Santé prison to demonstrate solidarity with those who had been jailed or sentenced for their part in the demonstrations of the preceding days. It crossed through the working-class neighbourhoods and then swerved to return by the rue Monge and the boulevard St Michel.

This was a demonstration the like of which Paris had not seen in a long time. About thirty thousand strong at the beginning, it visibly swelled; and towards the end it had clearly doubled. It had an enthusiasm and a youthful character matching the spring revivification that had brought leaves back to the trees on the boulevards. The demonstration was made up in large proportion of university and high-school students and striking professors. However, it was joined by many young workers, who every day in growing numbers had been taking part in the strikers' demonstrations, as well as by revolutionary workers and militants who had suffered for long years from the Stalinist gag on the organized workers' movement. At last, Paris again saw demonstrations planned without police participation, held without prior authorization, and not subjected to the control of marshals from the CP and CGT (Confédération Générale de Travail—the communist-controlled union), who barred all slogans and banners considered 'subversive'. At last there was a demonstration that gave free-rein to the initiative of the masses.

This demonstration of fifty thousand persons, comprising an overwhelming majority of young people, had a very strong political disposition. There were red flags, a black flag, the flag of Vietnam, but not one tricolour. The *Internationale* and other old revolutionary songs were sung. Revolutionary slogans were mixed in with the strikers' immediate demands: 'Against the Police State', 'Against the Bourgeoisie and Bourgeois Education'. In the working-class districts, the demonstrators called for worker-student solidarity.

Once it returned to the Latin Quarter, the demonstration again found itself facing a Sorbonne surrounded by several tight ranks of police troops, gendarmes (paramilitary police) and above all by the gangsterlike CRS (Compagnies Républicains de Sécurité, the semimilitary élite security police). Hatred against the 'forces of order' took extraordinary forms; there was a rain of angry shouts and insults. The UNEF marshals could hardly restrain the demonstrators. Now a confrontation, a clash seemed inevitable.

Unable to enter the Sorbonne, the demonstrators decided to stay in the streets of the Latin Quarter until their demands were met. After a few clashes, they began to construct barricades. Anyone there could see how spontaneous this action was. If you check a map of Paris, you can see at once that any 'specialists' in guerrilla warfare and street-fighting would never have dreamed of a deployment so easily encircled. No 'specialists' were there. Spontaneity and popular initiative were.

In quick succession automobiles were taken, materials and tools found in nearby construction sites, even pneumatic drills being used to loosen the cobblestones in the streets. Workers were particularly helpful to the students in the latter operation. A single fact will illustrate how well this activity expressed the general anger. The quarter where the barricades were built is essentially bourgeois or *petit bourgeois*. Yet when the demonstrators used automobiles to build the barricades, the public did not protest. Everyone knows how much an automobile means nowadays to its owner. Furthermore, the same people gave demonstrators, who had been out since 5 or 6 o'clock in the morning, food, something to drink and transistor radios to follow what was happening over the air. Finally, when the police resorted to the most brutal measures during the night, for several hours large numbers of fighters on the barricades were given refuge in neighbouring apartments.

A few days later, when the giant demonstration of May 13th was passing by, a big contingent of 'barricade fighters' marching along the rue Gay-Lussac chanted, 'Thanks, thanks, Gay-Lussac'. And from the windows came an answering 'Bravo, bravo'. It was a most moving incident.

From the Barricades to the General Strike

It cannot be said that France woke up to all this on Saturday morning, because everyone had been following the events minute by minute throughout the night as they were broadcast over unofficial radio transmitters. Journalists on the spot described the savage repression as it occurred, their commentaries punctuated by the continued exploding of grenades. Anger swelled.

The evening before, the CGT and the CFDT (Confédération Française et Démocratique de Travail) had fixed a demonstration for the following Tuesday evening. They met again, because it was impossible to stand by that long and commit themselves no further. On Saturday afternoon, demonstrations broke out again in the Latin Quarter, where many streets already resembled a battlefield—remnants of barricades, burned automobiles, macadam torn up. . . . Would the struggle in the streets be resumed?

In the evening, around 9 o'clock, Premier Pompidou made a

statement on TV and radio. Pale, his features drawn, with a nervousness in sharp contrast to his usual manner, he offered some generalities and then in substance indicated that the Government was capitulating on the three conditions laid down by the striking students and teachers. All the demonstrators were to be released, the police were to be withdrawn, the Sorbonne would be reopened on Monday. But things had already gone too far. The declaration had other consequences than avoiding new confrontations in the streets. The CGT and CFDT had already decided to stage a general strike and a big demonstration in Paris on Monday. They held to these decisions. Noting what the Government had conceded or promised, the UNEF and SNES stressed that this proved that the Government bore all the responsibility for what had happened in the previous days. They decided to continue the struggle until the promises were actually fulfilled.

Sunday was taken up in preparations for the general strike and demonstration on Monday. In the evening it was announced that the students and teachers were to assemble at the Gare de l'Est, that a parade would go from there to the place de la République where the workers' unions would assemble, that the unions belonging to Force Ouvrière (FO) in the Paris region would, for the first time, participate with the others. From the place de la République, a huge demonstration would cross Paris, going through the Latin Quarter to the place Denfert-Rochereau. It was akin to the victors paying a visit to the field of battle.

The discussions among the organizations had lasted for many long hours. We can reveal some inside information about this.

The Stalinist leaders of the CGT wanted the demonstration to leave from the place St Michel and go to the bourse du Travail on the place de la République. What they wanted was to avoid the Latin Quarter and end up at the address of the bureaucrats. The spokesmen of the UNEF and the SNES said that they could not accept this proposal, and that if the unions refused to change it they would organize an independent demonstration of their own from the place de la République to Denfert-Rochereau. The heads of the CGT had to assent just as, the evening before, the Government had had to acquiesce. On top of this they likewise had to accept the leader of the 'March 22nd movement', Daniel Cohn-Bendit, who only on May 3rd had been called 'the German' by l'Humanité. The marshals had to be made up of one-half workers from the unions and one-half students from the student organizations.

It should be added that on that Sunday, the heads of the Stalinist organizations—particularly the marshals, who, until then had never been used against the police (the organizations bowing to police orders) but against the 'leftists'—were warned by their chiefs that they must not do anything against the 'leftists', even if they were insulted by them. It was noted that they had to restrain themselves many times during the demonstration. But it would be a mistake to conclude from this that the Stalinists will be inclined to respect workers' democracy in times ahead. They staged this demonstration against their will, and one can be almost certain that they will seek revenge at an opportune moment.

It is impossible to describe the demonstration in a few words. We can only indicate a few features. Most of the workers who marched with the unions were certainly not up to the political level and militancy of the groups assembled around the students and teachers whose slogans were predominantly anti-capitalist, revolutionary, against the bourgeois State, for the socialist revolution, for workers' power, for internationalism ('Rome, Berlin, Warsaw, Paris!'). But the political temper of the workers was of a considerably higher level than in the past. No longer were there unworthy slogans such as *des sous, Charlot* ('some pennies, Charley').

The main feature of the demonstration was its anti-Gaullism. Inasmuch as the demonstration took place exactly ten years to the day since the military *coup* in Algiers that brought de Gaulle to power, a slogan heard everywhere was, 'Ten years, that's too much'. The leaders of the political parties (Fédération de la Gauche Démocrate Socialiste and Parti Communiste Française), who were excluded from the front ranks upon the insistence of the UNEF and the SNES, marched in the ranks of the crowd. They received but faint applause.

For the revolutionary militants it was a day that aroused great hopes. Their groups swelled in size as the demonstration progressed through the city. They did not even have to suffer the tricolour in the demonstration. Even more—a demonstrator climbed up the annexe of the Prefecture of the Police to pull down a flag floating from the windows. Likewise at the Palais de Justice, a demonstrator tore down the tricolour and replaced it with the black flag of the anarchists. The effigy of a member of the CRS suspended from a rope was carried by the Surrealists. There were only revolutionary slogans and spectacular actions. At the place Denfert-Rochereau, the CGT leaders called through a loudspeaker for the crowd to disperse. The vanguard groups (March 22nd movement, JCR, etc.) decided to continue the demonstration. Some groups under the leadership of sectors such as the anarchists went towards the Elysée —a move that was both utopian and adventuresome. But most went to the Champ de Mars, where a meeting was held of some 20,000 to 25,000 persons.

This meeting was by far the most important happening on May 13th, 1968. It was, in certain respects, on a much bigger scale, a continuation of the discussion that took place on May 9th, first at the boulevard St Michel, then at the JCR meeting. When the groups, some of a dozen persons, others of several hundreds or even some thousands, went from Denfert-Rochereau to the Champ de Mars, packing the pavements for several kilometres, bystanders thought that another uprising was under way. The truth was that most of the participants knew that this was not the time for new battles, but the moment to draw lessons from the events and to decide what to do the next day. For more than two hours there was a democratic tossing about of ideas, of proposals, prefiguring a kind of soviet assembly functioning democratically. Finally it was decided to continue the student strike and to occupy the Sorbonne the same evening, which was done. The university student movement has entered a new phase. It is not yet possible to draw a complete balance-sheet on what has happened, but a few conclusions can be drawn.

A New Period

We are not dealing with incidental events but with a break in the political equilibrium in France and the opening of a new period. It is possible, of course, to list the 'errors' committed by the Government (occupation of the Sorbonne, excessive repression, underestimation of 'grouplets' in the pattern of the Stalinists, etc.), but the movement would never have taken on the breadth it did, excited such sympathy, touched off a general strike by the unions (CGT, CFDT and FO), who had not even dreamt of such action only a few days before, if a situation had not developed in which many social contradictions had already reached a rather advanced point. In comparison with similar student movements in other countries, this one came late; but the delay, far from being due to the slower evolution of the French students, corresponded to the greater explosiveness of forces accumulating at a much bigger political level than elsewhere.

With a certain feverishness, the Government is at present preparing to take various measures. 'Today, I am appealing for everyone's co-operation, above all the students', and I will take the necessary steps,' Pompidou said before a Parliament which showed a little life precisely because the succession to Gaullism has been posed to a certain degree by the events.

Let us disregard the Gaullists and say a few words about the democratic and Social-Democratic opposition. These gentlemen of the FGDS, together with the Communist Party, will without doubt be the major beneficiaries in any elections that might be held in the near future. They would be carried into power 'legally'. During the uprising they hardly gave a sign of life. Now, on the parliamentary level, they are making all kinds of noise, without insisting on the fact that they have the possibility of coming to power via pressure from the streets.

The Communist Party is of particular interest. It is trying everything to 'recover' its leadership of the movement. On the day following the demonstration, it acted as if nothing unpleasant at all had been experienced by the bureaucrats in the march. It said not a word about the meeting at the Champ de Mars. A Political Bureau declaration, still based on unity with the democratic *bourgeoisie*, warned 'the workers and students against any adventurist slogans capable, under present conditions, of disrupting the broad front of struggle that has been constituted and giving the Gaullist régime an unlooked-for pretext to consolidate its shaky domination'.

These are not the words of other days, but the spirit has not changed. It is no longer a question of '*provocateurs*' but of the danger of an adventure. The politics of peaceful and parliamentary roads to re-establish a democracy, which is supposed to develop gradually into socialism, still lives on. Nevertheless, it would be rather surprising if the recent events did not shortly have some consequence within the Communist Party. The policies followed by this party among the youth are completely bankrupt. For around six years, the CP leadership expelled from the organizations and demonstrations under its control—often in a violent way—these 'leftists' who have now returned at the head of tens of thousands of youths. By an action that had nothing in common with parliamentism or pacifism, these 'leftists' forced the Government to capitulate, and all the bureaucratic machines set up in bourgeois society to stage a twenty-four-hour general strike.

For months the leadership of the Communist Party has been engaged in preparing for a new political combination with the factions of the *bourgeoisie*, aimed at assuring an alternative to take over from Gaullism. The role assigned to the CP was to provide a guarantee for the next régime against being bowled over by the Left. It played this role to perfection in 1936 and in 1945-47. It certainly does not doubt its capacity to do so once more. In 1936 and 1945-47, 'grouplets' (the term was accurate at the time) existed on the Left. The leaders enjoyed great prestige. (The Social Democrats were being challenged, but for a rather long time they were supported by the Stalinist leaders, which helped to smother the protests.) Without being unimportant, the development of the Left at no time reached such a level as to offer a practical challenge to these leaders.

The situation is quite different today. Even before the FGDS/ PCF combination was worked out, a force existed on the Left that could not easily be handled, owing to the fact that it had grasped the essence of classical reformism and post-Stalinist reformism. All the problems of French society, a combination of old problems resulting from worm-eaten structures dating back to the nineteenth century and new problems resulting from the modernization following the Second World War, became posed in an urgent way. The contending camps will have to define themselves, get organized and decide on their policies. The initiative taken by the students opened the way for a big mass-movement in the direction of socialism. One can be sure that, on the Right, political regroupments will take place and pro-fascist forces will be organized before long to defend the capitalist régime. Under such conditions, the construction of a mass-revolutionary Marxist party acquires decisive importance. Considerable forces are at hand to carry out this task, but they are fragmented politically and organizationally. Efforts must be made to overcome this state of affairs in order to succeed, as rapidly as possible, in attracting the numerous militants appearing among the youth as well as the many older people who for years have been awaiting better days.

We will return to all these problems, as well as to the consequences which this turn in the political situation in France cannot fail to have internationally—in the first place in Western Europe.

FRITZ TEUFEL

Prophylactic Notes
for the Self-Indictment of the Accused*

T. was born fifteen minutes before midnight on June 17th, 1943, in Ingelheim in the Rhineland. (Ten years later there occurred in East Germany a workers' uprising against Stalinist compulsion, set off by an increase of work norms in various branches of industry, which today is being unjustly praised or condemned in West or East Germany respectively as an anti-communist insurrection.)

Ingelheim was situated in the French occupation zone : there was nothing to eat there. In 1946 the T. family moved to Ludwigsburg in the US occupation zone, where it was almost possible to find enough to eat for a family of eight. T.'s father, an economics graduate, was initially an employee of the rural district office, but, after the currency reform, he built up for himself a practice as tax consultant.

* The following is a translation from the text, as published in the German weekly paper *Die Andere Zeitung,* of the statement made by the Berlin University student Fritz Teufel, to the Moabit County Court, when he appeared before it charged with having caused 'a grave breach of the peace'. This referred to the demonstrations in Berlin against the festive reception of the Shah of Iran on June 2nd, 1967, during which one student, Benno Ohnesorg, was shot dead by a CID policeman. The policeman, Kurras, had been acquitted shortly before the trial of Teufel began; Teufel was also acquitted. The name has given occasion to a good deal of 'humour' for 'Teufel' is the German word for 'devil'; perhaps this is why in the statement, drawn up while he was in custody awaiting trial, Teufel refers to himself as 'T'.

FIRST ANTI-AMERICAN ACTION

At the age of six, T. painted swastikas on houses occupied by Americans. His brothers had told him how Germany had twice fought against the whole world and nearly won, and would have done so if it had not been for the Americans. (Father T. was by no means a Nazi; but neither was he a Resistance fighter. He was a law-abiding citizen who sometimes railed against Church and State but always paid his taxes and Church contributions punctiliously.) At the time of his confirmation, T. was very religious and said his prayers every night. At the age of eighteen he read widely, including Tucholsky and Brecht. He was considered a bookworm. He wrote poetry. He abused his father because he did not vote for the Social Democrats—his father replying, 'These Reds with their unions ruin the economy.'

Up to the highest form but two, T. was a good scholar. Later on he felt school to be increasingly burdensome, boring and authoritarian—bad marks in Conduct and Co-operation; tried to do his school-leaving examination with as little work as possible—had to do it twice. In 1963 he received the testimonial of maturity. He was not eligible to defend his country because he was short-sighted; this suited him fine. (Many more rockets would probably have been stolen had T. been set to stand guard over them.)

When he had to enrol, T. was asked : 'What is it you want to study? . . . Journalism? Are you trying to pull my leg?' T. was not trying to pull the man's leg.

TO BERLIN

T. intended to go to Berlin, which not only had the advantage of being far from Ludwigsburg but was also, in his opinion, by far the most interesting place in Germany. (This is still the case.) T.'s father would have preferred to have had his son reading law at Tübingen University (near Ludwigsburg), but T.'s mother had always taken the part of her youngest son, who was thus for the summer term of 1963, admitted to the Free University of Berlin for studies in journalism, German language and theatrical knowledge. (These he had chosen according to his inclinations.)

When on the train to Berlin T. travelled across the German Democratic Republic for the first time, he stood at the window and waved. He thought : These poor brothers and sisters—still under Soviet occupation ! The brothers and sisters waved back; T. felt himself justified. He went on studying cheerfully on the principle, whatever is fun, be praised !

The question which at that time occupied him chiefly, was this : How can one make people laugh? It took approximately two years before he noticed, or slowly began to notice, or had increasingly pushed under his nose, the fact that the question had to be put differently : Why have people so little to laugh about?

PROPERTY AND FREEDOM

At one time, during the vacation, T. worked as an unskilled labourer with the Siemens electrical concern. He was depressed by the thought that he had only his social origin to thank for his good fortune in not having to do this sort of work for the whole of his life. He made the acquaintance of a Spanish student called Jesus, who was very badly off. It seemed to him a paradox that the Spaniards, who had fought against fascism, still have to suffer to this day under the Franco régime, whereas the Germans were liberated from Hitler without having done much about it themselves. T. began to take an interest in fascism. When attending the trials of the Nazis, he discovered that the accused were not so very different from their judges; or from other people, for that matter.

Studying was not unalloyed joy since, in order to pass certain examinations, he had suddenly to occupy himself with matters in which he had not the slightest interest (for instance, Gothic language). A lecture, to be given at the university by the writer Kuby, was arbitrarily banned simply on the basis of the domestic authority vested in the rector. T. began to read the leaflets lying about in the canteen. The best arguments were contained in the leaflets issued by the Left (SHB, SDS, Argument Club). T. began to take an interest in the political discussions at the university without, however, at that time becoming active himself. T. decided to fill a gap in his education and therefore took part in a SDS working party concerned with Marxism and the history of the working-class movement. This turned out to have been the *decisive* gap in his education. For six months T. read with hardly an interruption : Marx, Engels, Lenin, Trotsky, Rosa Luxemburg, Lukács, Korsch, Reich, Marcuse, etc. Like lightning theoretical knowledge struck into his innocent, fallow soil.

T. began to understand things which, previously, he had only vaguely divined : for instance, that in bourgeois society, property and freedom are identical; that freedom exists either as a matter of form, as the free choice between different evils (like a student looking for a room) or, as a matter of content, as private property, which means privilege. As a student of journalism, T. had the opportunity of occupying himself, in his work for a seminar, with the ideology of newspaper publishers. On that occasion (about a year before the slogan 'Expropriate Springer' became popular), he saw with particular clarity the connection between property and freedom as it affects the consciousness industry. In actual fact, freedom of the press is nothing but the freedom of publishers to defend, tooth and nail, and to expand the institution of private property, which, after all, they exemplify—and nobody knows this better than the publishers themselves. The recent controversy between the magazine *Der Spiegel* and the exiled Persian, Bahmand Nirumand, shows clearly that the freedom granted by even the most liberal publication stops at the very point where the institution of private property is openly attacked—even if 'only' in Persia.

BASIC LAW AND REALITY

To be sure, the Basic Law of the German Federal Republic still embodies some socialist or social-democratic ideas, in so far as Article 14(2) mentions that the use made of property ought to benefit the community. However, in the context of the Basic Law as applied in reality since 1949, this formulation is nothing but pure ideology in the sense of false consciousness. It suggests that private property and benefit to the community can be reconciled, or are even identical. But the use made of private property in the Federal Republic since 1949 has served not the community but private interests; it has cemented differences in wealth and education; it has furthered waste, through armaments and advertising, and also corruption and the fattening of the State and Party bureaucracy as well as the general hoodwinking of the people through the consciousness industry, and the exploitation and general frustration of all movements towards emancipation, both at home and abroad—where necessary, by brute force, as it manifests itself every day in Vietnam and as it manifested itself in Berlin on June 2nd. The death of Benno Ohnesorg was no tragic accident; on that day, a system established its essence.

THEFT

T. has a previous conviction for what the comedian Nestroy calls an experiment in achieving greater equality in the possession of wealth—the judiciary calls it larceny. T. did what, in a rationally organized society, probably anybody would be entitled to do, even on the present-day level of the development of productive forces : he took what he needed without paying for it. This happened in January 1967. It concerned half a pound of butter, two pairs of socks and a box of shoe-spray. T. freely admits it would have been better if he had expropriated the means of production of the newspaper publisher Springer.

COMMUNE K1

In March 1967 T. began to establish a 'Commune', together with eight other people. The establishment of this Commune ('K1') was one of the results of a long discussion held both inside and outside the SDS. The dilemma shared by all participants in this discussion was the difficulty of bringing together theory and practice in a society in which the legacy of a thousand years of fascism, the perfected manipulation of consciousness, and the international level reached by class struggle and exploitation, have caused the masses to accept domination in an apathetic way.

The participants in the discussion suffered from the contradiction between their socialist theories and their bourgeois existence. Socialist students, too, are products of bourgeois society and are dominated by the 'furies of private interests' (Marx); they are orientated towards competition and career-making. It is necessary to change society in order to change oneself. Solidarity is a product of revolution but also its necessary precondition. The participants in the discussion agreed that an organization which intends to change society is doomed to suffer shipwreck if its own structure does nothing but reflect the structure of existing society (for this, there are many examples to be found in the history of the European workers' movement). This means that an organization that wants to reorientate society in the direction of a structure that is anti-authoritarian, egalitarian and anti-private, must organize itself upon an anti-authoritarian, egalitarian and anti-private basis. In order to achieve favourable conditions for collaboration, we wanted to solve in common all problems which can be solved in common (housing, reproduction). Within the Commune the division of labour was, as far as possible, to be abolished.

SEXUALITY

Even within the circle of our close friends, one encountered the strangest ideas, formed by philistine lasciviousness, regarding a collective sexuality practised by compulsion. In this connection it need only be said that the Commune sees it as a problem that, in this society, relationships between human beings very easily take on the character of property relationships which impede or prevent collaboration—probably one of the most difficult problems of the Commune.

IN THE MATTER OF VIOLENCE

Perhaps it would be a Christian act to recommend to the Vietnamese that they should turn the other cheek. Very often, however, the other cheek is already burned as well. T. thinks that it is necessary to distinguish in principle between, on the one hand, violence serving oppression and, on the other, violence serving liberation. In view of the arsenal of weapons held by the police and military in the Federal Republic and in West Berlin, it would be madness and suicide if a minority were to try to counter that violence by violence of their own. The Commune K1 has never used violence nor advocated the use of violence. K1 hates violence. It is no accident that the same politicians and newspapers which applaud the genocide practised in Vietnam, talk of terror when, in Berlin, a tomato is squashed against the wall of the manipulated consciousness. T. confesses that he advocates that sort of 'terror'. But he thinks that to throw stones and dynamite in the fashion of Russian anarchists of the nineteenth century would be senseless manifestations of powerlessness. That we are not powerless is proved by the growing strength of the political students' movement. Every time we succeed in denouncing and ridiculing the ruling powers, we prove that we are not powerless.

'LEFT FASCISM'

What do academic Marxists, whose revolutionary impetus has dried out on the altar of science, mean when they talk of 'Left fascism'? It is known what fascism is—namely, preventive counter-revolution. Bourgeois society pulls the emergency brake. In Germany, it was a passionate struggle for an irrational cause and correspondingly, therefore, one could give to the passionate struggle for a rational cause the name 'Left fascism', if one chooses passion and not irrationality as the criterion for fascism. This is exactly what is done by academic Marxists who love the resigned quietude of their university chairs, and thus do nothing but supply a new variant to the bourgeois theory of totalitarianism.

ASSASSINATION OF HUMPHREY

The assassins were arrested before they had had an opportunity of discussing their crime in detail. We were agreed that the action should be conducted in such a way that it could in no way be interpreted as an act of aggression. It was to be, and had to be, unambiguously an act of ridicule in the style of American film comedies. By way of illustration, in November 1966 a scandal occurred in Seoul, the capital of South Korea. A Member of Parliament—who, as the *Neue Zürcher Zeitung* expressed it at the time, had been elected by a mob of malcontents and sent from the street into Parliament—entered Parliament with a bucket of human excrement, which he emptied from the speaker's tribune over the Prime Minister and his Cabinet. Even an action of that kind would have been impossible and far too aggressive in the case of Humphrey.

Not every word uttered by the Commune at the press conference must be taken seriously, because they indulged in the luxury of answering in kind various particularly stupid questions. Thus T. said at the press conference that, should shooting result, the Commune had designated five people who had to let themselves be shot dead : in this connection, one must bear in mind the safety precautions taken by the Americans which excluded any possibility that, in the case of a real assassination, shots would be fired into the mass of spectators. Also, there was no danger that our action could be interpreted as an attempted assassination. Any would-be assassin would go into some ambush with his rifle with telescopic sights, but would in no circumstances rush into the street. Probably the CIA knows more about this than does Commune K1.

AMERICA HOUSE

At that time T. would have liked to throw an egg against America House. However, he was afraid to do so in view of the strong posse of police. The property of not being a hero is probably the only one he shares with the CID policeman, K. It is true that the Commune K1 had discussed all sorts of things, but it has never really done anything without satisfying itself in detail regarding all the possible consequences. Thus, in the case of the Humphrey action, it was clear to everybody that all participants had to be prepared to be charged with committing a grave nuisance and with offending the head of a foreign state. But that we should be charged with an attempt against the life and health of the American Vice-President—that was as much of a surprise to us as it was to the public.

SHAH'S VISIT

Those who wished to avoid giving the impression that they agreed with the imperialist complicity with which Bonn and Washington supported all régimes in the Third World that are inimical to emancipation, who wished to avoid giving the impression that they approved of illiteracy, hunger, disease and exploitation in Persia, had no alternative but to demonstrate when the 'greatest reformer of all times', the operetta gangster of Teheran, the Viceroy of the American oil companies in Persia, was received in Berlin with pomp and circumstance. Unfortunately, the Commune could not think of much that could be done apart from the demonstration paper bags which were, above all, to protect the Persian fellow students from the secret service of their country. Nevertheless, we took part in the demonstration against the Shah in order to see what would happen. After all, there had to be some occasion when somebody else besides the Commune produced the ideas.

One thing has become particularly clear in connection with State visits : official politics assumes more and more the character of a circus; the politicians become interchangeable with ham actors. It is no accident that we talk of the political stage. (Some actors, of course, are quite cute; for instance Heinrich Lubke, the West German President. One could hardly believe that, once upon a time, he designed concentration camps; one could, at most, think of him as a former head-waiter at the Führer's headquarters.) The population is being degraded to the status of a theatrical audience. T. thinks that the audience in a theatre has good cause to throw eggs and tomatoes if it does not like the play.

THE EVENING IN FRONT OF THE OPERA HOUSE

T. arrived some time after 7.30. He felt some misgivings when he saw the barricade through which the police were herding the demonstrators into a narrow gangway between a railing and a building-fence. In addition there was a gigantic police force. T. believed, however, that these preparations had been made to intimidate the demonstrators, but not in order to facilitate beating them up systematically, as was in fact done later. Clashes began at 7.45 when policemen, who had been placed on the building-site behind the fence, moved against the demonstrators who were sitting on the fence. Rubber rings flew over the fence on to the demonstrators —some fell on the street, since the gangway was so narrow. No stones were thrown. Some demonstrators threw things back. When the VIP appeared, eggs and tomatoes were thrown in front of the entrance to the opera house. Smoke-bombs were thrown on to the street, which were then thrown back into the tightly packed mass of demonstrators. T. can say with absolute certainty that he did not throw a single stone, still less did he incite others to do so; nor did he see any policeman or demonstrator throwing stones.

RELATIONS WITH THE POLICE

We have nothing against the police. On the contrary : in December 1966 we demonstrated in favour of the introduction of a thirty-five-hour week for the police. However, we do have misgivings when we see the police being misused for political purposes, or when the consciousness industry makes deliberate attempts to incite the police against students. T. believes that any normal policeman would vastly prefer kicking his superior officer's behind to beating up students. When one sees pictures of uniformed men using their truncheons to beat a woman who is lying in the street, it is understandable if stones are thrown, even if one does not approve.

However, one thing is certain : people who show themselves to be inhuman to such a degree cannot ever themselves have been treated as human beings. These were no free citizens of a democratic society, but rather bloodhounds trained to savagery, like the American élite troops in Vietnam.

TOMATOES, EGGS, SMOKE-BOMBS

T. declares his solidarity with all those who have thrown objects suitable for demonstration purposes (that means objects incapable of inflicting injury), such as eggs, tomatoes and smoke-bombs. Even though he cannot prove having thrown, for instance, a tomato, he would like to encourage the Court to treat him as it would those who have thrown tomatoes, eggs or smoke-bombs.

ARREST

Shortly after eight o'clock there occurred what has been referred to as 'driving in the main wedge'—a task-force of policemen used their truncheons to beat a gap into the mass of the demonstrators. In order to see more clearly what was happening, T. advanced some way towards the scene of action. After the 'driving of the wedge' had been achieved, the police began to drive the demonstrators like a herd of cattle towards Krumme St. In order to escape a similar fate, those demonstrators who were standing in the vicinity of Sesenheimer St. sat down. T. was sitting near the events, approximately half-way between the building-fence and the railings, facing in the direction of Krumme St.

When, a little later, a second 'wedge' was driven in the direction of Sesenheimer St., he turned round to see what was going on, so that he was facing the demonstrators. The police then began to advance against the sitting demonstrators as well. T. tried to ignore the policemen and continued to turn his back on them. Suddenly he was pulled by the hair, and somebody said, 'Move on, get up!' He did not get up and received blows from the truncheons, as well as kicks. He took no counter-action but confined himself to protecting his face with his arms, while attempting to put his spectacles away, which, however, were broken nevertheless.

T. was carried away. When he was carried over the middle of the road, he heard a man in civilian clothes (this appears to have been CID officer Böhme) call out as he approached the group, 'Why, that is Teufel'—followed by words to the effect that he was one of those who prepared a dynamite attack against Humphrey. While T. was still being carried across the road, he was beaten. He shouted loudly. The beating stopped.

T. was transported in a police car to Keith St. police station. He was accompanied by two policemen. One of them, who wore a white uniform jacket (T. later learned that this was Hessner), continued to beat him during the drive with both his fists and his truncheon, all the while demanding hysterically what sort of people they were who prepared dynamite attacks and threw stones—for each policeman, a thousand SDS swine should be done in, we should not imagine that the police did not know us, they had pictures of all of us. All this, and more besides, he shouted several times over. The other policeman (Mertin) sat there and pretended that the whole thing was none of his business. Once T. attempted to explain that he had not thrown stones; whereupon Hessner attacked him again and shouted that all of them had thrown stones.

T. was glad when the drive was over. In the writ of indictment it says : 'Nothing of note happened during the drive to Keith St. police station.'

VITTORIO RIESER

The Struggle against Capitalism in Italy:
A Political Manifesto

I

From the Fight against the University System
to Confrontation with Society

The struggle of the student movement in Italy (type of clash, assembly, slogans, political documents) shows quite clearly that we have moved a long way since our confrontation with the university system and are now aiming at political action against capitalist society as a whole.

This extension and radicalization of policy is not a decision imposed by a restricted policy-making élite. On the contrary, the movement's leaders have often held it back because of their own problems (perhaps justified), or else have ideologized it in terms incapable of making an impression upon the majority of the students involved in the struggle. Nor can it be attributed to the type of clashes which have taken place and that have led to repressive action on an increasing scale by society. This has undoubtedly accelerated and concentrated the process, but has not been the cause of it.

The radicalization of the student movement shows therefore that there was latent, in the students, a *strong antagonistic feeling*, somehow linked with their objective position in society (and not exclusively produced by certain 'political stimuli' of one or another group). The Vietnam demonstrations in spring 1968 had already indicated its existence. But it is only recently that it has been able to outgrow its *roots* and succeed in escaping from the *forms of organization* and *immediate objectives* linked with the objective status of the student in education. These are merely starting points, which can quickly be left behind : but they alone are capable at present of guaranteeing the movement's *permanence* and the *continual outflowing of new forces* towards it.

The development of the movement beyond reformism (even of the most stringent and serious reformism) does, however, create two main *unsolved problems* :

(1) What proportion of the student base is prepared to follow the movement along this 'dangerous' revolutionary path?

(2) What can present-day strategic objectives of the movement *outside education* be?

The Fundamental Motivation and Its Relationship with the Student Masses

The common need to maintain a full, fighting and autonomous movement, which is free to make political choices inside and outside education, also affects the type of objectives it sets itself within the university. In the existing movement, none of the different proposals put forward in the various universities by groups of lecturers seems to satisfy this need : they are all centred upon the principle of 'coadministration' by which students become a (subordinate) component of the direction of the current system, which is technically a little improved and vaguely 'democratized'. It would not therefore seem that, *for the moment*, power relationships would allow the student movement to impose solutions upon the university which could guarantee it full political freedom and liberty of action. On the other hand, the acceptance of proposed compromises would mean its castration.

This situation may be temporary and the evolution of power relationships may soon result in more progressive solutions. However, at the moment, the student movement is faced with a drastic choice between the *acceptance of restrictive compromises* and the *refusal of any solution,* with all the attendant risks, *in order to maintain its own political autonomy.* This means that there is at present a *divergence* between the *satisfaction of certain immediate interests of students as a category* and the *politico-strategic needs* of the

203

movement. To give priority to the latter would mean being exposed to loss of examination sessions or of the whole academic year, without immediate material benefits.

This does not alter the fact that this drastic choice accentuates the difference between the *active nucleus* and the *majority of the students*; to the extent to which they agitate only as a 'category', and do not first and foremost utilize the unusual conditions in which they find themselves, in order to leave behind their 'role' as students. The students are subjected to the double pressure of their *social provenance* and *professional destination*, and will not be prepared to take actions which jeopardize their careers. As long as direct action and immediate improvement of the student status in the university coincide, the distinction between *'avant-garde'* and student 'mass' is hazy : when such action offers no immediate possibilities of material improvement, the difference between them increases.

This problem must be recognized, but it should not restrict our action. Because of the ambiguous class situation of the students one cannot apply to them criteria of action which would be valid for the working classes : a struggle potentially acceptable to *the masses* is a valid criterion for the working class, but cannot be a guiding criterion for students. However, there do exist other relevant problems and other needs which must be respected :

(a) The fact that the severity of the fight is now restricting the potential basis of the movement is a risk that must be taken; but we need not run the risk of a politically recoverable basis being relegated to the background by over-ideological speech or lack of material for discussion. There are continual opportunities for widening the basis, which can be exploited without abating the political line, that sometimes seem dangerously underestimated.

(b) The availability of a wide basis for the current radical line of confrontation does not automatically solve the problem of a permanent organization and its strategy. This is the fundamental problem of the movement which is still to be solved, and not only in Italy.

Lack of Objectives and of Strategy

In the student movement at present there is a relative lack of immediate tactical objectives, due more to the *objective conditions* surrounding it than to insufficient political elaboration.

On a university level such objectives exist (we will return to them later) : but they do not seem immediately attainable and, more important, cover only a part of the movement's activity.

The basic lack is of extra-university objectives on a level with the rest of society. This is inevitable at present, since the student movement as a force is simply not self-sufficient enough for a confrontation with the system, and since the other forces which would be decisive in such a confrontation (the working class and its organizations) are not currently taking up such a radical line of confrontation. (We are not concerned with analysing *why* this state of affairs exists : we merely state that it does.)

This situation forces revolutionary students to function on a much wider political basis than would 'normally' be expected of them and than they can currently cope with, given their present standards of power and organization. For example, they cannot limit themselves to challenging those facets of society which are directly linked with education : they are forced also to cover a field a good deal farther from educational problems, which has no clearly visible symbol for the purpose of a confrontation. But the fundamental consequence is that the student movement—like other, less numerous, 'revolutionary minority groups' before it—is trapped in a sort of vicious circle by which the only object of its action is 'itself', in which *the only objective of the movement is the growth of the movement itself*; and in which the strategy to which these forces will be directed is not—nor can it yet be—defined.

The student movement must accept this position, contradictory and 'projected into space' as it is.

It must accept it for its internal logic : because the development of its basis impels it in this direction; it is therefore its 'self-limitation' which is of an artificial nature, and not its forward expansion.

It must accept it for more general political reasons : in that it represents a stimulus to formation and generalization of revolutionary forces in other sectors of society.

*Relationships with the Working Class and the Organized
Working-Class Movement*

The existing situation also conditions the method of establishing a
relationship between the student movement and the working class.
The following are therefore ruled out as insufficient and unacceptable :

(a)   A relationship, based on 'institutional division of labour',
with the official organizations of the workers' movement, by
means of which the student movement delegates may approach
the working class.

(b)   A relationship in which the student movement has an autonomous but circumscribed right of approach to those problems
which specifically link school and factory : that is, the *right to
study* and *professional formation.*

This formulation is theoretically correct, and both these problems
(though not seen quite as the Italian Communist Party sees them!)
constitute a solid and important permanent field of action for the
student movement.

The prevalent situation, however, creates an exceptional interest
on the part of the workers in the student struggle, which they often
see as an example of the kind of severe, open struggle which might
become necessary for them. This attitude, which is often falsified
or oversimplified, is certainly not capable of constituting by itself
the basis of a mutual political action; but it does open up opportunities for communication (leaflets, newspapers, discussions, etc.)
and for communal action (student picketing during strikes, working-
class participation in student demonstrations).

The development of these relationships must be regarded as
flexible and not rigidly predetermined, in relation both to forms
of organization and to political content. On the level of forms of
organization, the need for an autonomous right to approach the
working classes instead of delegating everything to the official working-class movement must not lead to absurd theorizing by the
student movement in its capacity as a 'revolutionary *avant-garde*'
and consequently a futile attempt to oust, for example, the trade-
unionists. One must therefore evaluate on its own merits each
type of relationship with the trade unions.

On the level of political content the most important elements must obviously be the subjects developed by the student movement in recent months : both the more general ones of authoritarianism and those relative to the right to study, to professional formation, etc. But wherever direct relationship with a working-class situation is established, the *merits of the problems of the working-class struggle* must be explored.

Risk of Opportunism and 'Adventurism'

The first type of risk, among the problems of an action of confrontation by the student movement, is that of *opportunism*. This obviously does not take into account the opportunism founded on *political refusal* of the policy of confrontation : this type of opportunism has now been defeated in most if not all Italian cities, although it could of course reappear in the context of new and apparently more advanced 'offers of dialogue' and of negotiations. But apart from this there are risks of opportunism *within* a 'confrontation' policy. The principal one is that already referred to, the subordination of political developments to the need for adherence by the *mass* of the students. From this follow unnecessary precautions, which often prove obstacles to any extension of the movement, such as a tendency to restrict the movement on the part of its political management.

As the movement achieves more and more radical forms of struggle and discards opportunities for compromise solutions, so opportunism becomes the lesser danger (its supporters are in fact often on the fringe of the movement); and the risk of *adventurism* becomes much more real.

What are the characteristics by which adventurism may generally be known?

The basic characteristic is *underestimation of long-term prospects* and therefore of *strategic content* and *permanent problems of organization* of the movement.

Methods of struggle are often mistaken for *political content* : thus, a clash with the police is found to be an 'advanced political objective', when it is merely a method of fighting (even though at this moment it is of crucial importance).

This leads to measuring any *encounter with the enemy in purely tactical terms*, to taking a short-term view and ignoring the wood for the trees : a pause in the 'tit-for-tat' fighting is seen, wrongly, as a strategic defeat for the movement; and, vice versa, a minor tactical success is hailed as a strategic advance.

The tendency is thus to create a *divergence* between *development of the immediate action of the movement*, on the one hand, and its *political and organizational growth*, on the other. The former is considered enough to guarantee the latter and all efforts are concentrated upon it alone. Analysis and political debate on strategical subjects take second place or are considered merely forms of opportunistic evasion.

We are obviously not speaking of already crystallized positions, of a sort of 'organized tendency' : these are adventuristic attempts which continually arise in present fighting conditions, and are the more dangerous in a student *milieu* with facile tendencies towards verbal extremism unhampered by *objectively antagonistic conditions*, such as prevail in a working-class environment.

The more they prevail, the more these attitudes hinder a clear-sighted view of the basic political problem : if the student movement genuinely wishes to inspire the formation of a revolutionary force, it must draw up long-term plans; present-day conditions of conflict are therefore not sufficient to keep its organization going, since a continuation—uninterrupted for a long period—of the conflict in its present form, is unthinkable. Periods of acute conflict would alternate with periods of relative calm. It is necessary to form an organization capable of surmounting both; moreover, an organization which must develop for a while with a relative lack of objectives (since it is 'more advanced' than the rest of the political situation) demands a good deal more political maturity than is common within itself. The immediate organization of the conflict is merely a temporary surrogate of such maturity; and while possibly helpful in developing this maturity, it is unfortunately not enough (and can also develop it unevenly and misleadingly). The central task is therefore one of political amplification and strategic elaboration, to be executed on the *current basis of the movement*. It should be carried out, from now on, in the thick of the conflict, primarily because the conflict is the first and most efficacious criterion of political selection of the real basis of the movement;

and second because, if it does not begin at once, the movement will find itself unprepared and powerless in the face of developments (repressive and reformistic) created by the conflict itself.

2

Current Goals of the Struggle in the University

The present political homogeneity of the student movement has not sprung from a common starting point; rather, it has developed during the struggle, in forms of organization and methods of conflict, which have become more and more alike, influenced by a basis expressing mutual needs.

On the level of political objectives, the positions are (and partly were) various : they range from the refusal on principle of all negotiations to plans for university restructurization, which would be perfectly feasible within the existing system.

A unification of the movement is needed at this point even on the level of politically agreed objectives. It is necessary on a *tactical* level, so as to gain strength in the current struggle against the adversary. The national extension of this struggle has of late been our strong point. To counter this, however, the enemy attempts *divisive tactics*, trying a little of both *repressive intervention* and *'offers of talks'* : here trying to provoke through massive repression, there trying to neutralize the situation with offers of negotiation. Until now the only effect of repressive intervention seems to have been to intensify the movement (Turin is the best example). But there is still the danger that in situations where the struggle has not been radicalized to this degree, a manoeuvre towards integration based on offers—and consistent ones—of negotiation will succeed. Such manoeuvres must be countered by a national policy.

But there are also strategic reasons that make a common revendicative elaboration necessary. Precisely because it is projected forward in a struggle against present-day society, a struggle which for the moment has no concrete political aims, the movement needs to retain its roots in education and to formulate immediate concrete objectives, whose only criterion should be that they extend and consolidate its margin of action instead of limiting it. To gain a 'space' in the university means to create a permanent field of political action capable of continuing even when there are no overt clashes, and capable of attracting new proselytes and gradually elaborating a strategic prospect.

It is obvious that, seen in this light, some claims are automatically excluded : the aim is no longer abstract 'restructurization' of the university, but the creation within *education* (not only within the university) of a space in which the student movement can carry out its political work in complete freedom and with specific advantages, on the subjects and in the ways which it thinks fit. Seen thus, any solution of 'coadministration' fails : not only because it would imply a position distinctly subordinate for the student movement, but because it would concentrate its action upon an essentially didactic field. In this sense, even a solution of universal 'self-administration', such as that proposed in the Turin plans, would be unacceptable. Apart from the impossibility of putting it into practice with existing power relationships, it would lead the student movement to concentrate its forces upon matters of university education.

Therefore, the most practical solution seems to be to divide the university into two areas. The first, completely controlled by the student movement, would carry out all its political activities therein; some of these activities will take the form of *anti-courses* (but the number and subjects of these courses will be decided on the basis of political needs of the student movement and not on the basis of having to correspond on every point to a study plan). These anti-courses—though not the other activities—must be recognized as genuine methods of seeking knowledge, but *not subjected to supervision by lecturers*. The rest of the university will continue to function without student participation in its administration, but if necessary the students will be able to impose, through their own organized action, certain conditions which may have no particular value of principle but which will reduce the burden of traditional university activity in student life, for instance : streamlining study plans, examination guarantees, facilities for working students, right to discussion and intervention in all didactic activities. Thus the student movement can avoid the fundamental dangers : (a) of making university administration its aim, and (b) of accepting institutional forms of collaboration with the teaching body.

The movement is guaranteed freedom of political work by its

existing basis, and permanent possibilities of recruitment from the student masses (both through the attraction which its own activities will exercise and through material improvements which it will obtain in the 'traditional' sphere of university activity).

It is necessary that in following such a policy the student movement should present a united national front. In particular : it must refuse any localized solution which does not pass the test of fixed political criteria (and any negotiation whose basis would automatically exclude solutions based upon them); even when immediate acceptable solutions are reached, these must in no way imply that there should be any restriction on the action of the movement, which must be free to continue its activities even if only because of the needs of national interconnection.

Extra-University Objectives and Connections with Other Forces

SOME QUESTIONS OF METHOD

Unattainable 'Objectives'

In the student movement, as with previous 'revolutionary' minority groups, a curious tactical naïveté tends to reappear : the aiming at *seemingly* immediate objectives, which in fact could only be attained by overthrowing the entire system. Sometimes this is merely an unsuccessful attempt to make a policy 'more realistic' when objectively this is impossible at the present moment. But at other times the reasoning behind it is carefully worked out : a struggle which is concentrated upon immediate, specific, but unattainable objectives is seen as the only means of maintaining a continuous state of tension. This hypothesis is based upon a curious illusion of 'Machiavellian' relationship with the masses (or with whatever corresponds to them in a particular case : for example, the student base). Implicitly, it is supposed that they are not politically mature enough to undertake a long-term revolutionary struggle, with no prospects of intermediate gains; therefore, they are presented with a concrete, immediate objective, but one which is unattainable in the context of the existing system. Fighting for this objective, they will find themselves waging revolutionary warfare *sans le savoir*.

Such a tactical hypothesis is totally unrealistic : it is an ingenuous and illusory means of escape from the problem of relationship between immediate objectives and revolutionary prospects. This problem cannot be solved by universally valid formal schemes. In certain cases, a movement with revolutionary aims may be capable of mounting an action against immediate *attainable* objectives and making the attainment of these objectives an integrating factor in the growth of revolutionary power. In other cases this is not possible, and the only outlet is therefore to make the destruction of the system the central objective of the movement. Specific objectives, which can be attained only by means of such an overthrow, can then be valuable purely as exemplification, as propaganda, to show what the existing system is blocking and what its revolutionary overthrow would make possible.

The student movement is, therefore, from this point of view, in a composite situation. On the level of education, it can set itself *attainable* and *unintegrated* objectives, even if these require power relationships and a degree of political maturity which have probably not yet been achieved. On the level of society, the situation involves such a divergence between available forces and the degree of revolutionary awareness that it is difficult to find immediate objectives for which to fight.

But there are no 'short-cuts' out of this impasse. The only way out is by explicitly facing the problem of the *content* of a revolutionary strategy and of the forces that can undertake it.

One concrete example is that of the relationship with the working classes, and the function relative to them of a right to study, formulated in the most radical terms (salary guaranteed to all young people up to a certain age). In the abstract, this claim is correctly set out, in that it corresponds to specific subjects of the student movement, is designed to overcome certain class limits in education, and also stands for an 'overthrow' of the current general system. In reality, it does not solve the problem of relationship with the working classes. Its immediate unattainability is so evident that it would be no inducement to fight; it is rooted in the more general problem of revolutionary struggle. It would be more useful for such a problem to be examined from every angle, linking it with all the problems of the workers' condition, instead of from just one angle.

SOME LIMITED FIGHTING OBJECTIVES ON AN INTERNATIONAL LEVEL

In distinguishing possible objectives of the movement, one must view the student movement on an international level. On a Western European level at least, it is not too idealistic to hope for co-ordinating action towards analogous objectives. If one looks for extra-university objectives on a purely national scale, one forfeits what is possibly the movement's greatest long-term advantage : the fact that its roots lie in objective conditions which tend to be similar in the various European countries, and it therefore assumes some analogous political characteristics in the various countries *even before* any political co-ordination is organized.

By distinguishing traits which are common, or tend to be common, to the various European student struggles, one can suggest a series of possible objectives or 'lines of action' which on the one hand are 'too one-sided' with regard to the universal contestative force of the movement, and on the other 'too general' with regard to the specifically student stamp of the movement, but which nevertheless roughly correspond to its current stage of political development.

Authoritarianism

The struggle with authoritarianism is the general context of the student movement. At the present moment it can, however, be translated into various specific objectives. On the level of Western European society, one of these could be the fight against the various 'authoritarian laws' which flourish continually; emergency laws in Germany, restriction of the right to strike in England, laws of public security in Italy. The student movement can act as an incentive and a guide in the struggle against these laws, thus removing this struggle from the influence of the prospects and methods of orthodox communist or similar parties (wherever it runs the risk of being monopolized by these forces or channelled into a jaded prospect of 'democratic alliance').

VITTORIO RIESER

The Problem of Information

The student movement appears to be the best equipped to organize 'counter-initiatives' against the capitalist monopoly of mass-means of communication : whether by counter-attacks and direct polemic (anti-Springer campaign, the Dutch *'telerat'*, various kinds of 'anti-press') or by the creation of new ways and means of information, concentrated upon political subjects chosen by it. The field of information seen as a central element in any labour or political formation seems to be that in which the student movement could, in the most practical and permanent way, take political initiative, even on subjects of international politics (such as Vietnam and anti-imperialist wars in general), and partly also in relationships with the working classes.

Relationships with Working-Class Struggles

Here, too, there are analogous phenomena in the various European countries : on the one hand, a capitalist policy of integration (at the moment largely unopposed) which weighs more and more on the working-class organizations; on the other, a working-class reaction, which sometimes finds no organized means of outlet but at other times finds them within the trade-union organizations themselves (in which the integration process, politically accepted at the summit, is rendered more contradictory and difficult by the lack of opposition and by the consequent risk of loss of any basic agreement). Some experiences of the SDS, and some indications of the Italian situation, show that the student movement can have a function in this context : by providing, through example and direct communication, a stimulus to fight; by promoting specific forms of information and political debate, within the trade unions or outside them; by acting informally as an element of international communication (lacking to a high degree in the current stage).

It remains to be seen what the long-term outcome of this action will be : that is, if it will be purely transitory, if the student movement as such will assume a permanent function in this field, or if it will contribute to the formation of new organized forces on a working-class level. Working along the lines indicated above does not imply an *a priori* choice of one or other prospect of a long-term outcome.

Political Formation of Technicians and 'Other Intermediate Groups'

This problem is linked with that of the 'transitoriness' of the student stage. The movement can overcome this transitoriness either by becoming a political movement which extends beyond scholastic limits, or by forming people politically so that their influence will be transmitted to the next stage. At the moment it is perfectly possible to follow the first alternative (that is, not merely on the level of individual political formation), which is obviously the more interesting; but it still remains necessary to take action at the same time in accordance with the second alternative. The more so, since the nucleus of the current movement is made up of people from the humanistic faculties, with the risk that people from the polytechnic (in other words, those who are in fact going to end up in production) will remain on the fringe of the movement, limited to technicistic revendication.

It is therefore necessary to concentrate the work of political formation in these sectors of education, so as to create groups of technicians capable of reacting to the 'antagonistic stimuli' produced by the factory structure and of acting methodically in their professional destination. (This is a field in which one could usefully co-operate with the trade unions.) Even in the humanistic faculties there is a problem of 'orientation and political control' with regard to professional deployment, in the form of preparation and political organization of future teachers (so as vastly to exceed the limits in which the majority of left-wing teachers move at present).

Some Concluding Considerations

In the more advanced stages of struggle of the student movement, there exists, or there is a risk of, a growing divergence between the practical development of the conflict (more and more radical, and with a more and more general and political counterpart) and the development of the discussion and political organization of the movement (which often stagnates 'due to *force majeure*', in that all the power of discussion and organization is expended in the day-to-day organization of the conflict).

This divergence was, and is, partly inevitable : but it must be recognized as a negative element and one to be combated. Instead, however, the tendency seems to be to accentuate it : in other words, after every forward step in the practical conflict, to elaborate a new and 'more advanced' theorization of the movement, a theorization elaborated by a small handful of people and in general passively accepted by the ranks.

The strategic development of the movement thus takes place in the minds of the leaders, who attribute this or that significance to this or that conflict.

Now, however, a strong effort at political elaboration must be made by the *rank and file*, if the movement is to survive. If the political consciousness of the *whole* movement does not take a 'leap forward', the movement runs a double risk of disintegration : either the risk of progressive diminution of the number of those capable of enduring prolonged conflict, or the more probable one of disintegration as soon as there is any slowing down of or pause in the immediate conflict.

It is therefore necessary that, generally speaking, there should be homogeneity on a national level in the choice of central *methods* and *subjects* for this 'politicization' of the movement.

As for the *methods,* all 'intermediate organizations' between the individual fighter and the assembly are obviously essential : *work commissions, anti-courses.* It is clear that the subjects and means of functioning of these organizations must be decided mainly on the basis of political and not didactic criteria (without underestimating the usefulness of a whole series of studies, even long-term ones, so long as they are directly relevant to the political preparation of the militant members of the movement). These organizations are the only ones capable of basic political elaboration and discussion.

If these 'intermediate organs' remain crucial to effective political elaboration and discussion, other useful complementary methods could be co-ordinated and developed on a national scale. For example, the experiment of producing a *local agitators' newspaper* was successful (and would have been even more so had it been better utilized politically by the movement). This medium affords an adaptable means of communicating news and of widely disseminating political themes which are vital to the movement, reducing these to their basic essentials. Furthermore, as an instrument it is capable of development, on the level of the 'information reports' circulated by the prevailing mass-communications media.

In this sense, a local paper, which would be a direct, immediate, day-to-day expression of the movement, is more specifically useful than the proposed *national newspaper*. The latter can, however, be used for the incessant exchange and communication of documents, information and political hypotheses between one centre and another, which is of much importance at the present time to advancing the politicization of the movement.

As for the subjects central to the political work carried out by these methods, they are to some extent obvious : primarily the present choices of the movement, of permanent organizational forms to be established, of relationships with other forces. But, if we really mean to grapple with problems of strategy, we must try to make a wider and more 'objective' analysis of what the student movement is and what it signifies : we must place the student movement in the context of the social contradictions, old and new, of capitalist society. What positions do the students and their struggle hold in this context? What objective bases exist for connections with the working class? What hypotheses can be deduced on future developments of class warfare in this society?

These are obviously not questions which can be answered immediately. But one must put them in order to realize the true dimensions of the strategic problems facing one, and in order to escape from the facile intellectual dilettantism which fundamentally leads many students who clash with the police to think they are instigating a revolution. It is impossible to predict with any certainty the function of the student movement with respect to the eventual formation of a revolutionary force in our society. There appear to be three possibilities (not counting that of total failure) :

(1) The student movement directly discharges a long-term political function of confrontation, while keeping its student characteristics.

(2) The student movement limits itself to forming smaller groups.

(3) The student movement carries out its political function but loses its student characteristics, so that the short-term result is a much wider political formation.

The choice of one or the other of these would, at the present moment, be out of touch with the reality of the movement and with the concrete terms of the political elaboration developed to date. But there are some 'preliminary requisites' common to all three possibilities; while the starting point for all three types of development is *mass-conflict and the systematic and permanent organization of internal political debate.*

Without mass-conflict there is no hope of forming smaller active groups : since the number of activists decreases, and because there is a lack of concrete political consciousness which is necessary in a student *milieu* where there is a great risk of rhetorical extremism and practical inertia.

TONY CLIFF

The Struggle in the Middle East

I

IMPERIALISM

When speaking about imperialism in the Middle East, what comes to mind first and foremost is oil. Oil exploitation is fantastically profitable. The fixed-capital investment necessary to extract one barrel of crude oil daily is $190 in the Middle East compared with $730 in Venezuela and $1,500 in the United States.[1] The cost of producing one barrel of crude oil in the Middle East is only fifteen cents as against $1.63 in the United States.[2] The eight giant oil companies controlling world oil fix the prices in the world market according to the cost of production at the Gulf of Mexico. Middle East oil is really a gold mine. The rate of profit on Middle East oil, according to official figures (and these are, naturally, understated), averaged in the period 1948-60 67 per cent per annum on capital invested, as against 21 per cent in Venezuela and 10.8 per cent in the United States.[3]

If we were talking about Middle East oil before the Second World War, we would have spoken mainly of British oil imperialism. Then Britain controlled 100 per cent of Iranian oil and $47\frac{1}{2}$ per cent of Iraqi oil; the US interest was only $23\frac{3}{4}$ per cent in Iraq (equal to France's). Since then the situation has changed

[1] C. Issawi and M. Yeganeh, *The Economics of Middle Eastern Oil* (1962), p. 53.
[2] Ibid., p. 54.
[3] Ibid., p. 112.

radically : in 1959 the US share rose to 50 per cent of all Middle East oil, while that of Britain declined to 18 per cent (France had 5 per cent, the Netherlands 3 per cent, others, including local Arab governments, 24 per cent). Now oil imperialism is really United States imperialism.

Oil has had very little beneficial impact upon the development of the countries of the Middle East. The distortion of their economic, social and political development caused by feudalism and imperialism has been accentuated further. The employment in oil is very small : in Iran, only 1 per cent of the employed population earn their livelihood in oil; in Iraq 1 per cent; in Saudi Arabia 2 per cent; Kuwait 19 per cent; Aden 6 per cent.[4] Altogether, the total employment in oil in the Middle East is less than the employment in textiles in Egypt alone.

The richest oil resources are in countries with the most archaic social régimes. The imperialist divisions of the Middle East—and all the boundaries between the Arab countries were simply imposed by imperialism—placed barriers between the large population centres, which are also by far the more advanced socially and politically, and the main natural resources of the Arab region.

2

ZIONISM

A series of human tragedies brought the Jews to Palestine : pogroms in czarist Russia, persecution in Eastern Europe and the holocaust of Nazism. When they reached Palestine, they found that it was inhabited by Arabs. Whatever the motivation that brought the Jews in, an increasing conflict between Zionist settlements and the Arabs was unavoidable.

The Arab peasant on his very low standard of living, suffering from open or disguised unemployment, was there offering his labour and product for a very cheap price. How could a European worker, or prospective worker, find a job under such conditions? The only way discovered was to block the employment of any Arab workers by Jewish employers. In Tel-Aviv, which on the eve of the found-

4 Ibid., p. 152.

ing of the State of Israel had nearly 300,000 inhabitants, there was not one—I repeat, not *one*—Arab worker, nor one Arab inhabitant. Some time in 1944 a rumour spread that a couple of Arab workers were employed at the back of a café in Tel-Aviv. The result : a crowd of thousands went and smashed the windows and broke up the furniture. As the Arab peasant, out of sheer poverty, was ready to sell his produce for a much lower price than was asked by Jewish agriculturists, the Zionists prevented the *fellahs* from coming and selling their produce in the Jewish market. And when, under pressure of hunger, a *fellah* dared to break the boycott, he was subjected to beating and spoliation of his produce. Every member of the Zionist Trade Union Federation—the Histadruth—had to pay two special compulsory levies : (1) 'For Jewish Labour'—funds for organizing pickets, etc. against the employment of Arab workers, and (2) 'For Jewish Produce'—for organizing the boycott of Arab produce.

Not *one* Zionist party—not even the most extreme 'left' of Hashomer Hatzair, now Mapam—opposed the boycott of the Arab workers from going to work in Jewish plants, building-sites or orchards. They did not refuse the payment of the two levies to the Histadruth. In the whole Kibbutz movement there was not one Arab (since the establishment of the state the situation has changed radically : in the Kibbutz En-Dor there is one Arab member !). Not *one* Arab child was allowed into any Jewish school or kindergarten.

The boycott of the Arabs was inherent in Zionism : without the boycott no European worker or farmer would have survived economically. In opposing the local Arab population, Zionism had to try and serve the ruling imperialist power. The guiding principle of Zionist diplomacy has *always* been to affiliate itself with the world power in whose sphere of influence Palestine happened to be. Herzl, the founder of political Zionism, courted mainly the Turkish Sultan and the German Kaiser. After the First World War Zionism was orientated towards British imperialism. After the Second World War Zionism switched its attachment to United States imperialism.

It was not accidental that the Hagana—the main military Zionist organization in the 1920s and even more so in the 1930s—worked hand-in-glove with the British Army of Occupation and the police. For example, in the spring of 1936, the Auxiliary Police Force was established. By means of this force, an important part of the

Hagana, as well as some members of Etzel (the other Zionist military organization), became a legal armed force. In the spring of 1939 this force numbered some 21,000 men. Of course not *one* Arab was allowed into it. Moshe Dayan was one of the leading men active in terrorizing Arab villagers, summarily executing 'suspects', razing peasant huts and even whole villages. A year or so later, fifty thousand Zionists were taken into the British Army. The present Israeli Army is the natural continuation of the old British-controlled Auxiliary Police Force.

Even the 'left' Hashomer Hatzair did not at the time hide the connection between Zionist colonization and Zionist militarism. One of their spokesmen, Epstein, in an Arms Trial on June 28th, 1944, stated :

'You who come from England will surely know how to appreciate the difficulties and dangers involved in development and colonization undertakings in backward countries. No colonisatory undertakings in the history of mankind have taken place without being met by the hatred of the natives. Years, and sometimes generations pass, before these men become capable of appreciating and understanding the blessing inherent in the undertaking also for their future. But the British people did not recoil from developing these backward countries, knowing that by doing so you were fulfilling an historical and humanitarian mission. The best of your sons you sacrificed on the altar of progress.'

Is the State of Israel a colonial nation? The following features characterize a colonial state : (1) Being a backward nation, whose economic development is hampered by foreign imperialist rule, while being at the same time super-exploited by that imperialism. (2) Being in need of agrarian revolution to transfer the land to the peasants. (3) Needing to overcome artificial boundaries resulting from imperialism and a feudal past, in order to create a unified and free national state.

The Israeli economy is not a backward economy, suffering from exploitation by Western imperialism, but on the contrary it is subsidized heavily by Western capitalism. One need only think of the hundreds of millions of reparations paid by West Germany. This is not the product of Bonn's contrition over Nazi crimes against the Jews; after all, twenty million Russians were killed by the Nazis and still not a single mark was paid to Russia by Bonn ! It is because Washington willed it that Bonn paid up to Israel. Altogether, between 1949 and 1964 nearly $6,000 million came to Israel via German reparations, economic aid from the United States Government and from Jews in the United States and elsewhere.[5] This sum comes to some $3,000 per head of the population of Israel, or more than £1,000. This is a fantastic sum : even at the height of Empire, the net profit per average Briton from investments in the Empire did not come to £10 per head per year! Even in a year of economic depression, with hardly any immigration at all (1966), capital imports into Israel reached $505 million, or some £72 per head.[6]

Is Israel interested in agrarian revolution, in radical land reform? Of course not. Zionism got rid of the Arab *fellahs*. Agrarian revolution—that is, the restoration of the land to its original cultivators—is the last thing Israel would wish for.

Lastly, does Israel have an interest in the unity of the Arab countries into one state? Of course not.

Israel is not a colony suppressed by imperialism, but a *colon*, a settler's citadel, a launching-pad of imperialism. It is a tragedy that the sons of the very people who had been persecuted and massacred in such a bestial fashion should themselves be driven into a chauvinistic, militaristic fervour, and become the blind tool of imperialism in subjugating the Arab masses. In the same way that the existing social order is to be blamed for the calamity of the Jews, so it is to be blamed for the exploitation of their catastrophe for reactionary, oppressive aims. Zionism does not redeem Jewry from suffering. On the contrary, it imperils them with a new danger, that of being a buffer between imperialism and the national and social liberatory struggle of the Arab masses.

Israel naturally supports and is supported by imperialism everywhere. It supported the French war in Algeria during the years 1954-61, supplied arms to the Portuguese Government in Angola, and went so far as to accept feelers from the Saigon Government which asked it to help in advising on how to control the Vietcong. On March 20th, 1966 the Jewish Telegraphic Agency (ITA) cabled

[5] S. Zarhi, 'Peace and the Israeli Economy', *New Outlook* (Tel-Aviv, February 1967).
[6] Ibid.

the details of an exclusive interview granted to ITA reporter Milton Friedman by the South Vietnamese ambassador to the United States, Vu Van Thai. The report was given prominence by the press in Israel; and not in Israel alone. The ambassador revealed that negotiations were being conducted on Israeli aid to his country, specifically the dispatch of Nahal inspectors (Nahal is a combined military/civilian unit which has established a series of settlements along outlying sections of Israel's border). 'No one is better equipped than the Israelis to teach our people how to set up defence settlements to develop the country, unify the people and combat infiltrators and aggressors,' said Ambassador Vu Van Thai. In other words, Israel was requested not merely to supply aid, but to participate, however indirectly, in Saigon's war effort. The ambassador even went so far as to reveal that US Vice-President Humphrey had discussed the matter with Israeli diplomats in Bangkok (Israel has diplomatic ties with Thailand). This was a clear hint—if any such hint were needed—that this was not a 'private affair' between Jerusalem and Saigon.[7] One may well wonder what Moshe Dayan was doing in South Vietnam when he stayed there as a newspaper 'correspondent'. Was it to learn the use of napalm, or was it to teach the Americans and Marshal Ky the use of Palmach and Nahal?

Lesson from 1956

One argument used by Zionists is that Israel's opposition to the Arab national movement is simply a product of the Arabs' opposition to Israel. But the causative connection is very different indeed. Look at the case of Israeli aggression—in collusion with Britain and France—on Egypt in 1956. At the time of the nationalization of the Suez Canal by Nasser, the Egyptians seemed to be in a conciliatory mood. On August 6th, 1956 a Hebrew broadcast of Cairo Radio 'warmly congratulated Israel for her restrained attitude on the Suez issue and for refusing to let herself be used as a tool of the Western powers in the present conflict'. Twenty days later, President Nasser's Minister of State Ali Sabri surprisingly declared at Geneva that 'as long as there is no shooting war, Egypt will

[7] *New Outlook* (Tel-Aviv, May 1966), pp. 15-16.

allow Israeli vessels to pass through the Suez Canal as long as they carry no war materials.[8]

But Israel, the 'gendarme' of imperialism, did her duty by her master, and launched an attack on Egypt.

Can Colons Be Revolutionary?

The Jewish population in Israel is divided into classes and a class struggle rends the country. But this in itself *does not* mean that any significant number of Israeli workers are ready to join forces, or will be ready to join forces with, the Arab anti-imperialist struggle. The white workers of South Africa have gone on strike many times. One need only remember the 1922 white miners' strike, which was suppressed only after Smuts used planes to bombard the strikers. But the white workers never joined the Negro workers in the struggle against their oppression! The poorer the white workers, the greater their hatred of the black workers : the unskilled white workers on the railways are the most fanatical supporters of Vorster, previously of Verwoerd and before him Malan.

In Algeria, the attitude of the one million European settlers was much the same. The majority of them were workers and artisans. Before the FLN rebellion in 1954, many of them supported the Communist Party. 'The suburbs of Bab el Oued and Belcourt, in Algiers, were immediately after the Second World War unmistakably "red"; the large Spanish element in Algiers and Oran had unquestioned sympathy for the Spanish republicans, and provided the core of European communist membership.'[9] But all this changed with the Arab national rebellion : '. . . the further down one went in the social scale, among Algeria's Europeans, the greater the fear of the Moslem masses, ready to step into unskilled jobs and deprive even the poorest Europeans of their living'.[10]

While the Jews were the underdogs of Europe, in the Middle East the Arabs are the underdogs, and the Israelis the privileged and oppressors, the allies of imperialism.

[8] *Le Monde* (August 28th, 1956).
[9] E. Behr, *The Algerian Problem* (1961), p. 227.
[10] Ibid., p. 214.

The Question of Refugees

When the State of Israel was established in 1948, some 900,000 Arabs fled or were driven from where they and their fathers and forefathers had lived for more than a thousand years. The Zionists say this flight was simply a result of the Arabs' following the leaders who called upon them to flee. What is overlooked is the massacre in Deryasin (in this village all the inhabitants, men, women and children—without exception—were massacred by an extreme Zionist military organization), and that in the towns of Ramle and Lydda, Moshe Dayan forced all the inhabitants to leave at gun-point (guns were actually fired, too). Above all, how can one explain why the overwhelming majority of the Arabs fled unless they were *really* frightened of the Zionists? If, let us say, Cardinal Heenan called upon all Catholics to flee from Britain, does anyone really believe that any would respond to his appeal? If the Arab masses ran away simply because they heeded the call of their leaders, what a condemnation of Zionism!

Will Israel solve the question of the Arab refugees? Since the establishment of the State of Israel the number of Jews in the country has increased by $1\frac{1}{2}$ million. The number of Arab refugees and their children is $1\frac{1}{3}$ million. Will a capitalist Israel sacrifice many economic resources—first of all the land that belonged once to the Arabs and is now being settled by Zionists—to resettle the Arab refugees? The settling of Zionists in the years 1949-64 cost $6,000 million in German reparations, American-Jewish funds, etc. Maintaining the Israeli economy today, costs about $600 million in aid from abroad per year. To return the Arab refugees—even assuming the Jewish population of Israel remained static—would therefore need something like $1,200 million per year. Does anyone really believe that Jewish big business in the United States or Britain will spend all their resources to help the Arabs?[11] To create a subversive 'fifth column' of the Arab national movement? One

---

[11] A fund-raising dinner took place at Claridge's in London on June 8th, 1967. The host was Lord Rothschild; the number of guests was thirty; the money raised for Israel £7 million, of which £500,000 was for two *kibbutzim*. (*Daily Telegraph*, June 9th, 1967). Imagine such a collection for resettling Arab refugees in Israel!

can well understand Michael Assaf, an Arab expert of Mapai, when he says : 'I believe that with a 20 per cent Arab minority . . . and with our country as small and surrounded by hatred as it is, the State of Israel could not continue to exist.'[12]

One can judge how successful Zionist propaganda in the West has been when one notices how the question of the Arab refugees has been deflated : hardly anyone noticed that the number of Jews entering Israel was only marginally larger than the number of Arabs evicted.

3

THE ARAB NATIONAL MOVEMENT

The rulers of the Arab countries are divided, by and large, into two separate groups : first, the feudal kings and sheiks—King Feisal of Saudi Arabia, King Hussein of Jordan, the Sheik of Kuwait and other rulers of Persian Gulf dukedoms. They, together with the State of Iran, are reliable allies of imperialism. The other countries with relatively more progressive social and political régimes are Egypt, Syria, Algeria and Iraq. Of course no Chinese Wall separates the régimes of the two groups of countries, but there is a significant difference between them. The first group can get (together with Israel) arms from the United States and Britain, the second do not. It is not an accident that the Adeni workers—probably the most advanced section of the Arab working class—do not keep pictures of King Feisal or the Imam of Yemen in their homes, but of Nasser. (It would be trite to say that it would have been far better if they had the pictures of Marx, Lenin and Trotsky.)

However inconsistently, haltingly, Nasser moves, he has carried out some measures against imperialism and feudalism. In 1956 Nasser nationalized the Suez Canal. In February 1960 Bank Misr and the National Bank of Egypt were nationalized. In June 1960 the press was nationalized, and the Cairo bus services were municipalized. But the really big step was taken in June and July 1961. All banks and insurance companies were nationalized, and about

[12] 'Solving the Arab Refugee Problem', *New Outlook* (Tel-Aviv, July/August 1962), p. 21.

three hundred industrial and trading establishments were taken over either wholly or partly by the State. Between October 1961 and February 1962, six hundred of Egypt's wealthiest families, a high proportion of them Copts and Jews, had their property sequestered by the State. In August 1963 there was a further series of nation-alizations covering some firms which had already been partly nationalized, some companies in part privately owned under sequestration, and private companies. About three hundred con-cerns were affected, including the Dutch-British Lever Brothers, fourteen partly nationalized shipping companies, and twenty-nine land transport companies. In April 1964 there was a laconic Govern-ment announcement that Shell-BP interests in the UAR had been nationalized.[13]

Regarding land reform : in 1958 a maximum of three hundred *feddans* (1 *feddan* = 1 acre) for family holdings was decreed; and in July 1961 this was further reduced to one hundred *feddans*. The result was that while peasants who had less than five *feddans* owned 33.2 per cent of all cultivated land in 1943, in 1964 their share rose to 54.7 per cent. However, the land reform—although it eliminated the very big landlords—was far from being radical enough. Two million peasant families remained with less than one *feddan* each, while many landlords remained with one hundred *feddans* (some found loopholes even in this law of the maximum). The number of landless agriculturists has not decreased at all, but since 1952 has increased.

Other reforms were also introduced by the Nasser régime. For lack of space, I shall quote only some of them. In 1951-52 the Egyptian Public Health budget was £E10.1 million. In 1963-64 it was £E31.2 million, and in 1964-65 £E44.3 million. In 1951 there were 5,200 doctors, or one for every four thousand inhabitants. In 1964 there were thirteen thousand, or one every two thousand inhabitants. In 1962 there were over 57,000 beds in all the treat-ment establishments in the country, or one to every 482 inhabitants, compared with one to every six hundred inhabitants in 1952.[14] The Ministry of Education's budget has risen from £E1,600,000 in 1920 to £E40.2 million in 1951 and £E96.5 million in 1964.[15]

[13] P. Mansfield, *Nasser's Egypt*, pp. 137-40.
[14] Ibid., p. 111.
[15] Ibid., p. 120.

In Syria, the Ba'ath régime has been more radical than Nasser's in the field of land reform. But neither Nasser nor the Ba'ath régime can ever become revolutionary, can ever grow beyond their middle-class social basis, which is made up of army officers, civil servants and teachers, sons of merchants and prosperous artisans, better-off peasants and small-scale landowners. This section of Arab society stands in between the feudal lords and the high *bourgeoisie* on the one hand, and the workers and peasants on the other. Actually the lower-middle class is as far from the latter as from the former. In 1958, the class division of the urban population in Egypt was estimated as follows :[16]

	percentage of total population	average annual per capita income (in £E)*
Bourgeoisie and aristocracy	3	845.8
Lower strata of the middle class		
a. Middle-officials, professions	8	133.5
b. Artisans (employees)	9	122.7
c. Low-grade officials	14	105.6
Proletariat		
a. Industrial and transport workers	10	60.8
b. Craftsmen	5	40.0
Lumpen-proletariat		
a. Permanently-employed unskilled	2	26.8
b. Domestic servants	12	21.4
c. Permanently unemployed	37	–

* Unit not mentioned

The gap between the middle class—the social base of Nasserism —and the workers and peasants is as wide as between it and the big *bourgeoisie* and landlords. From the equivocal position springs the specific characteristics of 'Arab socialism'.

Nasser and the Ba'ath accept a criticism of feudalism, imperialism and monopoly capitalism. They reject bourgeois parliamentary democracy as a fraud. They accept the need for radical changes in order to break the power of the landlords and the big capitalists.

[16] Sources: *Tiers Monde* (July-September 1960); A. Abdel Malek, *Egypte-société Militaire* (Paris, 1962); C. Issawi, Egypt in Revolution (1963).

They advocate the transfer of key positions in the economy to State ownership and are enthusiasts for planned economy. They differ from real socialism in two central aspects : Nasser and the Ba'ath reject the agency of the working class and they reject internationalism.

Because Nasser rejects in practice the agency of the working class, his State ownership and planning have little to do with socialism.

The attitude of the middle class to State enterprise and planning is very ambivalent indeed. As part of the State bureaucracy they are interested in a rapid advance of State enterprise. However, as sons, brothers and cousins of small property-owners they are quite willing to let the private sector milk the State sector. Hence the Egyptian economy suffers from both the bureaucratic inertia of State capitalism and from the speculative working of private capitalism. To give only one example of State mismanagement, one enterprise required, according to the plan, an estimated investment of £E2 million; when its construction was completed, it was found to have cost £E32 million.[17]

The social position of Nasser has prevented him getting rid of the old bureaucracy inherited from the Farouk period. On top of this bureaucracy a new expanded one has arisen. Army officers have expanded their control into more and more spheres of economic, social and political life. Thus about fifteen hundred officers were appointed to the upper ranks of the non-military establishment between 1952 and 1964.[18]

Because of its really very shallow roots in the masses, Nasserism is very brittle, very prone to factionalism (hence the break-up of the UAR—the secession of Syria from Egypt—in 1961, the bitter conflicts with Kassem's Iraq, and so on). Because of its social base, Nasserism vacillates between republicanism and the obscene embrace of 'our Arab brother' King Hussein of Jordan, or King Feisal of Saudi Arabia. Nasserism also vacillates between an attack on the 'Moslem Brotherhood', including the execution of a number of their leadership, and Islamic fervour.

One of the main lessons from the collapse of Ben Bella in Algeria and Kassem in Iraq (as well as Nkrumah in Ghana and Sukarno in

[17] *Rus el Yussuf* (July 6th, 1964).
[18] A. Abdel Malek, 'Nasserism and Socialism', *The Socialist Registrar* (1964), p. 45.

Indonesia) is that the Bonapartist régimes in backward countries, trying to balance between the working class and the peasantry on the one hand, and imperialism on the other, as well as between the Great Powers (the policy of 'positive neutralism'), are extremely unstable. For a really successful anti-imperialist revolutionary struggle, Nasserism is found wanting : it is far too removed from the self-initiative of the masses. For such a struggle it is necessary for the national revolution to be intertwined with the social revolution, for the workers to take over the oil fields, factories, railways, etc., and for the peasants to conduct a revolutionary land reform.

4

THE 'COMMUNIST' PARTIES

One of the shabbiest roles in the situation in the Middle East was played by the so-called communist parties. The bankruptcy of the Arab communist parties was complete. Instead of keeping independent from the Bonapartist régimes of Nasser, the Ba'ath and previously of Kassem, they completely capitulated to them. The communist parties—following the Moscow guideline—accepted the peaceful transition to socialism in the 'Third World', and rejected the Marxist-Leninist analysis about the need to smash the bourgeois State machine. The communist parties followed the line of 'national unity', the line of separating the national struggle against imperialism from the struggle for social emancipation.

For decades, by far the most important communist leader in the Middle East has been Khaled Bakdash, the general secretary of the Communist Party of Syria. In a most important guideline on the general policy of Arab communists, he stated, as early as 1944 : 'It is evident that the problem of national liberation is a problem of the nation as a whole, and it is therefore possible without discussion to get the compliance of the whole nation around this great slogan for the realization of full national unity. National liberation is in the interests of the national landowners; it is in the interest of small and big merchants alike.'[19] And : '. . . our appreciation and honour

[19] *The Communist Party in the Struggle for Independence and National Sovereignty* (Beirut, 1944), p. 74 (in Arabic).

of the national capitalist who struggles faithfully for national liberation is not less than our appreciation and honour of the national
worker who struggles faithfully for national liberation'.[20] And without any shame he stated: 'He who reads our "National Programme", the programme which was adopted by the congress of the
Syrian and Lebanese communist parties (31. 12. 43-1. 1. 44-CT),
will find that it does not mention socialism. There is not one
expression or demand with a socialist colouring. . . . It is clear that
you cannot pose before a country which suffers from the yoke of
imperialism and from economic, agricultural and industrial backwardness the question of building a socialist order but only that of
national liberation from the remnants of the Middle Ages in its
economic and cultural life.'[21]

In accordance with this line, the Communist Party in Syria and
Lebanon has long since done away with the Red Flag as the flag of
the parties and the *Internationale* as their anthem. The flag of the
Syrian party is now the Syrian flag and its anthem the Syrian
national anthem; and the flag and anthem of the Lebanese party
those of the Lebanon. And in order to be worthy of sitting together
with national capitalists and landowners their form of address
changed from 'Comrade' to 'Mr'. Bakdash then sets out to reassure
these gentlemen :

We assure the landowners that we do not demand and will not
demand in Parliament the confiscation of their estates and lands,
but on the contrary we want to help them by demanding the
construction of large-scale irrigation enterprises, the facilitation
of the import of fertilizer and modern machinery. . . . All we
demand in exchange for this is pity on the *fellah*, that he be
taken out of his poverty and illiteracy and that knowledge and
health be spread in the village. . . . These are our economic, or
if you can say so, our social demands. They are democratic and
very modest. . . . All we demand . . . is the introduction of some
democratic reforms that all speak about and all agree are necessary. Our demand is not nor will be, and it is not on our programme, to confiscate national capital and the national factories.
We promise national capital and the national factory-owner that

[20] Ibid., p. 75.
[21] Ibid., p. 73.

we will not look with envy or hate at his national factory, but on the contrary we desire its progress and flourishing. All that we demand is the amelioration of the lot of the national workers and the realization of a democratic labour legislation which will regulate the relations between the employers and the workers on the basis of justice and national solidarity.[22]

So as regards the class struggle of the workers, too, we are very modest, very conciliatory, ready with all our hearts to defend capital, Arab *bourgeoisie*! You, too, be modest and conciliatory! Such is the way of arguing which repeats itself time and again in the Stalinist propaganda.

This line has led the Syrian Communist Party to cringe before the Ba'ath in Syria. It led the Iraqui 'communist' leaders to support General Kassem uncritically until he suppressed them in 1959, and his heir, General Aref, massacred many of them and imprisoned and tortured many others. The same opportunist policy led the Egyptian communists to splits and vacillations and at last to the dissolution of the most important of the communist splinters which joined Nasser's 'Socialist Union'.

5

THE SIX-DAY WAR

The war between Israel and her Arab neighbours followed an illuminating sequence of events. The anti-imperialist struggle in Aden had been rising. This, together with the revolutionary struggle against the Imam of Yemen, threatened Feisal, the King of neighbouring Saudi Arabia, one of the richest oil fields in the world controlled by the United States as well as the oil dukedom of the Persian Gulf. To add oil to the flames, in Syria a dispute with the Iraq Petroleum Company blew up. After nationalizing all the oil fields in Syria itself (December 1964), the IPC suffered a further blow at the end of 1966. Damascus demanded (and obtained) 5s 10d per ton instead of the previous 4s for the thirty million tons of oil flowing annually through the pipeline. In addition, Syria

[22] Ibid., p. 23.

wanted to raise the loading tax from 1s 1d to 2s per ton. The IPC would only agree to 1s 7d. Everything seemed close to agreement. Syria also claimed that payments on the basis of the former agreement of 1955 had been wrongly calculated and that she had lost £S110 million (Syrian pounds). In the course of the negotiation the Syrian authorities reduced their demands to £S40 million for the years 1956-65. IPC, however, apparently agreed to change their calculations for the future but adamantly refused to discuss the payment of arrears. As a result, the Syrian Government stopped the flow of oil. It is true a compromise between the Syrian Government and IPC has since been reached, but the threat to the oil companies still rankles.

In reply, the United States and Britain poured fantastic amounts of arms into Saudi Arabia; an Islamic League made up of Iran, Saudi Arabia, Kuwait and Jordan was formed; and on May 15th the Prime Minister of Israel announced that if raids on Israel continued the Israeli Army would march on Damascus.

The next steps followed suit in the terrible tragedy. The Egyptian Army concentrated in Sinai, and a *Jihad* (holy war) of all Arab states—republican and monarchist alike—was declared. The rest is history. One thing never threatened Israel (whatever Arab Zionist and imperialist propaganda claimed)—complete annihilation. The United States and Britain would certainly have marched in if the Egyptian Army had invaded even a few miles into Israel. One is reminded of the scare about the Mau-Mau going to kill all the whites in Kenya; the actual balance-sheet was a couple of dozen dead whites and thousands upon thousands of African massacred. The British capitalist press described the Mau-Mau as threatening 'genocide'; the white settlers and the army were only protecting the peace, defending the '*status quo*'.

Who benefited from the Israel victory? Above all Western imperialism. At the beginning of the war Christian Pineau, French Foreign Minister at the time of the Suez war in 1956, wrote in an article entitled 'From Suez to Aqaba' : '. . . present events justify to a great extent British and French attempts, eleven years ago, to put an end to Nasser's power'.[23] A concurrent *Daily Telegraph* editorial entitled 'Middle East War' dotted the i's and crossed the

[23] *Daily Telegraph* (June 6th, 1967).

234

t's : 'Britain has, indeed, certain quarrels with President Nasser; over the Tiran Strait, the Yemen, his campaigns of subversion against Arab governments friendly to the West and in areas where there are British interests and responsibilities. . . . An Egyptian success . . . would constitute a totally unacceptable defeat for the West in the Middle East and would mean the end of all Arab governments well disposed to the West.'

On June 9th the London *Daily Telegraph*, in an editorial entitled 'Israel's Triumph', made it clear why the West benefited from the defeat of the Arabs : 'As a result of Israel's amazing victory, the whole balance of power in the Middle East has decisively changed. . . . On the whole the West must be profoundly grateful to Israel. . . . President Nasser has long been a danger to the West and to world peace. He may not be so much longer.'

On June 10th *The Economist* came to the same conclusion in these words : 'It is not only Israel's chestnuts they have pulled out of the fire; it is those of America and Britain as well.'

On June 11th, in a political and historical generalization, Peregrine Worsthorne really waxed poetic in an article in the *Sunday Telegraph* entitled 'Triumph of the Civilized' : 'Last week a tiny Western community, surrounded by immensely superior numbers of the underdeveloped peoples, has shown itself able to impose its will on the Arabs of today almost as effortlessly as the first whites were able to do on the Afro-Asian natives in the imperial heyday.'

Sam White wrote from Paris in an article published by the London *Evening Standard* of June 9th : 'The traditionally anti-Semitic French extreme right became passionate Zionist overnight. Veterans of the "Keep Algeria French" campaigns paraded the boulevard chanting "Israel Will Vanquish" to the same rhythmic beat as they once chanted " *Algerie Francaise*".'

And the City of London reacted in consonance : sterling has been stronger than for a long time. As *The Economist* of June 10th put it so well : 'The brilliant speed of the Israel advance saved the pound.'

6

THE WAY AHEAD

Only people who wholeheartedly support a colonial people in rebellion against imperialism are justified in being severe critics of their leaders, politics and tactics. It is right to be very severe in criticism of the Arab national movement as led by Nasser.

The strength of any anti-imperialist liberatory movement is in the masses of workers and peasants being mobilized, in their self-activity, on the one hand, and in their making the correct choice of the weakest link in the imperialist chain, on the other. Hence the NLF in Vietnam are absolutely right in relying on mass-guerrilla bands and armies, and harassing the US Army and its hangers-on —the army of Marshal Ky—mainly in the countryside, while avoiding a stand-up struggle around the cities, above all Saigon.

The potential strength of the Arab anti-imperialist movement lies in the mass of workers and peasants. The targets of attack should be the oil fields, the oil pipeline and refineries. The peasants should start revolutionary land reform, thus creating the base for a guerrilla war. Nasser's military confrontation with Israel is exactly the opposite of the policy and tactics of the NLF. Israel, being modern and privileged, is an even stronger bastion of imperialism than Saigon. Furthermore, an anti-Israel campaign quite easily degenerates into a *Jihad*, in which the most reactionary régimes save themselves by channelling the struggle into racial currents.

Nasser of Egypt and the Ba'ath of Syria, whose social base is the lower-middle class, are of course incapable of following the policies of the NLF in Vietnam, not to speak of the Bolsheviks in Russia. Hence no guerrilla war or workers' attack on the oil fields can be led by the Nasserites; hence the latter's reliance upon tanks and aeroplanes, while the NLF rely upon guns and mortars. The Kosygins, as leaders of a highly bureaucratic society, are hardly good friends for a mass colonial liberatory movement. Their tanks, planes, missiles and technicians supplied to Nasser were no help at all to the Arab national movement, but an impediment, helping the Nasserite military caste to divert the movement to a wrong path.

The Arab workers and peasants who have suffered oppression over a long period of time need both social and national revolutionary policies. National emancipation and social emancipation are inseparable. The theory of Nasser, Khaled Bakdash and their ilk about stages separating the one from the other, is completely reactionary and utopian. Only when the workers take the key industries and the peasants take into their hands the land, can a really victorious struggle against imperialism and its hangers-on be carried out, however long, bloody and tortuous that struggle may be.

The only possible solution to the needs of the Middle East is the workers' and peasants' revolution aimed at the establishment of a socialist republic, with full rights for Jews, Kurds and all national minorities.

CHENHAMO CHIMUTENGWENDE

Zimbabwe and White-Ruled Africa

Defenders of imperialism and fascism in Southern Africa, Angola and Guinea-Bisau have clearly shown how determined they are to hold State power in their hands. The aim is to maintain the present capitalist system through racialist methods at the expense of Africans. Vorster, Caetano and Smith, who are heavily backed by international capitalism via NATO and international trade, are prepared to fight to the last to prevent the advance of the forces of progress. The oppressed peoples of Zimbabwe (i.e. Rhodesia), and the rest of white-ruled Africa have, as a last resort, decided to adopt the road of armed struggle to freedom, independence and socialism.

Britain and her Western allies who are directly or indirectly involved in the situation in Zimbabwe are trying to dodge the real issue at stake in Southern Africa and the rest of oppressed Africa. They remain passive or deal with side-issues such as UDI, while the African people are being oppressed, kept in bondage and mass-acred by the fascists. The African people of Zimbabwe, like their brothers in so-called Portuguese Africa, South-West Africa and South Africa, have realized that they are their own liberators. Because of their financial interests in white-ruled Africa, Western nations cannot be relied upon or expected to help.

There are about two hundred British firms and companies operating in Rhodesia. Over a hundred of these have all their personnel paid from earnings accrued from Rhodesia. Most have subsidiaries or associates or even headquarters in South Africa and are still owned by British financiers. Wall Street subsidizes many of these firms. The approach to international investments today is one of sharing risks. A closer look at many of the companies with British labels reveals that they are jointly owned by the Anglo-American world and its counterparts in the big six EEC countries. The problem in Rhodesia is imperialism, supported as it is by Anglo-American finance. Western imperialists are determined to ensure that any political system in that part of the world should safeguard their economic interests. Capitalism is made dependent upon the exploitation of the African people.

In Rhodesia, under the Land Apportionment Act of 1930, the European community which numbers 230,000 in a population of more than $4\frac{1}{2}$ million, possesses more than one-third of the land ($37\frac{1}{2}$ per cent). This land includes all the big towns and cities, and all the fertile land in this 151,000-square-miles territory. Eighty-five per cent of Rhodesian Africans live in rural areas as employees on European farms or as subsistence or cash-crop farmers. For Africans, education is neither compulsory nor free; in the case of Europeans, Asians and coloureds (mixed blood) the opposite is true. In the period 1967-68 the estimated average non-African earnings were £1,361 ($3,267) and for the African only £138 ($331) in cash and kind, which included food devoid of any nutritious value, and accommodation. Therefore a white man's average earnings are about ten times those of an African. But the school fees for a white child are only three times more than those for an African child.

Since the 1959 emergency, when the African National Congress of Southern Rhodesia was banned, one bill after another has been enacted in order to suppress the rebelling Africans and to muzzle their political aspirations. Petrol-bomb throwing or the use of any other explosives against people or buildings, even if empty, makes the death sentence mandatory if the culprit is found guilty. African nationalist parties have been proscribed, one after another. If the leaders have not committed any specific crime before the law, they are not tried but sent to detention or suffer restriction under the notorious Law and Order Maintenance Act of 1960.

No African nationalist organization worth its salt can be allowed to function normally, under the present laws of Rhodesia. One nationalist party formed at the end of 1964, called the Zimbabwe

African Democratic Union, was banned within twenty-four hours of its formation, before its leader, Advocate Herbert Chitepo, had even had the chance to hold a proper press conference to explain in detail the principles of his party.

The African people have been denied the opportunity of participating effectively in the government of their country through a qualitative franchise system. All voters require literacy, educational and property qualifications to register in Rhodesia. It would take over fifty years at the present rate of progress for the majority of Africans to meet the requirements. But again, the qualifications are always raised higher and higher as Africans progress. The idea is to keep only an insignificant number of Africans on the voters roll, so that they do not take over the country or even occupy a position where they could be a force to reckon with. Strikes and all other forms of protest against the system are illegal. For Africans to be good, law-abiding citizens they have to live as mere drawers of water and hewers of wood. They are expected to build a prosperous capitalist society whose wealth they are not allowed to share.

The pattern of oppression and exploitation has been the same in formerly colonized countries of Africa. The principle is one, and only tactics differ from one country to another. Vorster talks of *apartheid* as the only solution to South Africa's racial troubles and propounds that what is good for South Africa can be good for South-West Africa. Salazar spoke of his policy of assimilation and Smith goes for separate development. But in practice one finds that these supposed three philosophies are in essence identical. All the governments based upon these nakedly wicked philosophies deprive the African people, solely because of their colour, of the most elementary human rights : of the right to work and live with their families where they want; to take part in the running of the state machinery. They are in effect denied the basic right to live as human beings. In South Africa not even liberal African intellectuals are considered civilized enough to be allowed to find their way to the Cape Town Parliament or take part in the national administration of the country. The same situation applies to Rhodesia; not even the most conservative African reactionary or traitor is allowed to join the Rhodesia Front, Smith's party. Such people are simply dismissed as clever savages who are still not worth absorbing into the white man's society.

While Salazar preached his hollow philosophy of assimilation, Africans in Portuguese-ruled territories faced a savage and equally cruel system of exploitation and suppression. They have put up with forced labour, slave wages and the deprivation of educational opportunities.

When African organizations try to adopt non-violence, they are always blocked by ever-increasing repressive measures. Peaceful demonstrations are broken up and the fascists seize the opportunity to use their guns, jets and Saracen armoured cars against peaceful people demanding their rights. Yet, in the face of such frustrations, the oppressed people and their leaders are confident of winning the struggle, since theirs is a popular cause supported by the majority of the masses and freedom-loving people the world over.

THE NATIONALIST MOVEMENT

The African liberation movement really started as a mere vehicle through which African grievances could be channelled to the authorities. It combined trade union, cultural, economic and political activities. The multi-purpose associations did not speak of majority rule or of taking over the Government, or of revolution and armed struggle.

In South Africa, the African really became politically conscious at a national level much earlier than in most other African countries. As a result of ever-increasing racial pinpricks, oppression and exploitation, Africans began to form semi-political associations. This process culminated in the formation of the African National Congress of South Africa (ANC) in 1912, the African National Congress of Southern Rhodesia in 1957 led by J. Nkomo, and the Mozambique National Front led by E. Mondlane in 1962.

Africans had realized that the authorities could pay more attention to their grievances if they organized themselves on a national scale. In tone, spirit and intent, the objectives of ANC of South Africa and ANC of Rhodesia were the same. The following objectives were set forth when the South African ANC was formed :

(1) To unite all the various tribes in South Africa.

(2)   To educate public opinion on the aspirations of the black man of South Africa.

(3)   To be the mouthpiece of the African people and their chiefs.

(4)   To advocate on behalf of the African masses equal rights and justice.

(5)   To represent them in the Union Parliament, and generally to do all such things as are necessary for the progress and welfare of the African people.

Africans of South Africa, as was also the case in Rhodesia, soon learned that no outsiders would come to their rescue and that they had to fight for their rights entirely on their own. Futile delegations were sent to the British Government over some of the early manifestations of *apartheid*, such as the Land Act of 1913. Acts of civil disobedience, boycotts, strikes and other forms of non-violent passive resistance were organized. Other freedom movements in colonial Africa were also employing these forms of protest campaign. They had not thought of overthrowing the political system as a whole : the nationalist leadership was still reformist; the nature of the African struggle was not viewed as a protracted one; therefore the round-table conference method was believed to be the only right and possible one. But to the shock of the African leaders, that approach to the problems was found to lead to yet another cul-de-sac. Nationalist leaders were constantly arrested, imprisoned and physically tortured; more racial legislation was passed. As more and more Africans became politically conscious, the whites became tougher and more ruthless towards them. New strategy and tactics on the part of the nationalist movement became imperative.

In South Africa and Rhodesia, as was not the case in the Portuguese-ruled countries, Africans were allowed to organize themselves politically, though under extremely difficult conditions. But the leaders did not politically educate or prepare the masses for a tougher and different struggle against the capitalist, white ruling class.

The Youth League of ANC of South Africa initiated an action programme which was endorsed by the ANC in 1949. This was a turning point in the ANC tactics. The ANC began to see itself as a dynamic and more practical organization. However, the action programme was still based on the non-violence principle.

In 1955 the Freedom Charter was issued as a communiqué by the Congress Alliance, representing the Indian Congress of South Africa, the Coloured People's Congress, ANC and the Congress of Democrats (a European organization). The Freedom Charter incorporated the principles of a future non-racial society as envisaged by the Congress Alliance.

The ANC began to develop some cliques and other groups according to difference in principles and methods of application. The cleavage really came out into the open when the militant members of the Youth League broke away from Luthuli's ANC and formed the Pan-Africanist Congress (PAC) under Robert Sobukwe, now confined in Robben Island. The PAC charged that the ANC had become a decadent and multi-racial organization, while the struggle was strictly black-white conflict, and that a new approach to the liberation of the country was necessary. The PAC said that Coloureds, Indians and whites could not honestly identify themselves with the sufferings of the African people because the non-Africans were not oppressed or underprivileged to the same extent.

A similar story was true of Ghana when Nkrumah and Dr Danquah broke up. It also held true for Rhodesia and other African countries. The old and more conservative leadership was left in each case by the militant African nationalists who wanted definite and more meaningful programmes of action to follow. They saw the need for new tactics and they wanted to achieve immediate results towards realizing the liberation of their countries.

In Rhodesia, the nationalist leaders split while they were in exile in Tanzania. The more progressive nationalists led by Sithole and R. Mugabe wanted action, but Nkomo seemed to be too slow for them. They returned home, sacrificing their personal safety, and formed the Zimbabwe African National Union (ZANU) in 1963. Nkomo continued to lead ZAPU under the name 'People's Caretaker Council' (PCC).

In South-West Africa there are SWANU and SWAPO; in Angola, MPLA, UNITA and GRAE. In Mozambique there are two main parties, COREMO and FRELIMO, led by Mondlane. There are also two or more parties in each of the white-ruled territories. These divisions have done a terrible disservice to the struggle for freedom.

In all the parties there are conservative and progressive nationalists, reactionaries as well as Marxists. One finds a party supported by Peking, and yet some of the top officials of the same party are on the regular pay-roll of the American CIA. In fact the split in the liberation movement in Southern Africa and the Portuguese territories is due to a clash of personalities rather than intrinsic ideological differences. Self-interest, lack of dedication to the struggle and the absence of one clear ideology are the things that have really helped to maintain the cleavage in the liberation movement. In the fighting people's guerrillas rests the only hope for Zimbabwe and white-ruled Africa. They understand the struggle better, because they are directly and physically involved; and they speak the same ideological language, even if they belong to different parties.

The ANC of South Africa, which has had endless and unpredictable alliances since its inception, has entered into another alliance of convenience with ZAPU of Rhodesia. The idea is to fight and take over Rhodesia first and then use it as the initial guerrilla base against South Africa. The idea itself is considered sound by many practical and progressive politicians in Africa, but the ANC-ZAPU alliance is denounced for being too narrow and selfish. A wider alliance of the nationalist parties, which would include ZANU and PAC, is considered the most appropriate affiliation. Such an African united front would be in a better position to confront decisively the 'paper concrete wall' on the Zambezi River. If Lisbon, Pretoria and Salisbury can form an alliance to face the revolutionary whirlwind from the north, then Africans should respond accordingly.

NATIONALIST LEADERSHIP AND THE ARMED STRUGGLE

The African people have explored and exhausted all peaceful avenues to political change. They find the whites adamant and prepared to hold State power with the aid of a gun. The Africans have been pushed against a wall. They are human enough to feel the pinch of oppression and exploitation; and they are natural enough to revolt, using the appropriate means demanded by the situation. They realize, as has been said, that political power stems from the barrel of a gun. They have had to resort to armed struggle as the only sure means of attaining true freedom.

The Zimbabwe people's guerrillas, under the leadership of ZANU, first tested the method on April 29th, 1966 at Sinoia, an engagement that proved stern but nevertheless tactically manageable. A fierce battle that shook the Rhodesian white community took place on this day and there were heavy casualties on both sides. More people left Rhodesia for military training in independent progressive African states and other socialist countries of the world under the auspices of ZANU and ZAPU. The freedom fighters were charged with the duty of going back to intensify the armed struggle. They were to return home and train their brothers and compatriots in guerrilla warfare and to educate the masses politically.

Guerrillas followed up the Sinoia battle with violent measures taken against the Smith régime throughout the country, among them being : the shooting to death of a white couple on a farm near Hartley (*Zambia Times*, May 18th, 1966); the shooting to death of a security officer by the guerrillas in a midnight clash in the Zambezi bush on July 17th (*Zambia News*, September 4th, 1966); the shooting to death by the guerrillas of a white farmer near Gatooma on July 19th (*Rhodesia Herald*, July 19th, 1966). These and other incidents marked the beginning of a people's war for independence.

Smith's information department tried to give the impression to the outside world that all was well in Rhodesia and that the majority of Africans did not support the nationalists. News of battles in the Zambezi Valley and other parts of Rhodesia, between Smith forces and ZANU-led freedom fighters, was suppressed. But the battles became too frequent and more fierce in intensity, so that news of most of them could hardly be withheld indefinitely.

On August 13th, 1967 the young and militant fighters of the ZAPU-ANC alliance united with the guerrilla forces for a free Zimbabwe. A fierce battle which lasted for three weeks broke out in Wankie and heavy casualties on both sides were reported. This was an escalation of the war to perturbing proportions—of the hitherto 'mini-war of liberation'. Indeed the freedom fighters became so active and powerful that South Africa's participation in this fast-escalating war of liberation could not be kept a secret any longer. As usual, news of the war was heavily censored.

The Government-controlled radio and press and the Western media kept on trying to emphasize the false hypothesis that in these territories there are not sufficient jungles and mountains essential for the successful operation of guerrilla-type warfare. But people who have studied the art of guerrilla warfare, and cared to consider the victories of other countries by armed struggle, can understand well enough that jungles and mountains are important but not essential. It is the people and the people alone who are essential for success. The real difficulty besetting the guerrilla movement as a whole is that many of the engagements take the form of modern positional battles, which to the guerrillas is suicidal. As a result, many of the heroic freedom fighters are permanently and prematurely deprived of the chance of really contributing to the armed struggle. There can never be a true armed struggle when the guerrilla movement is subject to military ineptitude and led by conservative nationalists.

A protracted armed struggle can only be successfully waged by true revolutionaries with a correct political ideology. The major prerequisite of guerrilla warfare is that the guerrillas should be the leading part of the struggling masses. The guerrillas should support the cause of the ordinary man in the street. They should work with him hand-in-hand, for in fact they are one and the same people. And as long as there is oppression and exploitation of the masses by a reactionary capitalist clique, armed struggle will triumph. It is fallacious to suppose that the people can be happy with and accept willingly the exploitation and segregation imposed upon them by a bourgeois minority.

At the initial stage of the armed struggle, anybody and any organization can claim to be the true representative of the people. Any power-hungry demagogue without a correct ideological orientation can claim to lead the people to the desired destination. But as the struggle becomes more serious, bloody and bitter, the fighting forces and the people themselves will provide the proper leadership. *Petit-bourgeois* minded leaders and self-seekers will be wiped out. A Protracted and bitter armed struggle will help the people to discover why they want what they want, how to reorganize themselves and how to head for their goal. Whosoever does not believe in total guerrilla warfare or believes without taking a practical part in it, and yet claims to lead the masses, will end up a traitor. Those of us who prove to be the best practical exponents of armed struggle, will be accorded by the people—and only the people—the title 'vanguard'; and it will be this vanguard that leads them on the path to freedom.

In most liberation movements, progressive elements are out-numbered by reactionaries. Since this is a protracted war of libera-tion, their number is bound to increase, while that of the unpro-gressive dwindles. The intensity of the struggle and time itself will lead to the realignment of forces : progressives with proper political orientation, the activists or guerrillas, all on one side; and reaction-aries of all kinds on the other. The issue will become openly ideolog-ical : armed struggle and socialism, or capitalism and reformism.

BRITAIN AND NEO-COLONIALISM

The economic sanctions story drafted by Whitehall fiction writers and sub-edited by members of the United Nations Club in New York has failed to achieve its original aims. If toppling the Smith régime was the purpose, and not just hurting the Rhodesian economy, then the sanctions story will end in the expected anti-climax.

Portugal and South Africa, as was anticipated, have come to the rescue of the bunch of fascists reigning in Salisbury today. Smith decided to 'go it alone' and follow up to the hilt the policy of *apartheid* without officially subscribing to it. He had Vorster and Salazar—his 'brethren-in-crime'—on his side, and also Harold Wilson's promise that he would not use force. The quarrel between Britain and much of the capitalist world on one side and the Smith régime is the question of the 'legality of his Government', and not that of the exploitation of the black people. Smith and his 'cowboy' gang did not want to recognize the authority of the Wilson Government. They wanted to rule Rhodesia in a way which would best suit their local tastes, without acceding that any world power has the right to question them on some aspects of their legis-lation—even if that right were never exercised.

The African people have lived in bondage before and after UDI; so it is not UDI but the political system as a whole which they seek to overthrow. To the freedom fighters and the masses UDI is meaningless and not their business. It is a mere act of discourtesy to the Queen of England. If UDI had been crushed, another white group of capitalists and reactionaries would have been asked to form a government. It is therefore the system as a whole and not specifically UDI that Africans are struggling against.

The Labour Government would like to see a white liberal government rule the territory for about a decade or more. Such a government would pave the way for a multi-racial government under the dominance of the white man. The principle is that Western investments should be protected at all costs. The British Government would tolerate or be prepared to accept, after some resistance, a moderate nationalist government such as that in Kenya. In short, a neo-colonialist puppet régime is what would be acceptable. But South Africa is not prepared to tolerate anything of that nature on her doorstep. Such a state of affairs would be considered a threat in itself. Liberal ideas would infiltrate more easily into South Africa. A strong racialist ally would be preferable to a weak one—or worse still, to a neutral neighbour, which, by its lack of commitment, might be subject to anti-South African influence. For this reason, South Africa has gone all out to help her fascist sister Rhodesia. Pretoria is prepared to swim or sink with Salisbury.

Because Western investments and capital are vast in Southern Africa, fascist white capitalist régimes are preferable in Western capitalist eyes to nationalist governments, which could well be subject to some socialist ideas. They could of course be neo-colonialist régimes, but their ability to guarantee the safety of Western wealth would not be as certain as that of white racialist régimes. African leaders such as Sithole, Mandela, Nkomo and Sobukwe cannot be relied upon by foreign capitalist powers. They may be merely patriotic nationalists with little or no Marxist influence at all; nevertheless, they are unlikely ever to work openly for imperialists, as did Tshombe.

African leaders are only accepted as a last resort and as a desperate, but deceitful, gesture of goodwill. So far as African leaders of a country are concerned, the colonial power always has a choice which allows it freedom for manoeuvre. In Rhodesia a Banda, Kenyatta or a Kaunda has not yet emerged. A popular, strong and firm nationalist leader whom the imperialists can handle easily has still to emerge. Nkomo and Sithole may be popular, but they have leftist elements in their ranks and they are not considered firm or strong enough to be able to suppress the 'unacceptables'. On that score, such leaders are not considered good enough to serve foreign interests satisfactorily.

It is Rhodesia and South Africa with which the Western powers are deeply concerned. Socialist Asia and Eastern Europe have their eyes on Southern Africa as a whole, too. Guinea-Bisau, Angola and Mozambique are important, too, in that their being taken over by Africans will mean a big step nearer to the capturing of South Africa and Rhodesia. Once free, Mozambique would serve as an excellent base for toppling the criminal and reactionary political set-up in Rhodesia and South Africa. The border is even more difficult to control than the three-hundred-miles long Zambia-Rhodesia border where the Zambezi River helps the fascists.

The political climate in Swaziland would easily become more progressive if her powerful neighbour, Mozambique, became free. Angola could be used as a very good initial guerrilla base against South-West Africa. Botswana would find it easy then to change from being a mere South African satellite to a neutral state. After South-West Africa is freed, Botswana could then easily move to join the rest of progressive black Africa if she chose to.

If Guinea were freed, that would be enough to shock the obstinate, power-drunken Portuguese to reassess their situation. They would know it is possible to be defeated by people's guerrillas even in Angola and Mozambique, although they too would also fight harder to retain the *status quo*. However, without economic support from her Western allies, Portugal would fail to meet the expenses of wars in Africa. Her army is armed mainly with NATO weapons, without which she would be unable to conduct a war. Portugal, being one of the poorest nations of Europe, is very vulnerable to outside pressure—if only Britain, America, France and West Germany cared to exert such pressure.

The struggling masses find that their only friends in need are China, Russia, Cuba and some Eastern European countries. Some essential material support for the armed struggle comes only from these friends, while the rest of the supposed freedom-loving Christian world—understandably enough—is not concerned with the plight of the oppressed peoples of Zimbabwe and the rest of occupied Africa.

The British Government will not stand idle while a truly people's socialist revolution is on the verge of reality in Zimbabwe. Whitehall has affirmed that Great Britain would only intervene in Rhodesia if there was a breakdown of 'law and order'. In effect, this means that only a serious attempt to take over the State machine by the oppressed people would be considered 'lawlessness' by the British Government. The British will intervene either to save their 'kith and kin' or to make sure that, if an African government is to come to power at all, it should be a neo-colonialist puppet régime, not one like Sekou Toure's or Albert Karume's in Zanzibar.

CHARLOTTE NASSIM

Notes on the Revolutionary Students in Japan

Japan is not a revolutionary country. It has never been a revolutionary country, and on present evidence it is doubtful that it will become one. But, like every other major capital city from Paris to Peking, Tokyo has a very active student revolutionary movement. The term 'revolutionary Left' can really be applied only to the students in that movement.

There is much talk on the students' side about co-operation with the unions, but no evidence that it ever takes place. The unions are for the most part suspicious of these 'unruly young men'. It is not hard to see the reasons for the conservatism of most Japanese workers. All those with permanent jobs benefit greatly from the paternalistic system, and belong to the company unions which are staffed by company employees. On the other hand, temporary workers and workers in small industries often have a very hard time; their livelihood is precarious, they are underpaid, and the conditions in which they work are sometimes appalling. Nevertheless, the ambition of the temporary worker is to be taken on permanently by a large company—in other words, to join the system, not alter it.

The paternalistic system is peculiarly acceptable to the Japanese because of the emphasis upon hierarchy in the family, upon the importance of family loyalty and the necessity to meet family obligations which is part of the upbringing of every Japanese child.

Moreover, the Japanese child grows up accepting without resentment his place in the family, and his family's place in the community, an attitude that inevitably draws the sting from the notion of class struggle.

This having been said, it must be pointed out that there are many factors not inimical to revolution in Japan. There has been extremely rapid economic growth, there is a very uneven distribution of wealth, Western influence continues to challenge the traditional values and attitudes, and, most relevant at present, there has been a vast increase in the number of students.

The basic unit of student organization is the Students' Self-Governing Council of each university or college. Each council may or may not belong to one of the national federations, at which level the really active minority of student leaders is found. This minority is usually referred to simply as the Zengakuren, which stands for Zen Nippon Gakusei Jichikai Sorengo (National Federation of Students' Self-Governing Associations). The original Zengakuren was founded in 1948 with resolutions calling, among other things, for 'opposition to any new attempts to utilize education to further fascism and colonialism', and 'opposition to fascism and the defence of democracy'. Thus from the beginning the Zengakuren was not merely concerned with the field of student affairs, but also with the wider field of politics. The question as to which of these should take priority in Zengakuren policy has caused constant dissension ever since.

In its early years the Zengakuren was fostered by the Japanese Communist Party and encouraged to use violence. Also, some of the students were organized in 'Mountain Village Action Teams' which were to propagate political action in the more remote areas of the country and eventually to form the basis of an armed revolution. But in 1955 the JCP changed its tactics and, outwardly at any rate, adopted a more moderate line. This left the students high and dry, and the next year the Zengakuren broke away from the JCP, announcing its own policy : 'The prime aim of the student movement lies in the struggle to defend peace.'

Starting in 1958 there was a proliferation of revolutionary student organizations and these split up, collaborated or merged in a confusion which can only be explained by the Japanese custom whereby no decision is acceptable without unanimous approval. In any meeting of students, proposals are greeted with shouts of 'yes' or 'no'; there is no middle ground for discussion, and dissenters form their own factions and start recruiting members for themselves.

There are now three groups claiming to be the real Zengakuren. One of these is still influenced and supported by the JCP and is known as the JCP Zengakuren. Leaders of this group see themselves as the 'democratic intelligentsia'; they favour discussion, negotiation, and if necessary strikes against the faculty over university matters. The JCP Zengakuren occupies itself purely with student affairs—university regulations, fees and facilities—much more than the other organizations, whose *raison d'être* is more overtly political. This explains why it has a large following—at least on paper—of Students' Self-Governing Councils. But in reality, many of the members scorn the JCP Zengakuren's passivity in off-campus politics. Of the 829 student councils in the Japanese universities and colleges, only 510 (in July 1968) are committed to the support of any of the Zengakuren factions, and of these 330 support the JCP Zengakuren. Some of the students express uneasiness at a communist party that is so 'quiet and gentle', others join in demonstrations organized by other factions. The chairman of the JCP Zengakuren, Katsu Hirata, remarks that there are people with many different ideologies in his organization; thus they can adopt policies that in one way or another satisfy a high percentage of the student body of Japan. Inevitably this weakens the JCP Zengakuren's image, and prevents any cohesive leadership.

The Sampa Zengakuren (Three-Faction Zengakuren) is an uneasy coalition of three factions: the Chukaku-ha (Core Faction), the Shagakudo (League of Socialist Students) and the 'Liberation Faction' of the Shaseido (League of Socialist Youth). The Sampa will almost certainly split up in the not too distant future: in 1968 they did not succeed in holding a single convention. The Chukaku-ha, long the most influential of the three, has alienated the other two factions by sticking obstinately to its own line; so these other two factions held a separate convention in the summer of 1968. Each of the three factions has all along continued to publish its own paper. The Sampa Zengakuren is supported by 107 Students' Self-Governing Councils (in July 1968), and it has been the most prominent group in the public eye because of its violent clashes with the police. The Sampa Zengakuren's policy is that students should act as 'co-ordinators with peasants, citizens and labourers' in the struggle against imperialism and capitalism. A fourth group, the Marx-Lenin Faction, is now considered to be part of the Sampa Zengakuren.

Strongly opposed to the other two Zengakurens is the Kakumaru Zengakuren (Revolutionary Marxist Zengakuren). This group claims to be the heir of the original Zengakuren, but although it is in possession of the original official Zengakuren stamp and has the right to send delegates to the International Student Federation, it controls only thirty Students' Self-Governing Councils. However, its members regard themselves as a revolutionary élite, their theory being that revolution must begin with a mass student movement, so that, unlike the other Zengakurens, they have no policy of co-operation with the unions or political parties. The Kakumaru-ha is strongly influenced by the ideas of an enigmatic, gurulike figure, Kanichi Kuroda. Kuroda is about forty years old, is always seen in sun-glasses (being almost blind) and is said to be very witty. Certainly he arouses strong feelings of allegiance among some of the students who refer to him as 'Kurokan', or even 'momoku no kyoso', which means the blind founder of a religious sect! Others, notably the Sampa students who were formerly influenced by him, criticize him severely for his 'narrow, over-theoretical' views.

There are other organizations of students which do not claim the title Zengakuren. The most noteworthy of these is probably the Kozo-Kaikaku-ha (Structural Reform Faction), which controls thirty-eight Students' Self-Governing Councils. It proposes an anti-monopoly socialist revolution, brought about by peaceful means.

With all the interfactional and ideological disputes going on, it is not surprising that the student leaders have become rather distant from the main student body. Some of the students feel this acutely, but it is still not the main reason why only a small minority of students can be mobilized for demonstrations or violent protests. This minority is estimated to be twelve thousand on a nation-wide basis, of which about six thousand are in Tokyo. The average student approves of this minority, but feels unable to take part in violent action. This reluctance is only partly due to fear of jeopardizing future employment prospects (and most students consider it their duty to their family to get a good job); brought up to conform and obey, the young Japanese is usually unwilling to stick his neck out and commit himself in action.

The students have plenty of grievances on their own campuses, and here a larger number can be persuaded to take part in strikes and the occupation of buildings. At present there are internal disputes in more than fifty colleges, mostly in protest against increases in tuition fees, inadequate facilities and lack of contact with teaching staff. They have had some success in preventing certain increases in fees, and in forcing the resignation of some faculty and governing members of universities. Usually the authorities refrain from calling in the police; so far there have been only two instances of police intervention on university campuses.

On the whole, the authorities and the police have been very weak in their attempts to curb student violence. They try to prevent the students from reaching their objectives by blocking them with a numerically superior force. The police are extremely sensitive to charges of brutality because of the deplorable record of the Kempeitai (prewar military police). They are also aware that in some instances public sympathy is with the students, as was the case at Sasebo in January 1968—the last occasion of serious street fighting.

At Sasebo the students were trying to prevent the USS *Enterprise*, a nuclear-powered aircraft carrier, from entering the port. They resent America's special claims on Japan and are vigorously opposed to the Vietnam war. In this they are not unrepresentative of general public opinion which, having as it does a pathological fear of contamination, is also blindly opposed to anything associated with the term 'nuclear'. Public sympathy was openly expressed when the police surrounded the students and beat up those unable to escape. As usual, the students were fitted out with helmets like those worn by construction workers, and with long, thick wooden poles and cotton gloves. This get-up they call 'gewalt wear'. They had come to Sasebo by train and, to avoid detection and confiscation, the poles had been loaded on to the train, unseen by railway staff, at an intermediate stopping place.

The confrontation took place on the bridge leading to the US Naval Base, where the police were waiting with a barricade and armoured cars. Later, tear-gas and water hoses were used and the students retaliated by throwing stones and wielding their poles. The students were surrounded and over a hundred of them injured.

To a people who abhor violence, this was an appalling state of affairs. The day after the incident the citizens of Sasebo criticized the police and began to contribute generously to the students' campaign funds.

Since students arrested after such incidents are charged indiscriminately with a variety of offences, the upshot for them is often no more severe than a suspended sentence. That the serious charge of rioting and the tough Anti-Subversive Activities Law have not been applied is evidence of the extent of the Government's indecision in dealing with the students. However, much more serious rioting is expected over the Japan-US Security Treaty which may be revised for the first time in ten years in 1970. It has been predicted that over a hundred thousand students will then be spurred to action in protest against continuation of the treaty, and the Government has called for conferences with top police representatives to discuss how the expected violence should be handled.

Apart from specific issues such as the Security Treaty, protests such as occurred at Sasebo and the attempt to prevent Sato, the Prime Minister, from leaving the country to visit Saigon in October 1967, what are the students' aims in resorting to violence? First, they want to challenge the 'capitalist deception' behind the present Government's desire to develop Japan as a mass-consumer society. Second, they wish to expose what they consider to be the failure of the left-wing establishment in Japan. Third, they feel that, in the physical clashes with authority, they can somehow advance their ideological understanding and purity. Their ideology is mostly Marxist and drawn particularly from the earlier works—*Economic and Philosophic Manuscripts of 1844* and *German Ideology* being the most frequently quoted. The established Japanese intellectuals are also predominantly Marxist, but are often strongly critical of the students. Their criticisms are : that they do not read enough, and therefore their ideology is crude; that they are unaware of their historical position; and that they over-emphasize the subjective approach so that, lacking objective standards, their actions are determined by immediate circumstances. Finally, they are critical of the sexual laxity of the modern student.

Given the similarities between students' movements throughout the world, the Japanese revolutionary students are remarkable for their apparent rejection of anarchism, their extreme subjectivism, and the fact that they sometimes exhibit an almost religious fanaticism. There is a great contrast between the well-organized, well-equipped demonstrators and the interfactional dogfights. However, some form of unity may be achieved in time for the 1970 Security Treaty protests. It seems unlikely that the students will continue to be treated leniently : the mood of the 'gerontocracy' that governs Japan is becoming grimmer.

MALCOLM CALDWELL

Indonesia: The Struggle Continues

Predictably, the massacre of communists and their sympathizers in
Indonesia since the army *coup* in October 1965 has failed to
extirpate communism. On the contrary : the Communist Party of
Indonesia (PKI), rudely and painfully disabused of its constitu-
tionalist illusions, has turned and fought back. Since the major
policy statement issued by the PKI Central Committee 'somewhere
in Central Java' on August 17th, 1966 (the twenty-first anniversary
of the Indonesian declaration of independence) Maoist armed
struggle has been the official Party line.

Circumstances are not unpropitious. Indonesia is a huge archipelago, sprawling more than three thousand miles along the
Equator. Logistical problems are immense—more so for regular
troops than for guerrillas. The inland reaches of the biggest islands,
such as Kalimantan (Borneo) and Sumatra, afford the kind of
seclusion and inaccessibility required of base areas.

The country has a long revolutionary tradition. Sir Stamford
Raffles (who governed Indonesia from 1811 to 1815 when it was in
British hands) wrote of the Javanese : '. . . ever since the arrival
of the Europeans, they have neglected no opportunity of attempting
to regain their independence'. In the major uprising of 1825-30,
known as the Java War, eight thousand Europeans lost their lives,
while the Javanese suffered 200,000 casualties (largely due to disease
and starvation). Under Prince Diponegoro, Sultan of Jogjakarta,

258

the peasants rose *en masse* in the areas of Banjumas, Bagelin, Madiun and Kediri and proved adept at guerrilla warfare until they were deprived of their leader by Dutch treachery. In only half a dozen years of the nineteenth century was Java free of peasant uprisings, and expressions of social and economic grievances progressively figured alongside appeals to religion and tradition among the peasant revolutionaries. Nor was resistance to the Dutch confined to Java, for there were major revolts elsewhere (for instance, in the Moluccas from 1816 to 1818). Subjugation of the northern Sumatran state of Atjeh, which took the Dutch over thirty years and cost them many lives, was never absolute.

The twentieth century, which saw the birth of the modern Indonesian nationalist movement with the formation of nation-wide political organizations, witnessed further armed peasant uprisings. During the First World War Dutch troops had to be sent in to quell Kediri and the sugar districts around Jogjakarta and Surakarta. The Communist Party of Indonesia, founded in May 1920, is among the most long-established of communist parties in the world. In the period 1926-27 it staged insurrections in Java and Sumatra, armed clashes occurring in Priangan and Bantam (West Java), in Solo, Banjumas, Pekalongan, Kedu and Kediri (Central and East Java), and in Padang and Padangpandjang (West Sumatra). Guerrilla resistance continued longest in Bantam, which had always been a troubled area—a major peasant uprising against the Dutch had been staged there in 1888. Savage Dutch repression followed, and PKI leaders who were not killed in action or hanged on capture were imprisoned or exiled, many dying in the notorious penal colony of Tanah Merah in the malarial swamplands of West Irian (West New Guinea).

War and the Japanese occupation helped to prepare the people for armed resistance to the return of the Dutch. The Japanese themselves armed and trained paramilitary formations of Indonesian youth, while others went into underground organizations. Armed clashes with the Japanese were not frequent until towards the end of the war, for top priority was given to preparation for the coming struggle with the Dutch. Just after the war, in the ensuing chaos, there were spontaneous peasant uprisings in various parts of Indonesia, particularly in Sumatra, in which members of the traditional ruling class who had been too closely identified with the hated Dutch were murdered. But Indonesia's major experience of guerrilla struggle came with the long resistance to the reimposition of Dutch rule. After independence, dissident groups such as the Islamic organization, Darul Islam, and the 'Republic of the South Moluccas', waged armed resistance to the new government, and in 1958 there was a major rebellion in Sumatra. There are, therefore, ample precedents for the PKI's resort to armed struggle.

In the aftermath of the 1965-66 blood-bath, instigated and supervised by the present military rulers of Indonesia, the PKI had, in effect, no choice but to take to arms. Eighteen years before, in 1948, threatened by suppression and by the disbandment of military units sympathetic to it, the Party had staged an armed revolt in Surakarta as well as in and around the city of Madiun and neighbouring Ngawi and Ponorogo. It was a disastrous failure. In crushing it, the Republic forces captured and imprisoned 35,000 rebels, and killed many thousands, including most of the communist leaders. Writing later in prison, one of the leaders—Suripno—wrote : 'The lesson we learned, a very precious one, although very hard, was that the people did not support us.'

Precipitated once into premature revolt, the surviving PKI cadres were naturally reluctant to court a similar tragic sequel by injudicious militancy. In 1948 they had seriously miscalculated the strength of Sukarno's personal appeal, as the incarnate symbol of Indonesian nationalism, and—in challenging his régime—had crashed; and this despite the existence of genuine, widely felt economic and political grievances that could have won support to their side. Led by D. N. Aidit, the reviving PKI in the 1950s sheltered under the aegis of President Sukarno, seeking to strengthen him politically against reactionary political forces in Indonesia (Muslim groups advocating theocracy; the army), and at the same time to make capital out of the economic stagnation, political corruption and social disintegration that accompanied the failure of his régime's internal policies. While performing this delicate balancing act, the Party was seeking a truly mass-base that would make another 1948 impossible. Even when the PKI came much closer to the Chinese Communist Party in the early 1960s—parallel with Sukarno's move into the Peking orbit—it clung to Aidit's formulations of peaceful transition to socialism via a national, democratic and independent government.

There were some justifications for PKI optimism as well as for its caution. Its caution can be accounted for by the hostility of a very large and well-armed army. It is true that there were units sympathetic to the communists, and that they had support in the junior ranks. The air force, under Omar Dhani, and the marines (KKO) were in general sympathetic. But in firm control of the bulk of the army there remained a group of dedicated anti-communists of high rank, including General Nasution and General Suharto. At their disposal they had a number of crack anti-communist units specially trained in anti-guerrilla warfare, of which the best known are the RPKAD, the army's paracommandos, recently proudly described as 'trained to take on any task from assassination to intimidation, in or out of uniform'.

Caution was also enjoined by the realities of Indonesia's social structure. For historical reasons the Javanese, who had their heartland in East and Central Java, but who had also become numerous in Djakarta and its environs, and in enclaves on the south and east coasts of Sumatra, had evolved cultural forms sharply distinguishing them from both the non-Javanese on the island of Java and from the peoples of the other (Outer) islands. In particular, the mode of transmission of Islam to the archipelago had produced an important difference in attitude to it on the part of the Javanese and non-Javanese respectively. All were Muslims, but observance was stricter and more orthodox among the latter than the former. Islam came to the archipelago with trade from the Middle East and from Islamicized India. It tended to retain an association with trade and traders—in Sumatra, along the west and north coasts of Java and in many of the other islands to the east. (There were, and are, enclaves of Hinduism—in Bali—and of Christianity, notably in the easternmost islands, the Moluccas.)

This cultural dichotomy became reinforced by class differentiation for a variety of reasons. Dutch exploitation was at first most intense in the Javanese areas; they needed the irrigated rice fields for growing sugar, for example. Exploitation, administration, population growth and impoverishment went hand in hand. The problems of landlessness, excessive subdivision of holdings, and landlordism therefore presented their most acute aspect in East and Central Java. By contrast, in many parts of the Outer islands, which were in general lightly populated, it was possible for Indonesians themselves to claim a share of the international trade in locally grown commodities such as rubber, which transformed the archipelago in particular from the 1870s onwards.* The result was a 'proletarian-ized' peasantry in the heavily populated areas of Java; and a peasantry elsewhere, an important section of which was 'bourgeois-ified' by their becoming smallholders with an interest in and contacts with the international (capitalist) economy. In Java, those in the more orthodox Muslim tradition (known as *santri*) tended to sep-arate from and gain ascendancy over those in the more syncretic Javanese Muslim tradition (known as *abangan*). This was partly due to their association with trading, but also because where the former culture encouraged thrift and private enterprise ('Protestant' virtues), the latter laid stress upon social obligations, festivals and activities emphasizing social solidarity and mutuality. The result was a deepening split in Javanese society, with the poorest peasantry frequently *abangan*, and the better-off peasantry, traders, religious teachers, etc., *santri*. This was mirrored in the élites, where a man's roots were influential in orientating his political outlook : Sumatrans and others from the Outer islands were, for example, prominent in the 1958 revolt, the objectives of which were more 'rational' and capitalistic policies, while Javanese *priai* (literally, persons of rank) have been prominent among those who have favoured statism and 'solidarity-making' through political manipulation.

Finally, caution was prudent in view of relations with China and the Chinese. There were two and a half to three million ethnic Chinese in Indonesia (over a million of them citizens of the CPR), and—as elsewhere in South-East Asia—relations between the 'local' and 'alien' communities were subject to strain and, at times, break-down. Some of the Indonesian Chinese were supporters of the PKI, but the Party nevertheless remained predominantly non-Chinese in membership and support. However, its close relationship with the Chinese Party, and the prevalent popular belief that 'once a Chinese, always a Chinese' (which entailed regarding the Indo-nesian Chinese as ultimately a fifth column for Mao), meant that it was difficult for the Party to escape any odium attaching to the Chinese.

On the other hand, there were reasons for optimism. Until the

* See my recent book, *Indonesia* (London : Oxford University Press, 1968), *passim*.

last year or two prior to his fall, Sukarno had retained enough political leverage to shield the Party from the long knives of the anti-communist army leaders. Popular support was growing. The national elections of 1955 and the local elections of 1957 had demonstrated the extent of this. On the latter occasion the PKI won more votes than any other party in Central Java and came second in East Java. In most of the major towns the PKI emerged with absolute majorities—this was the case in Semarang, Surabaya, Madiun, Magelang, Malang and Surakarta, for example. Just prior to the decimation of the Party, PKI leaders estimated that it had between sixteen and twenty million supporters out of a total population of 110 million. However, support was disproportionately strong among Javanese *abangan* and *priai,* and weaker elsewhere (except for the special case of Kalimantan, where a largely Chinese Clandestine Communist Organization—CCO—operated against Malaysia in Sarawak, and had bases inside Indonesian territory, where many Chinese were agriculturalists). Such concentrated support automatically generated proportional distrust, fear and opposition on the part of devout, conservative and prosperous *santri.*

As Sukarno's physical health and political security began to show signs of weakening in 1964 and early 1965, the PKI found itself in an extremely difficult position. To make preparations for armed struggle, by propaganda and by securing arms, would inevitably trigger off army suppression. Yet it was now becoming clear that Sukarno's ability to stay the hands of the right-wing generals was drawing to an end, before the Party had succeeded in establishing and consolidating an absolutely impregnable mass-base. When, early in 1965, the PKI called for arms for the workers and peasants 'to defend the Indonesian Revolution', it was beyond Sukarno's power to comply; the army could not stand idly by while their ultimate enemy armed themselves to the teeth. Portents of what was in store were to be seen in the savage reactions of landlords and the local military to peasant attempts to enforce by direct action the provisions of the 1960 Sharecropping and Basic Agrarian Laws, notably in the peasant rising in Djengkol, Kediri district. Militant Muslim youth organizations were itching to grapple with the communist and Chinese unbelievers, and for months before the generals' *coup* there were drum bands in the streets. Their precarious position could hardly have been more sharply brought home to the PKI leaders than by such manifestations of military and religious strength and intentions.

This is not the place to subject the actual Untung *coup* of September 30th, 1965, and the generals' counter-*coup* to detailed analysis. The fact of Untung's known associations with the PKI, or with individuals in it, and the involvement of PKI youth and women's organizations in the kidnapping and murdering of the six generals, afforded the army a perfect pretext for what followed : suppression of the PKI and physical elimination of several hundred thousand of its cadres and sympathizers. The pattern varied from one part of the archipelago to another, but at first PKI armed resistance to the slaughters was surprisingly feeble. It appears that so long as confusion persisted, the PKI leaders still believed Sukarno could reassert himself and save them. They paid very heavily for this hesitancy, as the RPKAD paracommandos went from one part of the country to another in October, November and December supervising the killings, in places arming members of the Muslim youth organizations to facilitate the slaughter. Apart from those killed, between 200,000 and 300,000 'communists' or 'communist-sympathizers' were rounded up into hastily improvised concentration camps. Only in scattered instances did PKI armed resistance start at once. A pro-PKI army officer led a rebellion in Central Kalimantan, which the army succeeded in crushing. A number of units of the Central Java division of the army were sympathetic to the PKI, but put up little if any resistance when the RPKAD were sent into the area. Aidit himself was shot near Surakarta, having fled there to try to establish a base area in the Klaton and Bojolali region.

The important PKI policy statement of August 1966, endorsing Maoist armed struggle, which followed a painful reappraisal of former policies, was really only a recognition of necessity. Since then, sporadic reports of guerrilla warfare have reached the West, and an attempt will be made here to give a picture of the present situation. However, piecing together the early history of a people's liberation war is not easy. News is naturally sparse and often unreliable. The official agencies suppress as much as possible and minimize the scale of fighting. The guerrillas, on their part, seldom have regular channels of communication to the outside world. What follows has been culled from Western reports, Indonesian official statements and PKI sources available to me, both in English and the Indonesian language.

In Java, resistance has been strongest in the East and Central regions. Armed actions to kidnap and execute local landlords and reactionary officials have been reported in the last two years from the neighbourhoods of South Malang, South Blitar, Tulungagung, Bodjonegoro and Kediri. Clashes with security forces were reported from Ngawi, Malang and Banjuwangi. In March 1968 330 army officers and troops were reported to have gone over *en masse* to the PKI guerrillas, taking their arms and other equipment with them, in the Malang area, East Java. A journalist of *Kompas*, a Catholic newspaper, visiting East Java later in the year, reported that PKI activities had a political character and were well organized, and that in the countryside of Malang, Banjuwangi and Tulungagong there were armed incidents almost every other day. Such actions were also reported from Djember, Madiun, Magetan, Tuban, Bodjonegoro and Pandanarum. PKI guerrilla squads of from five to ten men, armed with automatic weapons and hand-grenades, struck particularly at those who had 'distinguished' themselves in the white terror of the late months of 1965 and early 1966—big landlords, reactionary local officials and right-wing military leaders. Other actions were aimed at capturing military equipment—rifles, grenades, machine-guns, etc. In the Surabaya region PKI guerrillas attacked and replenished their supplies from the ammunition depot of the air force (now purged of its pro-communist personnel, including former Air Marshal Omar Dhani).

Judging from the high-level administration consultations about the East Java situation, it seems clear that the authorities are seriously disturbed about developments. On August 5th, 1968 *The Times* of London reported that a band of six hundred PKI guerrillas had been caught and thirty killed during an army assault in South-East Java. Flame-throwers, sulphur and dynamite had been used to flush them from their hide-outs. A week later, the same paper reported that fifty guerrillas had been killed in an attack on a remote coastal area of East Java, and that a network of tunnels and caves of a 'communist stronghold' had been discovered. (It had previously been widely assumed that the PKI were seeking to establish a base area or areas in the southern parts of Central and East Java; circumstances, apart from these being the heartlands of their old support, were favourable, since there were mountains and dense primary forests available, as well as fertile wet-rice areas where peasant support was to be expected.) Meantime, the weeding-out of 'communists' from public life continues. At the beginning of August 1968 it was reported from Djakarta that a further eight hundred suspects had been arrested, including five senior army officers.

Incidents have also been reported from time to time from West Java, Sulawesi (Celebes) and Sumatra. In April 1968 fifty-two members of the armed forces were arrested and charged with plotting to set up an underground communist cell in South Sumatra. Since the end of 1967 peasants in North Sumatra who had tried to seize land from the big 'State' plantations (in reality, the private estates of the military men who run them) and had been brutally repulsed, have been in the hills, embarking upon armed struggle.

But it has been from the huge island of Kalimantan that reports of PKI armed struggle have been most persistent and substantial. Here, great stretches of primary forest and towering mountains favour the guerrillas. Moreover, since the bloody pogroms of November 1967 (conducted by the local Dyaks, with army connivance), in which hundreds of Chinese perished and tens of thousands were driven from their homes in the rural areas to emergency concentration camps near Pontianak and other ports, the entire Chinese population of Borneo—over a million all told in Sarawak, Sabah and Kalimantan—must be regarded as potential opponents of the Suharto régime. Both sides claim major victories in the fighting that has taken place, and the numbers involved indicate that this is another area where, as in East Java, the situation is well developed, and, for the Government, serious.

In October 1967, four months after the struggle had for the first time been officially admitted to exist, a clash in which 150 guerrillas were reported killed took place on Merabu Mountain, near the town of Bengkajan. Government troop reinforcements have been diverted to West Kalimantan, the focus of the rebellion, from elsewhere, notably from Sumatra. According to official estimates, the number of armed guerrillas is small—somewhere between seven hundred and two thousand, it is claimed. But this has been quite enough, if true, to cause the authorities great trouble and concern. The crack Indonesian Siliwangi Division has been sent in against the guerrillas, and in March 1968 a top-level meeting of military commanders discussed intensification of the pacification programme.

The West Kalimantan fighting is apparently commanded by Sofian, a PKI leader, now said to have his base in the Mount Slabu region. Clashes have been reported from Batu Hitam, Bengkajan, Sengkung, Melantjeu, Benua Martinus, Sambas, Seluas, Sanggau, Singkawang and elsewhere. Preparation for the struggle appears to have been thorough. Rice supplies have been cached in a score or so of semi-permanent training areas in the region between and behind Sambas and Pontianak, centring on Mount Niut, in a range which stretches over the border into Sarawak. Such supplies in remote and inaccessible areas would seem to indicate extensive local support for delivery, porterage and the subsequent silence. In the jungles the guerrillas themselves have also been able to clear land and grow crops.

By contrast, the security forces encounter serious logistical problems. Roads are virtually non-existent, and there are too few Russian helicopters as yet to give the army the mobility it needs if it is to cope with the rebellion. Government troops may take many days to reach suspect objectives, running short of food, medicine and other supplies on the way. Most of the regular troops dislike the Borneo jungle, which is unfamiliar to them. In carrying out reprisals against villages thought to be harbouring or supplying rebels, Government forces alienate the local population by burning down houses, pillaging and general maltreatment of people. To prevent the guerrillas finding sanctuary in Sarawak, the Indonesian authorities try to work closely with Malaysian security forces across the border. After an ambush by five hundred liberation fighters some sixty kilometres from the town of Bengkajan at the end of November 1967, the security forces realized they were up against well-armed guerrillas equipped with automatic weapons, heavy mortars, and other sophisticated equipment, and well entrenched in mountainous country advantageous to them. In a raid on the town of Singkawang, guerrillas got away with more than two hundred new automatic weapons. Bases vacated by the rebels and occupied by security troops invariably contain copies of the works of Mao Tse-tung, and there can be no question but that the guerrillas are preparing for a long, long struggle.

It is for these reasons that a certain amount of alarm at the deteriorating situation was expressed in the official Indonesian press during 1968. Recently the revolt spread to East Kalimantan, guerrilla groups having been engaged near Kerajan and Longawan.

It is too early to speculate on the likely development of this peasant guerrilla struggle for liberation in one of the biggest countries of the world. But certain factors must operate in its favour. The first is the continuing economic deterioration. Despite vaunted plans to put the economy on a sound footing, the right-wing military régime has as yet failed to halt the slide. Hunger and hardship remain the lot of the rural and urban poor, while the wealth of the élite has never been greater or more openly flaunted. There were mass-demonstrations demanding rice in Djakarta early in 1968. Corruption, once again despite loud promises of reform, is worse than ever. There seems no prospect of significant improvements in the economic field for the ordinary Indonesian, although a handful of the rich and powerful may for their part benefit from foreign aid and foreign investment.

Second, American intervention in Indonesia's affairs is certain to arouse a resentful nationalistic response. Apart from the United States Government wielding vital economic influence through international consortia of capitalist lenders and through international economic agencies, American business has led the field in the indecent scramble to take advantage of the new laws encouraging private foreign investment which America extorted as the price for emergency financial help. Naturally, to guard these investments and to help guarantee the correct 'climate' for further investment, an American military presence has been established. Ostensibly for innocent purposes, these rapidly expanding United States forces are headed by a colonel who, in the words of *The Times* reporter on July 8th, 1968 : '. . . is an experienced veteran of Special Forces and counter-insurgency in Asia'. New bases have been constructed and old ones renovated. Such a brazenly neo-colonial set-up must provoke local reaction, from which the PKI can only gain at the expense of the collaborators.

Third, the students, who played such an important role in allowing the army leaders to depose Sukarno, are turning sour on a régime which is revealing itself as venal as its predecessor and as impotent to improve the lot of the masses. Idealists and political realists among this influential group in Indonesian society can now only move in one direction—towards the PKI and armed struggle for a socialist society.

Fourth, the top leadership is by no means united and might well crack into factions, with one section backing the Sumatran Nasution and another the Javanese *santri* Suharto. It certainly looks incapable of healing the splits in Indonesian society that were so tragically exacerbated by the massacre they themselves presided over in the terrible winter of 1965-66. The records of régimes of this kind elsewhere—in Asia, Africa and Latin America—lead inexorably to the conclusion that they lead nowhere and solve nothing, except to serve the interests of international monopoly capital headed by the United States of America.

Fifth, the shocking pogroms to which they were exposed during the dark days of the anti-PKI violence can only have left bitterness and scars among the Indonesian Chinese community. One report claims that not a single Chinese was left alive in the west coast area of Atjeh in the north of Sumatra. In Java, too, violent repression was the lot of many of the Chinese communities. But reports claim that they have fought back and retaliated, parading with Mao badges and Maoist slogans in Kediri, Melang, Probolinggo, Pasuruan, Bondowoso, Situbondo, Panarukan and Besuki, and attempting to seize arms from local detachments of the armed forces.

Finally, the overall security situation in the region, from the point of view of the Americans and their string of client régimes, is deteriorating generally. The Malaysian Communist Party (MCP) has been active again in Northern Malaysia, and a base camp was recently uncovered in Southern Johore. Two-fifths of Burma is now, according to American sources, in the hands of the Burmese communists. Fighting is going on in north, north-east and southern parts of Thailand, and again on a significant scale in the Philippines. The Vietnamese continue to defy the full weight of United States military aggression. The national liberation movement in Indonesia must benefit from the extension of liberation movements elsewhere in the region, as United States power and attention become dispersed and distracted.

The peoples of the world will watch with intense interest the efforts of the Indonesian PKI to win, by armed struggle, elementary economic justice for the poor of this vast country, and final economic independence for their country from the exploitative neo-colonial net of the Western capitalist countries.

FIDEL CASTRO

Statement at the Solemn Tribute in Havana

'Revolutionary Comrades,

'I first met Che one day in July or August 1955. And in one night—as he recalls in his writings—he became one of the future expeditionaries of the *Granma*, although at that time the expedition possessed neither ship nor arms nor troops. And that was how, together with Raul, Che became one of the first two on the *Granma* list. And twelve years have passed since then; they have been twelve years filled with struggle and historic significance. During this time death has cut down many brave and invaluable men but, at the same time, extraordinary persons have arisen, forged from the men of the Revolution, and between those men and the people bonds of affection and of friendship have emerged which surpass all description.

'Tonight we are meeting to try to express, to some extent, our feelings towards him who was one of the closest, the most admired, the most beloved and, without doubt, the most extraordinary of our revolutionary comrades; to express our feelings for him, for the heroes who have fought with him and fallen with him and for his internationalist army that has been writing a glorious and ineradicable historical epic.

'Che was one of those people who is liked immediately for his simplicity, his character, his naturalness, his comradely attitude, his personality, his originality, even when one had not yet learned of his other characteristic and unique virtues.

'In those first days he was our troop doctor. And so our bonds of friendship and warm feelings for him were ever-increasing.

'He was filled with a profound spirit of hatred and loathing for imperialism, not only because his political awareness was already considerably developed, but also because, shortly before, he had had the opportunity of witnessing the criminal imperialist intervention in Guatemala through the mercenaries who aborted the revolution in that country.

'A man like Che did not require elaborate arguments. It was sufficient for him to know that there were men determined to struggle against that situation, arms in hand; it was sufficient for him to know that those men were inspired by genuinely revolutionary and patriotic ideals. That was more than enough. And so, one day at the end of November 1956, he set out on the expedition to Cuba with us. I recall that that trip was very hard for him since, because of the circumstances under which it was necessary to organize the departure, he could not even provide himself with the medicine he needed and, throughout the journey, he suffered from a severe attack of asthma with nothing to alleviate it, yet without ever complaining. We arrived, set out on our first march, suffered our first setback and, at the end of some weeks, as you all know, a group of those who had survived the expedition of the *Granma* was able to reunite. Che continued to be the doctor of our troop.

'We came through the first battle victorious, and Che was already a soldier of our troop and, at the same time, still our doctor. We came through the second victorious battle, and Che was not only a soldier but the most outstanding soldier in that battle, carrying out for the first time one of those singular feats that characterized him in all military action. Our forces continued to develop, and we faced another battle of extraordinary importance at that moment.

'The situation was difficult. The information we had was erroneous in many respects. We were going to attack, in full daylight—at dawn—a strongly, well-armed position at the edge of the sea. Enemy troops were at our rear, not very distant, and in that confused situation it was necessary to ask the men to make a supreme effort. Comrade Juan Almeida had taken on one of the most difficult missions, but one of our flanks remained completely without forces; one of the flanks was left without an attacking force, placing the operation in danger. And at that moment Che, who was still functioning as our doctor, asked for two or three men, among them one with a machine-gun, and, in a matter of seconds, rapidly set off to assume the mission of attack from that direction.

'On that occasion he was not only an outstanding combatant but also an outstanding doctor, attending the wounded comrades and, at the same time, attending the wounded enemy soldiers. After all the weapons had been captured and it became necessary to abandon that position, undertaking a long return march under the harassment of diverse enemy forces, it was necessary for someone to stay behind with the wounded, and Che stayed with the wounded. Aided by a small group of our soldiers, he took care of them, saved their lives and later rejoined the column with them.

'From that time onward he stood out as a capable and valiant leader, the type of man who, when a difficult mission is pending, does not wait to be asked to carry it out.

'Thus it was at the battle of El Uvero, but he had acted in a similar way on a not previously mentioned occasion in the first days when, following a betrayal, our little troop was surprise attacked by a number of aircraft and we were forced to retreat under bombardment. We had already walked some distance when we remembered some rifles of some farmer-soldiers, who had been with us in the first actions and had then asked permission to visit their families at a time when there was still not much discipline in our embryonic army. And right then it was thought that possibly the rifles were lost.

'I recall that the problem was not brought up again, but during the bombardment Che volunteered. Having done so, he quickly went out to recover those rifles.

'This was one of his principal characteristics: his willingness instantly to volunteer for the most dangerous missions. And naturally this aroused admiration, and twice the usual admiration, for a fellow combatant fighting alongside us who had not been born here, a man of profound ideas, a man in whose mind stirred the dream of struggle in other parts of the continent and who was, nonetheless, so altruistic, so disinterested, so willing always to do the most difficult things, constantly to risk his life.

'And that was how he won the rank of major and leader of the Second Column organized in the Sierra Maestra. Thus his prestige began to increase, and he began to gain fame as a magnificent combatant who was to reach the highest posts in the course of the war.

'Che was an incomparable soldier. Che was an incomparable leader. Che was, from a military point of view, an extraordinarily capable man, extraordinarily courageous, extraordinarily aggressive. If, as a guerrilla, he had his Achilles heel, it was this excessively aggressive quality, his absolute contempt for danger.

'The enemy believes it can draw certain conclusions from his death. Che was a master of warfare. He was an artist of the guerrilla struggle and he demonstrated this an infinite number of times. But he showed it especially in two extraordinary deeds. One of these was in the invasion in which he led a column, a column pursued by thousands of enemy soldiers over flat and absolutely unknown terrain, carrying out—together with Camilo—an extraordinary military accomplishment. He also showed it in his lightning campaign in Las Villas Province, especially in the audacious attack on the city of Santa Clara, entering, with a column of barely three hundred men, a city defended by tanks, artillery and several thousand infantry soldiers.

'Those two heroic deeds stamped him as an extraordinarily capable leader, as a master, as an artist in the skills of revolutionary war. However, now, after his heroic and glorious death, some attempt to deny the truth or value of his concepts, his guerrilla theories.

'The master may die—especially when he is master of an art as dangerous as revolutionary struggle—but what will surely never die is the art to which he dedicated his life, the art to which he dedicated his intelligence.

'What is so strange about the fact that this master died in combat? What is stranger is that he did not die in combat on one of the innumerable occasions when he risked his life during our revolutionary struggle. And many times it was necessary to take steps to keep him from losing his life in actions of minor significance.

'And so it was in combat—in one of the many battles he fought —that he lost his life. We do not have sufficient evidence to enable us to deduce the circumstances preceding that combat, to imagine to what extent he may have acted in an excessively aggressive way, but—we repeat—if, as a guerrilla, he had an Achilles heel, that Achilles heel was his excessive daring, his complete contempt for danger. And this is where we can hardly agree with him, since we consider that his life, his experience, his capacity as a seasoned leader, his prestige and everything his life signified were more valuable, incomparably more valuable, than he himself perhaps believed.

'His conduct may have been profoundly influenced by the idea that men have a relative value in history, the idea that causes are not defeated when men fall, that the powerful march of history cannot and will not be halted when leaders fall. And that is true, there is no doubt about it. It shows his faith in men, his faith in ideas, his faith in example. However—as I said a few days ago—with all our heart we would like to have seen him as a forger of victories, to see victories forged under his leadership, since men of his experience, men of his calibre, of his really unique capacity, are not common.

'We have a full understanding of the value of his example. We are absolutely convinced that many men will strive to live up to his example, that men like him will emerge from the heart of the peoples. It is not easy to find a person with all the virtues that were combined in him. It is not easy for a person, spontaneously, to develop a personality like his. I would say that he was one of those men who are difficult to match and virtually impossible to surpass. But I would also say that the example of men like him contributes to the appearance of men of the same ilk.

'In Che, we admire not only the fighter, the man capable of performing great feats. And what he did, what he was doing, the very fact of his rising, with a handful of men, against the army of the ruling class—trained by Yankee advisers sent in by Yankee imperialism and backed by the oligarchies of all neighbouring countries—in itself constitutes an extraordinary feat. And if we search the pages of history it is likely that we will find no other case in which a leader with such a limited number of men has set about a task of such import, a case in which a leader with such a limited number of men has set out to fight against such large forces. Such proof of confidence in himself, such proof of confidence in the people, such proof of faith in men's capacity to fight, can be looked for in the pages of history—but their like will never be found.

'And he fell.

'The enemy believes it has defeated his ideas, his guerrilla concepts, his points of view on revolutionary armed struggle. And what they accomplished, by a stroke of luck, was to eliminate him physically; what they accomplished was to gain an accidental advantage that an enemy may gain in war. And we do not know to what degree that stroke of luck, that stroke of fortune, was helped along, in a battle like many others, by that characteristic of which we spoke before, his excessive aggressiveness, his absolute disdain for danger.

'This also happened in our War of Independence. In a battle at Dos Ríos they killed the Apostle of our Independence. In a battle at Punta Brava they killed Antonio Maceo, a veteran of hundreds of battles. Countless leaders, countless patriots of our War of Independence were killed in similar battles. This, however, did not spell defeat for the Cuban cause.

'The death of Che—as we said a few days ago—is a hard blow for the revolutionary movement in that it deprives it, without a doubt, of its most experienced and able leader. But those who are boasting of victory are mistaken. They are mistaken when they think that his death is the end of his ideas, the end of his tactics, the end of his guerrilla concepts, the end of his theories. For the man who fell, as a mortal man, as a man who faced bullets time and again as a soldier, as a leader, is a thousand times more able than those who killed him, by a stroke of luck.

'However, how must revolutionaries face this serious setback? How must we face this loss? If Che had to express an opinion on this point, what would it be? He gave his opinion, he expressed that opinion quite clearly when he wrote in his Message to the Organization of Solidarity of the Peoples of Asia, Africa and Latin America that, if death surprised him anywhere, it would be welcome as long as his battle-cry had reached a receptive ear and another hand stretched out to take up his rifle. And his battle-cry will reach not just one receptive ear, but millions of receptive ears. And not one hand, but millions of hands will stretch out to take up arms. New leaders will emerge. And the men—of receptive ear and outstretched hand—will need leaders who emerge from the ranks of the people, just as leaders have emerged in all revolutions.

'Those hands will not have available a leader of Che's extraordinary experience and enormous ability. Those leaders will be formed in the process of struggle; those leaders will emerge from among the millions of receptive ears, from the millions of hands that will sooner or later stretch out to take up arms.

'It is not that we feel that his death will necessarily have immediate repercussions in the practical sphere of revolutionary struggle, that his death will necessarily have immediate repercussions in the practical sphere of development of the struggle. The fact is that when Che took up arms again he was not thinking of an immediate victory; he was not thinking of a speedy victory against the forces of the oligarchies and of imperialism. As an experienced fighter, he was prepared for a prolonged struggle of five, ten, fifteen or twenty years if necessary. He was ready to fight for five, ten, fifteen, twenty years, or all his life if need be. And within this time perspective his death—or rather his example—will have tremendous repercussions. The force of that example will be invincible.

'Those who cling to the idea of luck try in vain to deny his experience and his capacity as a leader. Che was an extraordinarily able military leader. But when we remember Che, when we think of Che, we do not think fundamentally of his military virtues. No! Warfare is a means and not an end; warfare is a tool of revolutionaries. The important thing is the revolution; the important thing is the revolutionary cause, revolutionary ideas, revolutionary objectives, revolutionary sentiments, revolutionary virtues. And it is in that field, in the field of ideas, in the field of sentiments, in the field of revolutionary virtues, in the field of intelligence—apart from his military virtues—that we feel the tremendous loss his death means for the revolutionary movement. Because Che's extraordinary personality comprised virtues which are rarely found together. He stood out as an incomparable man of action, but Che was not only that; he was a man of visionary intelligence and broad culture, a profound thinker. That is, in his person the man of ideas and the man of action were combined.

'But it is not only that Che possessed the double characteristic of the man of ideas—of profound ideas—and the man of action, but that Che as a revolutionary united in himself the virtues which can be defined as the fullest expression of the virtues of a revolutionary : a man of complete integrity; a man of supreme sense of honour, of absolute sincerity; a man of stoic and Spartan living habits; a man in whose conduct not one stain can be found. He constituted, through his virtues, what can be called a truly model revolutionary.

'When men die it is usual to make speeches, to emphasize their virtues, but rarely can one say of a man, with greater justice, with greater accuracy, what we say of Che : that he was a pure example of revolutionary virtues. But he possessed another quality, not a quality of the intellect nor of the will, not a quality derived from experience, from struggle, but a quality of the heart : he was an extraordinarily human man, a man of extraordinary sensitivity. That is why we say, when we think of his life, that he constituted the singular case of a most extraordinary man, able to unite in his personality not only the characteristics of the man of action but of the man of thought, of the man of immaculate revolutionary virtues and of extraordinary human sensibility, joined with an iron character, a will of steel, indomitable tenacity.

'And because of this, he has left future generations not only his experience, his knowledge as an outstanding soldier, but also, at the same time, the fruits of his intelligence. He wrote with the consummate skill of a master of our language. His narratives of the war are incomparable. The depth of his thinking is impressive. He never wrote about anything with less than extraordinary seriousness, with less than the greatest depth; and we have no doubt that some of his writings will pass to posterity as classic documents of revolutionary thought. And thus, as fruits of that vigorous and profound intelligence, he left us an infinity of memories, an infinity of narratives that, without his work, without his efforts, might have been lost for ever.

'An indefatigable worker, during the years that he served our country he did not know a single day of rest. Many were the responsibilities assigned to him : as President of the National Bank, as Director of the National Planning Board, as Minister of Industries, as commander of military regions, as the head of political or economic or fraternal delegations.

'His versatile intelligence was able to undertake with maximum assurance any task of any kind. And thus he brilliantly represented our country at numerous international conferences, just as he brilliantly led soldiers in combat, just as he was model worker in charge of any of the organizations to which he was assigned, and for him there were no days of rest, for him there were no hours of rest. And if we looked through the windows of his offices we would see he had the lights on until all hours of the night, studying

—or rather, working or studying. For he was a student of all problems, he was a tireless reader. His thirst for learning was practically insatiable and the hours he stole from sleep he devoted to study.

'He devoted his scheduled days off to voluntary work. He was the inspiration and provided the greatest incentive for that work which is today carried out by hundreds of thousands of persons throughout the country; he stimulated that activity in which our people are making greater and greater efforts.

'And, as a revolutionary, as a communist revolutionary, a true communist, he had a boundless faith in moral values, he had a boundless faith in the conscience of man. And we should say that he saw, with absolute clarity, moral resources as the fundamental lever in the construction of communism in human society.

'He thought, worked out and wrote many things. And it is fitting to bring out, on a day like today, that Che's writings, Che's political and revolutionary thinking, will be of permanent value in the Cuban revolutionary process and in the Latin American revolutionary process. And we do not doubt that his ideas, as a man of action, as a man of thought, as a man of untarnished morals, as a man of unexcelled human sensitivity, as a man of stainless conduct have, and will continue to have, universal value.

'The imperialists boast of their triumph at having killed this guerrilla fighter in action; the imperialists boast of a triumphant stroke of luck that led to the elimination of such a splendid man of action. But perhaps the imperialists do not know, or pretend not to know, that the man of action was only one of the many facets of the personality of that combatant. And if we speak of sorrow, we are saddened not only at having lost a man of action, we are saddened at having lost a morally superior man, we are saddened at having lost a man of exquisite human sensitivity, we are saddened at having lost such a mind. We are saddened to think that he was only thirty-nine years old at the time of his death. We are saddened to lose the further fruit that we would have received of that intelligence and that ever richer experience.

'We have an idea of the magnitude of the loss for the revolutionary movement. But, nevertheless, here is the weak side of the imperialist enemy : they think that by eliminating a man physically they have eliminated his thinking; that by eliminating him physically they have eliminated his ideas, eliminated his virtues, eliminated his example. And so shameless are they in this belief that they have no hesitation in publishing, as if it were the most natural thing in the world, the by now almost universally accepted circumstances in which they murdered him after he had been seriously wounded in action. They do not even seem to be aware of the repulsiveness of the procedure. They do not even seem to be aware of the shamelessness of the admission. They have published it as if thugs, oligarchs and mercenaries had the right to shoot a seriously wounded revolutionary prisoner.

'And, even worse, they explain why they did it. They assert that Che's trial would have been earth-shaking, that it would have been impossible to place this revolutionary in the dock.

'Nor have they hesitated to spirit away his remains. And, be it true or false, they certainly announced they had cremated his body, thus beginning to show their fear, beginning to show that they are not so sure that by physically eliminating the combatant they can liquidate his ideas or liquidate his example.

'Che fell defending the interests, defending the cause of the exploited and the oppressed peoples of this continent. Che fell defending the cause of the poor and disenfranchised of this earth. The exemplary manner and the selflessness with which he defended that cause cannot be disputed by even his most bitter enemies.

'And, before history, men who act as he did, men who do all and give all for the cause of the oppressed, grow in stature with each passing day and find a deeper place in the hearts of the people with each passing day.

'The imperialist enemies are beginning to see this, and it will not be long before it will be proved that his death will, in the long run, be like a germ which will give rise to many men determined to imitate him, many men determined to follow his example. And we are absolutely convinced that the revolutionary cause on this continent will recover from the blow, that the revolutionary movement on this continent will not be crushed by this blow.

'From the revolutionary point of view of our people, how must we view Che's example? Do we feel we have lost him? It is true that we will not see new writings of his, true that we will never again hear his voice. But Che has left a heritage to the world, a great heritage, and we who knew him so well can become in great degree his beneficiaries.

'He left us his revolutionary thinking, his revolutionary virtues; he left us his character, his will, his tenacity, his spirit of work. In a word, he left us his example. And Che's example will be a model for our people; Che's example will be the ideal model for our people.

'If we wish to express what we expect our revolutionary combatants, our militants, our men to be, we must say, without hesitation : "Let them be like Che!" If we wish to express what we want the men of future generations to be, we must say : "Let them be like Che!" If we wish to say how we want our children to be educated, we must say without hesitation : "We want them to be educated in Che's spirit!" If we want the model of a man, the model of a man who does not belong to our time, the model of a man who belongs to the future, I say from the depths of my heart that such a model, without a single stain on his conduct, without a single stain on his actions, is Che! If we wish to express what we want our children to be, we must say from our very hearts as ardent revolutionaries : "We want them to be like Che!"

'Che has become a model of what men should be, not only for our people but also for people everywhere in Latin America. Che carried to its highest expression revolutionary stoicism, the revolutionary spirit of sacrifice, revolutionary combativeness, the revolutionary's spirit of work. Che brought the ideas of Marxism-Leninism to their freshest, purest, most revolutionary expression. No other man of our time has carried the spirit of proletarian internationalism to its highest possible level, as Che did. And in the future when an example of a proletarian internationalist is spoken of, when an example of a proletarian internationalist is sought, that example, high above any other, will be Che's example. National flags, prejudices, chauvinism and egoism had disappeared from his mind and heart. And he was ready to shed his blood spontaneously and immediately, on behalf of any people, for the cause of any people.

'And thus, his blood fell on our soil when he was wounded in several battles; and his blood was shed in Bolivia, for the redemption of the exploited and the oppressed. That blood was shed for the sake of all the exploited and all the oppressed; that blood was shed for all the peoples of America and for the people of Vietnam, because while fighting there in Bolivia, fighting against the oligarchies and imperialism, he knew that he was offering Vietnam the highest possible expression of his solidarity.

'It is for this reason, comrades of the Revolution, that we must face the future with optimism. And in Che's example we will always find inspiration, inspiration in struggle, inspiration in tenacity, inspiration in intransigence towards the enemy, inspiration in internationalist sentiment.

'Therefore, after tonight's impressive ceremony, after this vast, incredible demonstration of recognition—incredible for its magnitude, discipline and spirit of devotion, that shows that this is a sensitive, grateful people who know how to honour the memory of the brave who die in combat and to recognize those who serve them, that demonstrates the people's solidarity with the revolutionary struggle and how this people will raise aloft and keep ever higher aloft their revolutionary banners and revolutionary principles—in these moments of remembrance let us lift our spirits optimistically to the future, with absolute confidence in the final victory of the peoples, and say to Che and to the heroes who fought and died with him :

'EVER ONWARD TO VICTORY!
WE WILL WIN!'

PAUL ROCKWELL

How We Became Revolutionaries

INTRODUCTION

For many years university intellectuals conceived of academia as
a kind of sanctuary, divorced from the petty squabbles of mankind, though somehow in a position to influence them. Professors
lived in a quiet dream about themselves. To them, the university
was a neutral institution. Students could resist the draft; the
blacks could riot; workers could strike utilities. But the university,
it seemed to the professors, ought to stand above political confrontations.

Actually, what most professors call neutrality is inaction, and
ignorance of the class basis of their own society. When professors
say, 'We are the university,' their definition of the university ex-
cludes the maids who clean their offices, the workers who build
the buildings, the tenants who pay the rent, and the countless
millions who endure the effects of their imperial research. Such
people are part of the university only as victims. If the vast millions who build or unwittingly support the university were to control its uses and operations, many of the professors who now claim
a majority, and whose studies, paid for out of the public till, are
superfluous to the necessities of life, might be expelled, so useless
are they to the public good.

The intelligentsia is a social stratum within the framework of
bourgeois society. Its status, its ease, its privileges, the very divisions of labor implied by the term intelligentsia, are bound up
with the existing mode of production, wherein one class appropri-

ates the surplus produced by another class. Thus the American intelligentsia tends to preserve the present mode of production rather than transform it. Any major crisis in capitalism will naturally envelop the university. It is absurd to talk of neutrality in a period of intense class struggle, when the nation is beset by wars, resistance, and riots; when, in short, the vast exploited masses are rising to assert their historic rights. The university could not, even if it wanted, choose to be value-free. It can choose good values; it can choose bad values; or it can remain ignorant of the values on which it acts. The notion of value-free inquiry, of social research without reference to social ends, is the bugaboo of escapist science.

We cannot understand the conflict in American schools apart from the broad sweep of capitalist development. Crises and convulsions, which many people expected years ago, were postponed by a vast national debt, easy credit, and colossal military spending that, regardless of the moral issue, were parasitic on the State. The postponement of a crisis often makes it more violent when it comes. Today militarism, riots, strikes, wars, unemployment, needless bureaucracies, meaningless jobs, the diversion of energy into the production of waste, the increase in world privation—all these are the scourges of our society, and they squander the creative capacity of mankind. Capitalism has become too expensive and inhuman to be endured by humanity any longer. The collective character of production now contradicts the private appropriation of its results. The American intelligentsia is a privileged part of that appropriation and deserves to be attacked.

The American university is rightly a battleground for revolution. However, to explain the present ferment, it is not enough to note the class character of the university—maids have always swept professors' floors. We need to understand why the university has become a target for revolutionary struggle *in the present period,* and how middle-class students have become revolutionaries within middle-class institutions. These are the issues to which we should address ourselves. The first pertains to the destructive character of American education, the second to the transformation on consciousness within one part of the bourgeoisie itself.

I

WHY THE UNIVERSITY HAS BECOME A BATTLEGROUND

(a.) The University Is a Violent Institution

'Our colleges and universities,' said John A. Hannah, President of Michigan State University, in 1961, 'must be regarded as bastions of our defense, as essential to the preservation of our country and our way of life as supersonic bombers, nuclear-powered submarines, and intercontinental ballistic missiles.'

Though it maintains a physical distance from the harm it inflicts on men, the university under imperialism has become an especially violent institution. We cannot separate the modern forms of violence—Green Berets, the CIA, nerve gases, mace, chemical inventions, world strategies, and psychological techniques—from the cerebral character of modern imperialism. The most heinous crimes of our century are not the crimes of passion; they are crimes of intellect.

'Our problem,' Robert Sheer writes, 'has been that we expect the voice of terror to be frenzied, and that of madness irrational. It is quite the contrary in a world where genial, middle-aged generals consult with precise social scientists about the parameters of the death equation and the problem of its maximation. The most rational, orderly, disciplined minds of our time are working long hours in our most efficient laboratories, at the task of eliminating us.'

The 'death equation' is not a histrionic term. There is a sense in which murder has become a science. The man who wrote the following report for the IDA (Institute of Defense Analysis, the Pentagon Think Factory in the schools) would probably be considered normal in our society:

A model is developed for predicting the expected number of attacks to be made as a function of the target kill assessment (TKA) probabilities, the single attack kill probability, the confidence on the level of kill desired, and the maximum number of attacks available. The expected number of attacks is compared with the expected number of attacks required if no TKA data are available. Finally, the maximum number of attacks that might be required to achieve the desired kill confidence is computed. (U.S. Gov. Research and Development Reports, June 10, 1966, p. 61)

Columbia University, an exemplary case, trains troops for the American Empire (NROTC, Naval Reserve Officers' Training Corps), provides a base for the 432nd Military Intelligence Detachment, under the Department of the Army. It is contracted to the Army Chemical Center at Edgewood Arsenal for research in biological warfare. Entire branches of the School for International Affairs are financed and controlled by lawless organizations like the CIA, as it is contracted to the IDA. Such contracts may not seem concrete, if we divorce the wars abroad from the antecedents in civilian institutions. Yet if we view the imperial process as a whole, we see that NROTC, which trains at Columbia, actually kills peasants in Vietnam; the CIA, contracted to Columbia, actually helps rig elections in Latin America and overthrow elected governments; chemicals researched in the universities actually destroy crops and limbs in Asia.

Thus the violence in our society is far more grave than liberal professors, who chastize students for seizing buildings, realize. Many academics would rather see a million Vietnamese die from new inventions than interrupt the academic 'civil liberties' of two professors involved in war research. Liberals refuse to take severe measures against the *de facto* violence of the university, but willingly take police measures against popular discontent. They renounce violence when it comes to introducing changes in what already exists. But in defense of the existing order they will not stop at the most ruthless acts.

The term 'defense,' as it is used by the universities, is a euphemism. Much of what men call 'defense' today is violative, not only of provisions of the Constitution (Article I, Section 8; Article VI, Section 2), but of the codified values of mankind. Overthrow of elected governments, contamination of food, rigging of elections, bribes, coups, political blackmail, secret use of troops, secret aid to dictators, undeclared war, indiscriminate bombing, the political use of medicine, scorched-earth programs, forced transfers—the entire complex of anti-revolutionary wars in distant lands—go by the name of 'defense' in America. That is why defense science in American universities can be part of a criminal, violent process, and why many professors are implicated in the general crime. According to the research of Mike Klare (of the North American Congress on Latin America), thirty-eight American universities have institutionalized chemical-biological war research. Defense expenditures for research and development leaped from $652 million in 1950 to $7 billion in 1965.

Those who lay responsibility for anarchy and violence on SDS (Students for a Democratic Society) have entirely missed the point. To purport that a small outside group wants to wreck 'the university' is absurd. Under the present rulers, the university is wrecking itself.

(b.) Pluralism Is Really a Method of Control

The university is a pluralist institution. Its studies are divided into departments and courses, which in turn are chopped into tests and grades. Such pluralism, whereby the domains of thought are isolated from one another, is a method of control. The university is constructed in such a way as to prevent comprehensive understanding. Plekhanov once said, 'Men do not make several distinct histories—the history of law, the history of morals, the history of philosophy, etc.—but only one history, the history of their own social relations, which are determined by the state of the productive forces in each particular period.' Course education, the present division of labor in social science, dismembers the activity of social man and reifies various aspects of humanity into separate forces. Hence we study economics by itself, psychology by itself, law by itself, but achieve no synthetic view of the world. We take courses together in a cumulative, not an organic sense.

The university is an aggregate of experts. Each scholar may know and teach a part of knowledge; but no one may see the whole. Yet capitalism cannot be transformed except by men who

287

understand its structural operations and have an overview of history. Hence the very form of education is conservative. And the 'Sears Roebuck' catalogs of the schools are not accidental. Expertise is simply the mental form of 'keeping people in their place.'

The university is an anti-socialist force, not merely because of war research or anti-communist ideology in the courses. The university is anti-socialist in its very modes of thought. It presupposes that the measure of human achievement is individual, not collective. Hence, it grades individuals. Yet people create and produce socially. A group of twenty-five 'C' students working together on a common task may produce more wealth and value than twenty-five 'A' students working separately.

Ironically, the anti-social individualism implied in American education produces greater uniformity of management and labor in the large corporations. It is far easier to control large numbers of men if each person strives for his happiness *alone*, than if all persons work together to advance their common rights.

Erich Fromm, in *The Art of Loving*, describes the way in which 'individualism' leads to mechanical uniformity: 'Modern capitalism needs men who co-operate smoothly and in large numbers; who want to consume more and more; and whose tastes are standardized and can be easily influenced and anticipated. It needs men who feel free and independent, not subject to any authority or principle or conscience—yet willing to be commanded, to do what is expected of them, to fit into the social machine without friction; who can be guided without force, led without leaders, prompted without aim—except the one to make good, to be on the move, to function, to go ahead.' The American university calls upon us to study alone and to get ahead alone. As such, the university is the enemy of learning, the enemy of our freedom.

(c.) The Class That Controls Production
Also Controls Forms of Consciousness

The political significance of the university lies in one fundamental fact: that the class that controls production also controls the forms of consciousness. Keynesian economics, positivist philosophy, behaviorist psychology—these anti-humanities of the schools—are the mental forms of corporate enterprise. What J. A. Hobson wrote about British and American universities in 1909 is no less true today: 'The actual teaching is none the less selected and controlled, wherever it is found useful to employ the arts of selection and control, by the business interests playing on the vested academic interests. No one can follow the history of political and economic history during the last century without recognizing that the selection and rejection of ideas, hypotheses, and formulae, the moulding of them in the intellectual world, have been plainly directed by the pressures of class interests.'

Marx wrote in the *German Ideology*: 'The ideas of the ruling class are in every epoch the ruling ideas; i.e., the class which is the ruling material force of society is at the same time its ruling intellectual force. The class which has the means of material production at its disposal has control at the same time over the means of mental production.'

We have already seen in America that the men who run the monstrous corporations—from Allied Chemical to Lockheed Aircraft—also run the universities. The material basis of our schools lies in the hands of an entire class. The trustees of most universities are the giants of corporate enterprise. Consider some of the interlocking powers of recent trustees at Columbia. Grayson Kirk, former president, was also a director of Con Edison and Socony Mobil Oil, and sat on the board of the Institute for Defense Analysis. He has been a member of three CIA-conduit foundations. Trustee William Burden was a director of Lockheed Aircraft, Manufacturer's Hanover Trust, and Allied Chemical, and a chairman of IDA. It is natural for men like these to want the university to conduct defense analysis when their own interests are so involved in 'defense.'

We are not dealing here with any conspiracy, nor with deliberate subversion of the process of education. But we do confront a natural proclivity of men bred of empire to mold education to their needs and purpose.

Interlocking directorates are a means of concentrating power. They are a way by which corporate interests silently control the life of a seemingly free institution. The profit performance of the corporate system is the highest interest of the executives of American universities.

Its effect on education is direct. At Columbia, Keynesian economics counsels us to place the burden of debt on the posterity of working men. Behaviorist psychology amoralizes the social sciences and makes advertising possible. A behaviorist view of human affairs expects people to behave in a certain way. Positivist philosophy discredits the intellect that might otherwise dare to speak of general developments, and which could grasp the similitudes that interlock entire civilizations. As Tom Hayden notes: 'With administrators ordering the institution, and faculty the curriculum, the student learns by his isolation to accept elite rule within the university, which prepares him to accept later forms of minority control.'

The fragmentation within the curriculum of the university is based on world-wide concerns and interests. The international character of Columbia, the ease with which the university has been turned into a bastion of imperialism, is reflected even in symbolic performances. Every year the trustees, in the name of Columbia University, give the highest honorary degrees to anti-communists, dictators and reactionaries. These high honors are completely political. On November 5, 1965, Columbia awarded a Doctor of Laws to Carlos Castillo Armas, who, with the CIA, had just overthrown the elected government of Guatemala. Their tribute to the new military dictator proclaimed him a

> soldier who inspired his fellow citizens to overthrow the rule of a despot; a statesman who is their leader as they re-establish Constitutional and democratic government built firmly upon principles of liberty. The alien communist regime which would have smothered freedom in his native Guatemala found in him a resolute foe. In armed strife he was a gallant warrior. With peace restored, the free ballots of a grateful electorate made him

his people's guide . . . staunch advocate of inter-American friendship, he merits the honor of our constituents . . . This University, where many of his young countrymen have come to study, delights to honor him today for his dedication.

Actually, Armas had disenfranchised all illiterate Guatemalans. In May, 1965, Field Marshall P. Pibulsongren, the Prime Minister of Thailand (a military dictator who took away the new franchise of the Thais), was acclaimed by Columbia a

dynamic leader of an ancient people; trained . . . in the military sciences . . . fought and vanquished foes within and without . . . resolute in answer, with his battalions, to the U.N. call against aggression in Korea . . . His nation became the first to ratify the SEATO; stalwart friend in this day of the Free World as people of his area gird against those who would by stealth disunite and then enslave them.

On June 1, 1955, Allen Welsh Dulles, former director of the CIA, received this charming honor: 'He is a citizen whom his fellow Americans may never duly appreciate because they may never know the full extent of his service.'

We cannot review the long, sorry record of reactionary honors —the degrees which, with the acquiescence of the liberal faculty, were conferred upon Rusk, McNamara, Rockefeller, Premier Sato, and many others. Most of the leading financiers, dictators and reactionaries of the world exploit their own countries under a halo bestowed upon them by an American university.

The university is a sanctioning institution—marking, grading, passing, failing, providing credits and degrees. Such 'honors' are not superficial aspects of the learning process. They provide a focus, a glass through which the world must be viewed. They perpetuate falsehoods, as we see in the content of the degrees. They give an ideal glow to activities that are substantially inhumane. (It was just after the Bay of Pigs that Dean Rusk received the highest honor that Columbia awards.) Most important, sanctions coerce. University awards are crucial to winning or keeping a job. In creating struggles for tenure, fights for a grade in political science, mere instincts for self-preservation, the university guides students and faculty into reactionary channels.

The present university does for imperialism and corporate enterprise what the church once did for the feudal state. It protects imperialism from effective attack, provides its inquisitions with the glow of divinity, and makes real change impossible. Classified research, training of troops, defense analysis, reactionary honors, are but some of the defenses with which the university advances interests that lie outside its bounds.

In America, with an annual military budget of $80 billion, the war machine owns the universities. It buys minds, buys research, determines subject matters, and allocates the means of communication and influence to those men who support the Cold War. The material basis of intellectual output lies in the hands of a small elite. As long as its power exists, we shall not be free. That is why the university is one focus for revolutionary struggle.

Insofar as the American university has become a means of production—producing the mechanisms, the weapons, the research, the sanctions, and the reactionary modes of thought, all of which maintain the class character of capitalist society—and insofar as the university is controlled by a single class of men, the university cannot avoid the great political struggles of our age. Capitalism has reached a stage so desperate, so imperial, so consistently repressive, that few of us can remain aloof from the necessity to create a new society. Universities that so consistently make war on people cannot expect to remain immune from popular discontent.

II

REFLECTIONS ON THE COLUMBIA INSURRECTION

In times when the class struggle nears the decisive hour, the process of dissolution going on within the ruling class, in fact within the whole range of old society, assumes such a violent, glaring character that a small section of the ruling class cuts itself adrift and joins the revolutionary class, the class that holds the future in its hands.—Karl Marx.

We see why radicals attack the university, but it is more difficult to understand how students *within* the university are becoming radical. The middle class has begun to attack itself. Many universities, if not in a state of siege, have become polarized. In almost any crisis, liberal faculties become reactionary, while in the same crisis, students become radical and identify with the NLF.

We live in a special period of history, in which the ordinary laws of development and human behavior are superseded by a special set of laws, peculiar to what revolutionaries call 'the mass strike process.' In such times, the correlation of forces changes radically; class consciousness intensifies a hundredfold; fascism looms over the streets and threatens to possess the seats of government; masses that once felt homogeneous are polarized; liberals, who once participated in civil disobedience, become reactionary, side with 'law and order,' and discover in themselves a contempt for workers which they had not recognized before. In the dramatic ebb and flow of revolutionary passions, entire classes count their development in months and years where they had previously counted them in half-centuries.

The system of capital has become so taut that a single disturbance in one locus reverberates throughout the entire system. A crackpot shoots a black leader in Memphis, and mass riots immediately spread over a radius of two thousand miles. Students take over the Sorbonne, initially for student power, and ten million workers go out on strike. Assassinations touch off assassinations, which, though they may be the gestures of desperate men, come in waves only when there is a broad base of discontent. At the same time, in the midst of assassinations, hijackings and other public histrionics, a mass, savior politics develops, especially among the petty bourgeoisie, which gropes for a political Jesus to bring the country out of the morass.

It would be impossible to analyze here the antagonisms within the middle class. The dissolution of capitalist society, however, has already assumed a violent character in the universities. If we review a recent university crisis (Columbia, 1968), we can sense the intensity of the struggle and understand the initial development of revolutionary consciousness within the student Left. Consciousness does not develop evenly. Almost within a month, Columbia SDS became a revolutionary organization.

(a.) The General Malaise

When we seized five buildings at Columbia University, we had little more than our own ideals, our fears, and a vague but growing sense of outrage at the injustices of our society. Martin Luther King had just been shot, his memory demeaned by university officials who refused to pay a decent wage to Puerto Rican workers and who, after grabbing Harlem land for a student gym, offered a back door to blacks in the patronizing, be-grateful way of liberals.

For years our university had evicted tenants from their homes, taken land through city deals, and fired workers for trying to form a union. University trustees consistently lied to the community, as the record shows, and continued to publish CIA books under the guise of independent scholarship. For years the university had trained officers for Vietnam who, as ROTC literature indicates, kill Vietnamese peasants on their own land. By encouraging secret work for the IDA and the CIA, in chemical-biological research for the Defense Department, the trustees had implicated their own university in genocide.

The draft began to pick us off one by one. The military colossus, which the universities had helped to build, corrupted even our civilian lives. We lived in an institution that channeled us, marked us, failed us, and used us for purposes that were not our own.

We felt helpless in the history of our times. For years we had gone to frantic parties, read esoteric poetry, smoked pot, and arrayed ourselves in ornaments. We tried to remain aloof from the disasters of the world—fascism in Greece, starvation in India, ruin in Vietnam, and racism in America. Like the Indian rain dance, which never brings rain but makes the Indians feel better about the drought, our own sorceries did not really work. The war continued, the riots spread, and capitalism decayed before our eyes.

The incongruity between what we saw and what professors told us was, for a time, only vaguely felt. But as the draft hovered over the university, we saw that capitalism, especially in its military form, exploited us; that the trustees who ruled Columbia were part of the class that oppresses the world. The men who ran the monstrous corporations, allied with war and empire, were the same men who ran the universities. We began to perceive connections. Professor Hilsman, who helped to set up concentration camps in Vietnam, also taught students at Columbia. The military that bombed entire cities, uprooted populations, ruined crops, co-opted revolutions, and blackmailed tiny nations was the same military that confronted us at the university in the form of IDA, CIA, NROTC, and war research.

The collegiate wing of privilege could not shield us from the decay and violence in our society. The university was a proponent of the most violent system the centuries have created—the system of capital. It was that system that led to fascism, starvation, racism, and ruin, and it was that system from which our university drew its very existence.

Columbia, standing at the top of a hill, looks down on Harlem. At dusk, from Morningside Drive, one can see the soot, the appalling exhaust of human affairs hanging over the ghetto. People who survive in Harlem have been evicted from Morningside by the trustees, or still pay rent to Columbia. We walked to our classrooms across land that has been made private. Land, once public, on 116th Street between Broadway and Amsterdam had been purchased from the city by the trustees for a nominal fee. We studied in buildings that had once been homes in a city that is underhoused; in our classes we listened to apologies for the Cold War and capital.

In the early '60s we tended to look for immediate causes for our malaise—a bad President, a faulty decision. But the pressure of events forced us to be more discerning.

(b.) Not Local Disobedience, but World Revolution

There is an historic scope to the events of our times—the massive black rebellions in the cities, the constant strikes, the gigantic demonstrations against the war, the heroic acts of individuals in the draft resistance, the liberation of Cubans from foreign dominance, the cultural revolution of 700 million people, and unforgettably, the supreme fortitude of the National Liberation Front of Vietnam. Although these events are separate in time and place, they are part of a coherent movement directed against militarism and capitalist control of human material. In special times in history, and because of their special status in society, students become the precursors of social change. They first begin to study and make connections; they discover parallels; they gain a sense of history. Unlike other groups, students have time to articulate the struggle and to begin to provide it with a program.

We did not abandon our student interests, but we defined our interests in relation to the historic struggle that manifests itself throughout the world today. Vast populations, which had lived in poverty for centuries, began to demand an equal share in the resources of the world. Students in Spain, Mexico, and Italy began to expropriate their universities from the ruling elite, and, simultaneously with the Columbia insurrection, fought against the State police.

If the Vietnamese could withstand the force of bombs, if the blacks could withstand the onslaught of modern police, if Cubans could triumph over imperialism, could we not also, in some tiny way, join the struggle for liberation? We thought we could, and began the seizure of Columbia University, April 23, 1968.

The Strike did not follow the lines of civil disobedience. The Strike at Columbia was an insurrection. Unlike protestors in the early '60s, we refused to be tried by our accusors. For years the Left had wrecked itself through martyrdom, and we desired to break the trend of voluntary punishment. We would not submit to reprisals without a fight. We were convinced that capitalism could not be overcome by speech alone, that those who are in the right should not be punished, and those who, like the trustees, are criminal should not go free. Many professors claimed to agree with our ends, and even admitted the necessity of our acts, yet refused to advocate amnesty for the students. We had learned through hard experience that such professors are just as slippery as the administration. They 'agreed' with our goals only to deprive us of the right of winning them—like demented liberals who believe the Vietnamese should be independent, but on no condition should take arms against foreign occupation.

To be sure, we did not understand the explosive character of our demands at first. Only after violent confrontations did we realize that we had attacked the very mainstays of capitalism. The university was a landlord. But to us, rent, inflated income, was unjust. The university was an employer. But we did not believe in wage-slavery. The university was a war-maker, and to us imperialism was America's most heinous crime. The trustees, *unable to grant concessions,* appealed to the billy club against the manifestation of popular discontent. The repeated use of police brutality revealed the savagery to which the ruling class is prone when students assert their rights in conjunction with blacks, workers, and the dispossessed. Hence, the strike became far more than a fight for student power or local reform. We did not seize buildings to change current policy, only to leave a corrupt administration, representing the privileges of an entire class, in the seat of power. Rather, we challenged the capacity of the trustees to run the university at all. We wanted a revolution.

It seeemed, perhaps, that we had lost our common sense to conceive of a revolution in America. For most of our lives no idea had been more taboo, or seemed more absurd, than social revolution. To be sure, the insurrection was not a revolution. 'Revolution' explicitly refers to a process in which one class, joined by intermediate strata of society, takes away the control of production by force from another class. The insurrection, however, was touched by a revolutionary consciousness. New developments in the world had changed our modes of thought. The war in Vietnam, which first disillusioned us about America, finally dramatized man's capacity for revolution. In Vietnam, the punji stick somehow triumphed over the cluster bomb and jet. History was more than odds. Blacks in America, peasants in Asia, had chosen to liberate themselves or die, and that very choice was the beginning of a victory for mankind. Nothing is so terrifying, nor so heroic, as an entire people fighting against great odds for its survival and independence.

The Tet offensive was a major event in history. It seemed to transform our consciousness. We began to feel that if the U.S. military were to win in Vietnam by force or forced negotiations, if the struggle for liberation were crushed or compromised, something in us would die as well. Our rights and the Vietnamese struggle became inseparable.

In Cuba racism and illiteracy had disappeared; in China starvation had been conquered; in Vietnam the people's war seemed indefatigable. A period of contiguous revolution had come upon us, and men all over the world began to envision the new society. World history had somehow formed the ineffable motivations of the Columbia insurrection.

(c.) Law and Rebellion

Men should not have to fight in order to be free. Yet a social order that has outlived itself rarely yields to a successor without resistance. Social justice does not come as a gift from those in power; it comes through organized struggle against the class that controls the material of life. 'Liberty,' as Fidel Castro said, 'is not begged but is won.'

That we must acquire our rights at the hazard of civil peace is the fault, not of radicals, but of a social system that is already violent and creates the necessity of resistance. The ghettos, the appalling conditions around Columbia, are not accidents. They are inevitable results of absentee ownership, whereby the wealthy dictate to the poor the brute necessities of life, as Columbia rent collectors 'bargain' with tenants just before eviction.

The right to rebel against unjust authority has been recognized by philosophers, jurists, and citizens since ancient times. The city-states of Greece, the philosophers of ancient India, theologians from Aquinas to Luther, proclaim that when a power degenerates into tyranny, subjects are released from their obligation to obey its laws. The French Declaration of the Rights of Men proclaims, 'When the government violates the rights of the people, insurrection is for them the most sacred of rights and the most imperative of duties.'

That Columbia's city deals—eviction of tenants, seizure of land, nonprofit status—were 'legal' did not mollify us; it alarmed us about the class character of law in our society. We claimed that Columbia was a racist institution, that the powerful structure of trusteeship was inherently elitist. The conflict in the universities is not between those who believe in law and those who do not believe in it. Rather, the conflict pits two conceptions of law against each other: the law of Andrew Carnegie, whereby a minority of financiers administers the resources and lives of a working population; and the law of a socialist society, under which neither rich nor poor exist, and through which the working population controls the wealth, produced for its own liberation. We do not want to replace the present trustees with new trustees. It is not for us to create better individual men. No men themselves, but the relationships that force them to act coercively, are at fault in America. Trusteeship should be eliminated altogether. Forms and forces that men took for granted for decades, and that once seemed to determine the very nature of things, have now become repressive and must be abolished. Relations of landlord to tenant, debtor to creditor, employer to employee, trustee to student—relations that are inherently coercive—are some of the fetters which our movement has begun to break.

(d.) Distances Shall Be Broken Down

The creative, even joyful character of the Columbia insurrection has often been overlooked. Every building that we seized became a commune. In the communes we took up what Che once called 'the most important revolutionary aspiration: to see man liberated from his alienation. Man under socialism is more complete. His opportunities for expressing himself and making himself felt in the social organism infinitely greater.'

Before the insurrection, our education was systematically oriented toward isolating the individual, inducing him to follow the lonely track of material interest—getting a better grade from a superior, getting a degree, impressing the dean for a letter of recommendation, taking on a useless subject for a lifetime in order to avoid the draft for two years.

In the communes, distances were broken down. Our collective life released creative capacities in individuals and we began to glimpse the outlines of a new society. One communard described the Math Commune:

The delegated clean-ups and night watches were important in our society, but much more integral were the seemingly endless discussions which formed our collective thinking. News came to us through these meetings not in faceless broadcasts or as cool sheets of newsprint; we received news by voice and gesture. . . . Everything seemed tangible in that small society, events were close and real; duties were meaningful and human. We constantly touched one another with comfortableness born not only out of constant proximity, but also because we shared our political thoughts and our common danger. If we were led, we could touch our leaders. If we were in constant strain, we were not alone. If we were physically constrained in rooms, we were freer in our relations with one another. . . . Perhaps our small society was limited in scope; certainly it was temporary and probably unrealistic in relation to the great amorphous society around us. . . . But in the end, the lingering experience we still feel and yearn for is the experience of a society in which alienation is abnormal rather than normal. Briefly we smelled, tasted, and touched in a society which needed each of us totally, a society in which we were not fragmented, to which each of us was vital, a society in which our minds and our bodies equally were required of us, a society in which we were whole.

Some of us memorized a poem of Whitman:

I hear it was charged against me that I sought to destroy
    institutions.
But really I am neither for nor against institutions . . .

Only I will establish in Mannahatta and every city of
    these States inland and seaboard,
And in the fields and woods, and above every keel little
    or large that dents the water,
Without edifices or rules or trustees or any argument,
The institution of the dear love of comrades.

In our times, desperate romantics, bourgeois anarchists, and moralists, rather than build a revolutionary movement collectively, attempt to purge the body politic by some mad, dramatic act. Capitalism has its sorcerers.

But we are not sorcerers. The Columbia insurrection was not destructive; it was not romantic; it was revolutionary. We did not use sabotage or gimmicks, the kind of activism that is not only wrong, but futile, to stop the university. Any individual could shut down the university by stealth. Only a radical mass struggle can advance the cause of a humane society. The Columbia insurrection was a collective act, which represented many strata of society—blacks from Harlem (who took over a building with Students for an Afro-American Society), tenants from the community in Morningside (who took over a building at 114th Street), and high school students from the city (who lived with us in the communes). Out of our mass struggle came a Liberation School, a Community Action Committee, a Strike Committee representing thousands of people, and a sense of dedication that no repression can overcome.

It was the essence of the insurrection, and it will be the theme of our future activity, to include the vast, unrepresented masses of humanity in the definition of the university. The words of Che aptly express our view:

> Let it be clear
> that we have measured the scope
> of our actions,
> and consider ourselves
> no more than elements in the great army
> of the proletariat.
> What do the dangers or sacrifices
> of a man
> matter
> when the destiny of humanity is at stake?

TARIQ ALI

The Age of Permanent Revolution

'Force is the midwife of every old
society pregnant with the new one.'
—Karl Marx

'What distinguishes a revolutionary is
not so much his capacity to kill as his
willingness to die.'—Leon Trotsky

'We are not only good at destroying
the old world, we are also good at
building the new.'—Mao Tse-tung

Shortcomings in a symposium such as this are inevitable and will
no doubt be subject to criticism. In self-defence let me simply say
that it has not been possible to deal with all the potentially explosive
areas which exist throughout the world. That these exist, is in
itself a fact which should bring joy to the heart of many a revolutionary. In recent times revolutionary ideas have spread throughout
the world with a rapidity that would have amazed Lenin and
Trotsky. In the circumstances, therefore, I have concentrated on
those areas which in my opinion seem to be among the more significant in accelerating the revolutionary process.

There can be no doubt whatsoever that for revolutionary socialists
(and no less probably for monopoly capitalists) the most significant
event of the twentieth century has been the seizure of state power
in 1917 by the Russian Bolsheviks. In much the same way as some
of the leading Bolshevik theoreticians were obsessed by the French
Revolution and the personalities and currents involved in it, we
today are obsessed by the Russian Revolution and the reasons for its
subsequent degeneration. Differences on the subject are so strongly
adhered to that in some instances they result in a sterile dogmatism
and impede the work necessary for building a strong revolutionary

movement. Suffice it to say, however, that the influence of the Russian Revolution of 1917 and its leading ideologues still predominates within the Marxist movement throughout the world.

It was assumed by most of the early Marxists that the Revolution would first take place in advanced capitalist countries such as Germany, France and England. This did not happen. The first proletarian revolution took place in a relatively backward country, Russia, and there it stayed. Both Lenin and Trotsky had taken it for granted that the Revolution would have to spread throughout Europe if it were to be successful inside the Soviet Union itself, but the Revolution did *not* spread. The betrayals by the reformists led to the defeat of the German and Central European revolutions of 1918-21 and thus succeeded in isolating the victorious Russian Revolution. The failure of these revolutions was largely responsible for the degeneration of the Russian Revolution. From that point onwards the policy of the Soviet Union became counter-revolutionary. The communist parties of Western Europe were transformed, after their leading cadres were either expelled or assassinated, from revolutionary parties into frontier guards for the Soviet Union. They became the instruments of Soviet foreign policy and the twists and turns of their 'policies' resulted in the abandonment of all independent Marxist analyses. The Party line laid down by Stalin was transmitted to the various communist parties throughout the world, which in turn transmitted it to their respective followers.

At the end of the Second World War all pretence of internationalism was thrown to the winds by Stalin. He dealt directly with Churchill and Roosevelt to decide the fate of Europe in the classic fashion of a triumphant conqueror. Eastern Europe was Stalinized by the Red Army, with the exception of Czechoslovakia and Yugolavia, where the indigenous communist parties had mass-support. In Western Europe the communist parties of France and Italy faithfully followed the Stalinist line : class-collaboration became the order of the day. Communists participated in coalitions with bourgeois governments. In France there was a National Government, including two communists, which voted war credits for France to continue the aggression against Vietnam. In Greece a successful revolution was betrayed by the Stalinists. Stalin was keeping his side of the bargain with a scrupulousness that would have puzzled most of his left-wing victims. As a result of the failure of the two revolutionary movements in Europe after the First and Second World Wars the focus shifted to the colonial world.

Stalin had not believed that a socialist revolution was possible in China; his disastrous policies had resulted in the massacres of Shanghai and Canton. Perhaps he believed that since most of the leading communist cadres had been wiped out it was now fairly safe for him to deal with Chiang Kai-shek. Stalin had reckoned without Mao Tse-tung. It is not necessary to go into details of how Mao organized the Chinese Communist Party and led it to victory. What is important to note is that if Mao had followed Stalin's advice he would have disbanded the Chinese Party and merged with Chiang Kai-shek's nationalists and in the process would, no doubt, have been liquidated. Despite paying lip-service to Stalin, Mao in fact did exactly the opposite. He fought the most protracted civil war in recent history, with no material aid from Stalin. Unless, of course, one counts a manual on partisan warfare which Stalin sent him as a gift and which Mao handed to Liu Shao-chi with the inscription : 'Read this carefully if you want to end up dead.'

The success of Mao's armies came as a shock to Stalin; right up to 1948 he had been persuading the Chinese communists to come to some sort of agreement with the nationalists and this the Chinese steadfastly, and to their credit, refused to do. In October 1949, exactly thirty-two years after the Bolshevik Revolution, Mao's peasant armies marched into Peking and proclaimed China a People's Republic. Since the largest country in the world was now under a communist government, the Soviet Union had no option but to help it. This was the logic of its own historic legacy and this is as true today as it was then : if a revolution succeeds, the Soviet Union will be obliged to aid it—or it will be compelled to justify its own existence as a socialist country in completely different terms. The success of the Chinese Revolution coupled with the Vietnamese victories in the northern half of Vietnam provided the same sense of elation to Asian communists as had the Russian Revolution to European socialists. Moreover, Asian communism was to prove itself more human, more humane and more willing to admit its mistakes than its counterpart in the Soviet Union. The Chinese Revolution established Mao Tse-tung as one of the leading experts on guerrilla warfare, and while the excessive personality cult built around Mao today has alienated many revolutionaries, Mao's stature as one of the greatest revolutionary leaders of this century is beyond question.

In Latin America the record of Stalinism has been as bad as in Asia. The betrayal of revolutionary politics by the Stalinist parties in Latin America from 1930 to 1968 has been well documented elsewhere and there is no need here to discuss the tortuous arguments which the Latin American Stalinists have used to justify their position in the past and which they continue to use today. So far had the degeneration set in that one of the 'revolutionary functions' of the Mexican Communist Party was to organize and arrange the assassination of Leon Trotsky—a task to which they dedicated themselves with fervour. If only the international Stalinist movement had shown the same enthusiasm in combating world capitalism, the world situation today would be considerably different. Latin America was to remain in the doldrums until the Cuban Revolution. It was this revolution which seemed to break all the laws of Leninism, since in the first instance it was not a socialist revolution. Castro's revolution was organized without a revolutionary party, without a mass-base in the peasantry and, lest we forget, despite the Cuban Communist Party whose attitude to the Cuban guerrillas was one of ill-concealed contempt. The evolution of the Castro revolution is well known. Castro realized that it was impossible to be anti-imperialist and 'neutral' at the same time; that if anti-imperialism was to be the basis of the Cuban Revolution then the Cubans had to ally themselves to the communist world and socialize the property relationships within Cuba. When the Cuban leaders rejected the bogus concept of 'neutrality' and became part of the communist camp, they proclaimed at the same time the first communist state in the Western hemisphere.

Since then the Cuban Revolution has advanced and matured to an amazing extent—despite the economic blockade imposed by the United States and some of its satellites. As in China, illiteracy has been virtually stamped out; compulsory education is stringently implemented, and consequently the whole face of Cuba has been changed unalterably. Havana, once the brothel of Latin America, has now become its revolutionary furnace. The Cuban leadership has declared that the fires of the revolution must be stoked until they spread to the rest of Latin America and thus end the isolation of revolutionary Cuba. A revolutionary foreign policy, closely wedded to a domestic economic policy, is strongly opposed to material incentives or any other form of Liebermanism. The emphasis is upon building the new socialist man. Nevertheless, to paint Cuba as a Utopia would be misrepresentative. Admittedly there is total cultural freedom, but there are still considerable political restraints; there is as yet no real inner-Party democracy and the trade unions are too bureaucratized. However, the population is armed and the people's militias are still in force. Despite numerous attempts on the part of the CIA it has been impossible to overthrow the revolutionary government of Fidel Castro. Cuba has not merely paid lip-service to the cause of internationalism. One of the leading figures of the Cuban Revolution, Ernesto Che Guevara, gave up his post as the Minister of Economic Affairs to aid the Latin American revolution. Che's departure from Cuba has no precedent in history. No revolutionary leader has left the comparative comfort of a successful revolution to start from scratch elsewhere. The only other time that this might have occurred was when, not long after the Russian Revolution, the German Communist Party requested the Comintern to send Leon Trotsky to Germany, since it was felt that his presence would benefit the Party considerably. Trotsky himself was willing to go but Lenin refused him the opportunity, arguing that Trotsky was indispensable inside the Soviet Union.[1]

The effect of the Cuban Revolution on the rest of Latin America cannot be overestimated. In every Latin American capital the writing on the wall can be seen by everyone : VIVA CUBA, VIVA CHE, VIVA FIDEL. During the riots of October 1968, the students and workers of Mexico carried Che's slogan : 'Create Two, Three, Many Vietnams.' The Castroist current has upset the *status quo* so zealously preserved and guarded by the Latin American communist parties. In these parties themselves the rank-and-file militants have after vicious arguments left the Party and joined the Castroites. The parliamentary road to 'socialism' has been seen by many communist militants in Latin America to be simply a false substitute for real revolutionary work. Many socialists in Europe are not aware that 'legalism', so far as the exploited countries are concerned, is simply not possible. The choice is not between 'legal' work, during a transitional period, and underground activities, but between

[1] See Isaac Deutscher, *The Prophet Armed* (Oxford University Press).

underground work and annihilation. While it may be easy enough to hand out leaflets containing revolutionary propaganda outside factories in London, Paris or West Berlin, many militants have been killed for far less by the hired thugs of the oligarchies in Latin America. And it should also be understood that by 'underground activities' one does not mean guerrilla warfare alone, but organizing the urban militants within the cities as well. Both courses, however, imply that an armed struggle is inevitable for the seizure of power. There is no instance in history where a ruling class has handed over power voluntarily : and those who cite the Russian Revolution should not forget the civil war which followed it.

As I mentioned earlier in this summary, it has not been possible to include analyses of all the struggles taking place in the world. Nevertheless, it is essential to record, if only cursorily, some that have not hitherto been discussed—those which will escalate in the next few years. This volume does not have a chapter devoted specifically to Vietnam. The reason for this is NOT that the Vietnamese struggle is unimportant, but that the subject has already been covered many times elsewhere. Needless to say, that conflict colours the entire book, the NLF being one of the main inspirations to world socialist revolution.

In Western Europe there are two countries which stand out—way out on the Right. One symbolizes the old fascism, the other the new : Spain and Greece.

In Spain an armed rebellion has begun in the Basque provinces; elsewhere worker-student demonstrations are rapidly gaining momentum. Despite the fact that the Basque struggle is not a fight for socialism, it should in no circumstances be underestimated, because although the ETA—the organization conducting the struggle—is essentially a nationalist grouping, yet, according to Anton Achalandabaso, a leading Marxist opponent of the Franco régime, its leaders have understood :

(a) That not all inhabitants of the Basque country are Basque. Those of Basque origin may even be a minority.
(b) The industrial proletariat, which has the most militant tradition in the whole of the peninsula, will attach more importance to the class struggle than to nationalism.
(c) Given its present stage of development, Basque industry will

require more and more immigration from poorer areas of the peninsula.

(d) Any fight for national liberation which takes contemporary conditions into account must be Marxist in nature.[2]

While in Greece the colonels have managed to give the country a façade of stability, there are strong undercurrents which indicate that the complacency of the fascist régime may receive rude jolts in the not too distant futre. There is increasing evidence that the CIA was closely involved in the Greep *coup*, and that this was known to the State Department. A Greek revolutionary, in an interview with the editors of the *International Socialist Journal*, maintained that :

'In its time, Nazi Germany prepared its grand *coup* by means of a series of smaller *coups* here and there; and at this moment American imperialism is doing the same thing. . . . There have been a whole series of *coups* and all of them with more or less the same technique : Brazil, Ghana, Indonesia, Argentina, and now Greece. The colonels or "gorillas" take power in a few hours; they throw out the existing political powers and then instal themselves as a force which succeeds, at least up till now, in maintaining control.

'We must not consider Greece an isolated occurrence, a case which came about solely because there were internal imbalances. Greece, aside from the fact that it is in Europe, has a vital strategic position for American imperialism. . . .'[3]

Yet, while the underdeveloped countries of Europe are experiencing a nascent fascism, we are often told by social democrats that Scandinavia is a bright and shining model of social democracy. Sweden, in particular, is often cited as the example *par excellence*.

Has Sweden proved that capitalism can do away with the problem of 'private affluence and public squalor'? As Marxists we are not simply concerned with full employment. We are equally concerned with the question of alienation resulting from the capitalistic mode

[2] *The Black Dwarf* (September 22nd, 1968).
[3] *International Socialist Journal*, No. 21 (June 1967), p. 350.

of property relationships, and in that regard there is nothing to suggest that Sweden is an exception. It would be wrong to maintain that Scandinavia, or the rest of Europe for that matter, will necessarily experience a *high* level of unemployment and that this will pave the way to a socialist revolution. Indeed there is evidence to suggest that the more affluent society becomes and the more leisure time that workers enjoy, the more does the process of alienation begin to take root. For Marxists, socialism is not only a question of public ownership; we are as insistent on the question of control— workers' control on the shop-floor, students' control in the universities. This process is a necessary part of the withering away of the State, and the fact that no communist country has even begun to apply the 'control' section of Marxism does not invalidate it as a concept. It merely causes one to view the development of 'communist' societies with a certain amount of apprehension. Goran Therborn, a prominent Swedish New Leftist, accurately spelt out the corporate nature of Swedish social democracy thus :

> The relations between the employers and the unions in Sweden are a function of the relations between the political dominance of the working class and the corporative hegemony of the bourgeoisie. This has meant that the employers have explicitly acknowledged the sectional justification for organized labour; indeed in a society like Sweden they had no alternative. In exchange the unions have willingly accepted bourgeois hegemony and recognized the needs of the 'economy', that is the needs of Capital. In such a situation, the strategy of the employers since the middle 'thirties has been to press a kind of community of organized labour and organized capital—with the implicit supremacy of the last. This strategy has met the demands of union leaders for formal respect and has resulted in a bilateral co-operation working ultimately in the interests of the owners and managers of the 'economy'. The famous productivity-mindedness of the Swedish union leadership should be seen in this context.[4]

But if Swedish social democracy has so far managed to avoid the basic problems of capitalism, the same cannot be said for its

[4] Ibid., No. 7 (January/February 1965), p. 62.

counterparts elsewhere. The social-democratic leaders of Western Europe are in a state of crisis. (The British social democrat Wilson tries desperately to betray the Africans of Zimbabwe to the racialist white settler, Ian Smith. As a mediator he uses that well-known 'impartial figure'—Balthazar Vorster, the ex-Nazi who rules South Africa.) The social democrats have, to paraphrase Marx's description of Thiers,[5] become 'masters in small state roguery, virtuosos in perjury and craftsmen in all the petty stratagems, cunning devices, and base perfidies of parliamentary party-warfare'. It is their policies which are leading Europe to its second pre-fascist decade : and not only Europe but the United States as well. In his farewell address to the American people the then President Eisenhower expressed some curious views (no doubt the appropriate speech-writer was duly reprimanded by the FBI) in a somewhat uncannily prescient warning to Americans :

'Until the latest of our world conflicts, the United States had no armaments industry. American makers of plowshares could, with time and as required, make swords as well.

'But we can no longer risk emergency improvisation of national defenses. We have been compelled to create *a permanent armaments industry of vast proportions*. Added to this, three and a half million men and women are directly engaged in the defense establishment. *We annually spend on military security alone more than the net income of all United States corporations.*

'Now this conjunction of an immense military establishment and a large arms industry is new in the American experience. The total influence—economic, political, even spiritual—is felt in every city, every state house, every office of the federal government. We recognize the imperative need for this development. Yet we must not fail to comprehend its grave implications. Our toil, resources, and livelihood are all involved; so is the very structure of our society.

'In the councils of Government, we must guard against the acquisition of unwarranted influence, whether sought or unsought, by the military-industrial complex. The potential for the disastrous rise of misplaced power exists and will persist.

'We must never let the weight of this combination endanger

[5] Thiers was the butcher who drowned the Paris Commune in blood.

our liberties or democratic processes. We should take nothing for granted. Only an alert and knowledgeable citizenry can compel the proper meshing of the huge industrial and military machinery of defense with our peaceful methods and goals, so that security and liberty may prosper together.'[6]

Leaving aside his pseudo-liberal rhetoric, the warning given here by Eisenhower was a sound one and, as recent events have shown, the military-industrial complex has been exercising more and more influence upon the policies of subsequent United States presidents.

But while the social democrats and their equivalents in the advanced capitalist countries are being confronted by a series of recurring crises, their counterparts in the underdeveloped countries are being forced, more and more, to show their real, repressive side. In India, 'the world's largest democracy' (*sic*), a mass-movement is building up which, when it decides to unleash itself, will stun the world by its ferocity. The poverty and mass-starvation that exist in India and Pakistan are no secret. Contrasted with China the 'progress' achieved by the American satellites in Asia is virtually non-existent. In the Naxalbari region in West Bengal the peasant movement, led by Maoist peasant militants, started occupying the land and burning the estates of the landlords. The movement—though supported by Peking—was denounced by the pro-Peking section of the Indian Communist Party. The growing resistance of the workers in Calcutta and other industrial centres was also discouraged by the 'Left' Communist Party. In Kerala the 'Left' communists form the government and are behaving in classic social-democratic fashion. The bureaucracies which run the Indian communist parties are coming under extreme pressure both from their own rank-and-file militants and from the masses in general. Unless they decide on a genuine revolutionary strategy and lead the masses, the pendulum will swing sharply to the Right—which is offering its usual panacea of religious chauvinism coupled with free enterprise.

In Pakistan the Ayub régime is everywhere unpopular. It has managed to antagonize large sections of the native *bourgeoisie*, the students, intellectuals and the growing urban proletariat. A major railway strike in early 1966 was largely successful, mainly because

[6] Quoted in *The Nation* (October 28th, 1961), p. 278 (my italics).

of the spontaneous pressure from the young workers. It was a total and complete strike and the most effective in the whole history of Indo-Pak trade-unionism. Although it was forcibly brought to an end after a few days, some of the major demands of the workers were accepted. The 'Maoist' leaders of the trade union tried to get the strike called off on grounds that it was 'backed by the CIA which was trying to destroy the Ayub régime' and was 'preventing wheat supplies from reaching the peasantry'. It was not surprising that these leaders were spat on by the militants on the one hand and imprisoned by the Ayub régime on the other!

In other parts of Asia the struggle has taken more concrete form. In Thailand the north-eastern provinces are under martial law because of the activities of the Thai guerrilla movement. In the Philippines the Huk movement is gradually being reactivated and the Government has offered huge rewards for the two Huk leaders, Pedro Taruc and Commander Sumulong, dead or alive. In Laos the Pathet Lao continue their policy of harassment, and in consequence are gassed, bombed and napalmed by the United States Air Force. In Indonesia, as Dr Caldwell points out in the present volume, the guerrillas are gaining many more recruits. The Vietnamese resistance has excited the imagination of peasants throughout South-East Asia. It has shown the world that, while the march of history can temporarily be frustrated by napalm bombs and B 52s, it cannot be halted. And the lessons which the Vietnamese are teaching American imperialism are also being assimilated and learned by the liberation movements throughout the world.

In Africa the Portuguese-controlled territories of Mozambique, Angola and Guinea are rapidly being taken over by native liberation movements. In Portuguese Guinea the guerrillas hail every new Vietnamese victory as their own. They have been visited by NLF cadres from Southern Vietnam and have been told by them how best to protect themselves against bomber raids and napalm bombs. Yet, while there has been an increasing degree of co-ordination on the part of the national liberation movements in the exploited world, there have been no similar trends in the advanced capitalist countries.

The division between imperialism and the exploited world has become much greater. The gaps in the standards of living, productive capacity, resources and capital investment continue to widen. While after 1917 the exploitation was more direct, insofar as the peasants and workers of the colonies produced surplus value for Western capitalists, and while to a certain extent this is still the case, the emphasis now is on exploitation through trade by means of unequal exchange. As a result of this trade, considerable capital resources are transferred from underdeveloped to developed countries. Although most of the exploited countries are no longer colonies and have gained their 'independence', this has not really affected Western capitalism. Only in a few cases has the colonial revolution removed the opportunities for capital investment: China, Cuba, North Vietnam and North Korea. The rest are still part of the capitalist market. There has been a conscious attempt by the imperialists to free themselves from their chronic dependence upon raw materials, as is evidenced in the remarkable strides made in the production of synthetic materials. But the process is at best a partial one; key resources such as oil and iron-ore have still to be imported. Indeed dependence upon them has increased and even the United States counts on the import of oil and iron-ore, for which Brazil and Venezuela are vital. Undoubtedly there has been a relative decline in imports from the exploited world, but there is no question of total independence at the moment. It should be noted in this regard, however, that the Soviet Union and the Eastern European countries, in their trade relations with the exploited world, contribute towards maintaining the unequal exchange. The Soviet Union could easily pay more without harming its own economy. This would help break the imperialist trade-grip, but the ideology of 'peaceful co-existence' acts as a barrier.

In its final phase monopoly capitalism is beginning to generate more and more capital. This is done at a rate which cannot be absorbed by the underdeveloped countries. The result is, therefore, a tremendous divergence of capital export towards other monopoly capitalist countries. Sixty per cent of American capital is now exported to Canada, Western Europe and Japan, and this increase in the flow of capital from one imperialist country to others is a relatively new development. The rationale behind this is also self-evident. As long as there are different wage-levels and as long as there are different levels of productivity the effect is virtually the same. Whether the United States invests in Latin America or Britain it pays much lower wages. The result is the same surplus profit. The average wage in Western Europe is 40 per cent of that in the United States; in Japan it is 20 per cent. This disparity has created a situation that is immensely attractive to capital investment. The so-called multinational corporations which are springing up are in fact controlled by the United States. But this perverted internationalism on the part of monopoly capitalism has completely by-passed the official organizations of the workers. There have been no corresponding moves to 'internationalize' the trade unions. The trade unions are at least fifty years behind the development of monopoly capitalism. Efforts by some of the American unions for closer co-operation have been rebuffed on grounds of petty chauvinism by their European counterparts. During the French coal strike of 1963, when there was only one week's worth of coal reserves left, coal poured into France from Britain, Belgium and West Germany. The working class has at the moment no counter-strategy to pose against the international amalgamation of capital. Such a strategy is badly needed.

What is absolutely clear is that the revolutionary movement is in a period of upswing throughout the world. The war in Vietnam, the events of May 1968 in France and the invasion of Czechoslovakia symbolize this upswing. Vietnam is at the moment the battle-front against imperialism. France showed the extreme vulnerability of monopoly capitalism and the strength of the working class. Czechoslovakia has initiated the struggle for political revolutions in Eastern Europe and the Soviet Union itself. Trotsky's description of a Stalinist society is still valid :

> The basis of bureaucratic rule is the poverty of society in objects of consumption, with the resulting struggle of each against all. When there are enough goods in a store, the purchasers can come whenever they want to. When there are few goods, the purchasers are compelled to stand in line. When the lines are very long, it is necessary to appoint a policeman to keep order. Such is the starting point of the power of the Soviet bureaucracy. It 'knows' who is to get something and who is to wait.
>
> A raising of the material and cultural level ought, at first glance, to lessen the necessity of privileges, narrow the sphere of

application of 'bourgeois law', and thereby undermine the standing ground of its defenders, the bureaucracy. In reality the opposite thing has happened : the growth of the productive forces has been so far accompanied by an extreme development of all forms of inequality, privilege and advantage, and therewith of bureaucratism. That too is not accidental.[7]

Those of us who form the hard core of today's new revolutionaries are still Marxists, but we abhor Stalinism; we believe in Leninism but prefer the emphasis to be upon 'democracy' rather than 'centralism'; we are Guevarist but can appreciate and analyse the mistakes made by Che. We are puzzled by the tendency among many Left factions in the developed countries to devote as much time and energy to attacking each other as to attacking capitalism. The new revolutionaries fight against sectarian tendencies. And what is most important of all, we are not to be bought off by the State. WE mean business.

[7] Leon Trotsky, *The Revolution Betrayed.*

NOTES ON CONTRIBUTORS

TARIQ ALI, born in Pakistan of a well-to-do political family, came to Oxford to study and has lived in Britain for over five years. At the University, he was President of the Oxford Union. In 1966 he began working in London as a freelance writer, since when he has become prominent in the Vietnam Solidarity Campaign. He is editor of *The Black Dwarf*, a bi-monthly newspaper of the radical Left, published in London. (pp. 67-78 and 283-296)

MALCOLM CALDWELL, a lecturer on South-East Asia in the School of Oriental and African Studies in London, writes for the quarterly *International Affairs* and is one of the leading authorities in Britain on Indonesia. (pp. 258-270)

STOKELY CARMICHAEL, Prime Minister of the Black Panther Party, the most militant Black Power organization in the United States, is known internationally as a writer, revolutionary activist and spokesman for the oppressed minorities in his country. He has been banned from entering Britain by the Labour Government. (pp. 91-163)

FIDEL CASTRO, revolutionary internationalist, is Prime Minister of the Revolutionary Government and First Secretary of the Central Committee of the Communist Party of Cuba. (pp. 271-282)

CHENHAMO CHIMUTENGWENDE, for two years a guerrilla fighter in Zimbabwe (Rhodesia), was granted political asylum in Britain after his recent escape. Several members of his family remain imprisoned by the Smith régime, and for his own revolutionary activities he is wanted by the South African and Rhodesian police. He is presently engaged in journalistic studies in the University of London and as a journalist has contributed articles to *The Guardian* and various African papers. (pp. 238-250)

ELDRIDGE CLEAVER, President of the Black Panther Party, is, together with Stokely Carmichael and Huey P. Newton, among the most potent and explosive figures on the American Left. He has been sentenced several times to prison in San Francisco on a variety of charges and is at present an editor of *Ramparts* magazine. (pp. 79-90)

TONY CLIFF, himself a Jew, was expelled from Palestine in the 1930s by the Zionists for 'subversive activities'. One of the foremost Marxist authorities on the Middle East, he is well known on the British Left as a leading theoretician of the International Socialism group. (pp. 219-237)

REGIS DEBRAY, French Marxist philosopher and an associate of Fidel Castro and Che Guevara, has been a leading theoretician of the Castroite guerrilla movement in Latin America. His best-known book is *Revolution in the Revolution*. Arrested in Bolivia for his association with the Guevara guerrillas, he is at present serving a thirty-year prison sentence in that country. (pp. 11-46)

TOM FAWTHROP, a leading militant student in Britain, was active during the student protest at the University of Hull. He is the author of a controversial book on educational organization in England, entitled *Education or Examination*. (pp. 54-66)

PIERRE FRANK, one-time secretary to Leon Trotsky, is now leader of the French Trotskyists. He was twice prosecuted during the Algerian war and was the victim of two plastic-bomb attacks by the OAS. In the forefront of the May Revolution in France, he is on the United Secretariat of the 4th International, which was first established by Leon Trotsky. (pp. 159-175 and 176-189)

JACEK KURON, an activist Polish student leader of the Left, is at present in jail in Poland for his opposition to the Stalinist régime of Gomulka. (pp. 131-158)

BILL LUCKIN, a working journalist, spent a year teaching in Shanghai and was present in China on the eve of the Cultural Revolution. (pp. 115-130)

ERNEST MANDEL, editor of the Belgian left-wing weekly *Le Gauche* and author of *Marxist Economic Theory*, is known internationally as a leading Marxian economist and is on the United Secretariat of the 4th International (pp. 47-53)

KAREL MODZELEWSKI, a militant Polish student leader of the Left, is—like his compatriot Jacek Kuron—in jail in Poland for opposing the Gomulka régime. (pp. 131-158)

CHARLOTTE NASSIM, associated with Zengakuren, the main radical movement in Japan, is a British journalist who has lived and studied in Tokyo. (pp. 215-257)

INTI PEREDO, mentioned frequently in Che Guevara's diaries, is successor to Che Guevara as leader of the Bolivian guerrillas. (pp. 104-114)

VITTORIO RIESER, a leader of the Turin students, was a front-rank participant in the occupation of the University and has been active in bringing about the alliance between the Left unions and students in Italy. (pp. 202-218)

PAUL ROCKWELL is editor of *Gadfly* magazine, a columnist for *The New York Free Press*, and a graduate student in philosophy at Columbia University. As a member of Students for a Democratic Society, he was a participant in the Columbia insurrection of 1968.

FRITZ TEUFEL, a leading member of the Maoist section of the West German SDS (Sozialistischer Deutscher Studentenbund), has been prosecuted frequently in his country for political and cultural 'crimes'. He has been built up by the right-wing German press as a 'bogy-man', because of his libertarian attitude towards sex and morality. (pp. 190-201)